Beggars on
Golden Stools

Beggars on Golden Stools

REPORT ON LATIN AMERICA

by

PETER SCHMID

Translated from the German by

MERVYN SAVILL

GREENWOOD PRESS, PUBLISHERS
WESTPORT, CONNECTICUT

Library of Congress Cataloging in Publication Data

Schmid, Peter, 1916-
  Beggars on golden stools : report on Latin America.

  Reprint of the 1956 ed. published by Praeger, New
York.
  1. Latin America--Description and travel--1951-
I. Title.
[F1409.2.S3 1975]   918'.03'3   74-20278
ISBN 0-8371-7853-3

Originally published in 1956 by Praeger, New York

Reprinted with the permission of Praeger Publishers, Inc.

Reprinted in 1975 by Greenwood Press,
a division of Williamhouse-Regency Inc.

Library of Congress Catalog Card Number 74-20278

ISBN 0-8371-7853-3

Printed in the United States of America

CONTENTS

LIST OF ILLUSTRATIONS

LIST OF ILLUSTRATIONS—*Continued*

MEXICO

Murder in a bus

THE coat in which I began my journey has grown threadbare from use, and is full of holes. The bloodstain, too, on the left arm is growing paler, although I always tell the cleaner to leave this exciting reminder of my adventures alone. This little rust-brown stain reminds me of the craziest experience of my life—of a murder committed at my side. Such a thing does not happen every day, not even in Mexico where human life is cheaper than elsewhere. It was a murder such as one hopes only to meet in dreams, and yet it took place, I might almost say, as a kind of welcome during the first few days of my arrival. Murder in a bus!

It is ridiculous in this country (as incidentally it is anywhere else) to stay in luxury hotels and to travel in first-class buses. The latter are arrogant, brand-new chromium and glass cages which still look North American and unacclimatized. They glide almost noiselessly over the smooth roads: when an Indio hails one, it does not stop for him as the friendly second-class buses do. For the latter there are no recognized stopping-places. You simply stand on the kerb and wave, and the monster obeys your insignificant self or some barefooted drunken *peon*. He clambers in, sits down next to you in his bright-coloured poncho, his naked, cracked and calloused feet in sandals made of old tyres; and an odour of the soil assails your nostrils. Here you begin to learn what a foot actually is. We Europeans protect them artificially in leather sheaths and prevent them from coming in contact with mother earth. As a result our feet grow white. But how magnificent is the peon's foot! A foot with a destiny; moulded by the earth it tramples. And then again the poncho, that primitive garment woven into a thick cloth at your own spinning wheel from the wool of your own sheep. A cut in the right-hand corner, in the

9

middle of the square, large enough for the head to pass through, and it is ready without need of tailor or tape measure. It hangs down back and front and falls in pleats over the arms, making it a simpler and more beautiful garment than an Arab burnous, which is made of the same straightforward material.

And to complete the picture, a tall wide-brimmed hat; an age-old hat, you would be tempted to say, if you did not know that it was quite a recent innovation. You will look for it in vain in the old Indian picture books: the Aztec only covered his head for ceremonies. The Spanish conquerors, unused to the power of southern sun, must have introduced this headgear to the Indians. Its giant dimensions arose from the ignorance of its imitators, and yet it has grown to be inseparable from the Mexican face: such vital savagery needs this frame to mellow it.

Or perhaps a young Indian mother will come and sit beside you. She cannot enjoy the pleasure of leaning back comfortably in her seat because the baby is asleep, rolled up in its blanket on her back, its tiny head lolling to one side like a broken flower and its slit eyes closed. You have seen these mothers a hundred times before in the Far East and you will see them again as far south as Bolivia. The broadest and least frequented ocean lies between the two worlds and yet the people are of the same stock. The Mongolian hunters pursued their game over the ice bridge of the Bering Strait and pressed onwards to the warm south. If you were to undress one of these babies you would find the same spot on his back as the Mongolians use for decoration in early childhood. Nature herself proves the theory of their origin over which the anthropologists still puzzle.

Yes, it is a joy to travel second class! The turkey or the hens your neighbour carries in his lap may soil your trousers. You may have to clamber over sacks of maize or bundles of sugar cane when you want to get out. And you waste a tremendous amount of time. But this wasted time turns out to be your greatest asset: you have made contact with reality and Mexico has accepted you!

But to return to my murder and what actually happened. This young man who one night travelled at my side, or rather tried to travel, from Teotihuacan to Mexico City, must be transported

back into his true period. So first the reader must allow me to
lead him up the steep steps of the Sun pyramid on whose summit
for thousands of years—no one knows exactly how old it is—
sacrificial victims had the obsidian knife plunged in their breasts
and their still quivering hearts raised on high as an offering to the
image of the god. That is far more exciting and sinister than a
simple revolver shot in a bus. With the only difference that here,
in the bus, a woman's simple human despair guided the weapon,
whereas in the hands of the priests it was a question of a superhuman, metaphysical despair. That is what lay and still lies behind
so many human errors, both individual and collective: despair.
In the first instance the priests of the ancient tribes were driven by
a belief in magic: they believed that the strength of the god could
be rejuvenated by human blood; they strove to sustain the Sun
on his course through the sky, so that he might win his battle with
the host of stars and rise again in all his might over the human
world. It was despair that urged the barbarous young Aztec folk
to dip their hands in the blood of thousands of victims: it was a
terrible fear that there could never be enough blood, and that
despite all their sacrifices, the solar deity would lose his power
and that his adorers would be plunged into the darkness of
oblivion. Hence the need for a flood of sacrifices to counter the
expected disaster; the need for war to be carried far beyond the
frontiers on behalf of the flagging God, in order to compel the
subjected races to provide victims for the insatiable juggernaut.
Thus from metaphysical despair an empire was born. Although
they considered themselves masters of their world they trembled
ceaselessly, and they behaved ruthlessly to the vanquished because
they themselves felt that they were subject to a pitiless rule. One
has only to look at the images of these gods today in the Mexican
museums: Coatlicue the Earth Mother from whose womb everything sprang—gods, men, constellations, beasts and plants. She is
skull-headed, decked with serpents, more a conglomeration of
bodies than body itself, appalling, terrifying. . . . Terror was the
essence of the divine. A conflict of demons was being waged in the
world and above it; nothing good as regards the human race
could issue from it. There was none of the smiling geniality and

weaknesses with which the Greeks endowed the Lords of Olympus. It was invariably a question of the earth's preservation. Every fifty-second year a world cycle was supposed to end with the threat of an apocalypse. The fires were extinguished on the altars and the men broke their household utensils into small pieces. For five unhappy days they waited, fasting and trembling, expecting the end of the world. The priests, however, watched from the lofty temple to see if the fateful stars would reappear. And when the Pleiades sailed into the centre of the sky, heralding the continuation of the world, a new fire was kindled in the breast of a man whence it was carried by thousands of torches to light the extinguished altars of the land. A new lease of life became a miracle of heavenly grace in a land where, in the true sense of the word, there was no grace, in a world where man was merely a plaything of the immortals, where existence—that wretched span between birth and death—merely represented a flickering flame in the storm of transcendental powers. Of what value then was the individual? What mattered death with a torn breast where each breath was a painful sacrifice to savage fear? Wherein lay the bitterness of dying?

These were my thoughts as I stood alone on top of the Sun pyramid. Around me lay a scorched valley with no shady trees, bounded by blue hills and an extinct volcano. As soon as the Aztecs arrived in the Valley of Mexico this temple city was abandoned because the earth, wantonly plundered of the moisture-giving forests, had been transformed into this impoverished steppe. All that had served man vanished with him. No trace of secular buildings remained; the temples of his gods still towered to the sky. Only the edifices erected to the eternal survived.

Thus the flanks of the Sun pyramid have endured; they are of clay faced with stones, vaster than anything the Egyptians built. Romantic science has traced lines of influence from the Pharaohs to America, but this is pure fantasy. These edifices, with their terraces, gradually rising on an incline to a flattened peak giving an artificial perspective, are far more subtle than the Egyptian pyramids with their pure geometrical form. Although from a technical point of view the pyramids, constructed from cyclopean blocks of stone, may appear to be a greater marvel, from the æsthetic stand-point they are put into the shade by their South American brothers. They tower there, surrounded by smaller pyramids, like a mighty circumflex accent on a mighty ground plan. Not far away arches the smaller pyramid of the Moon. No enthusiastic archæologist has yet laid bare its crumbling sides which are over-grown with brambles. The broad street of tombs leads from it in a direct line to the oldest and most important sanctuary, the temple of Quetzalcoatl. This is the unpronounceable name of the god who brought the blessings of civilization and a code of human ethics to the Mexicans. One day when his pupils had learnt enough he left them with a fatal prophecy. He promised that he would return one day with a white skin and fair hair. Now, the Spaniards who landed at Veracruz with their horses and mur-derous weapons could be described as white-skinned and fair-haired. The Aztecs, ripe for extinction, fought only half-heartedly against them: what use was human might against the return of their vanished god?

Naturally, Quetzalcoatl appears in his temple, not in his human but in his mythical metamorphosis, as a plumed serpent with a huge, gluttonous mouth and lustful eyes, the most magnificent symbol for a conqueror that can be imagined. He stares from the parapet of the steps; stares from the friezes which surround the pyramid, actually stares no less than 365 times, once for each day of the year, alternately with one of his colleagues Tlaloc the Rain-maker, who can be recognized at once by the thick circles that surround his eyes like a pair of motoring goggles. They look out over a gigantic field covered with yellow pampas on to the most majestic temple courtyard I have ever seen. It is an enclosed rectangle like a castle wall. Everything here is geometry, pure superhuman mathematics. The altar cubes protrude from the surrounding wall: broad steps lead up to them. Above there is nothing but a platform under the eternal sky—a similar platform to the one that crowns the sun pyramid. No roof encloses the god: the sanctuary has no limitations. When the sacrifice rose it had to give the impression of winging its way to eternity.

But to return to the entrance—to return from the calm to the screeching of the hawkers. They have mingled their fakes with the true antiques which the soil yields in great quantities. An experienced eye can easily detect the swindle. Paradoxically the fake was usually more expensive than the genuine clay head which I usually bought for about 4 cents. The surplus and cheapness of these can be explained by the ancient custom, I have already mentioned, of periodically destroying all the household goods at the end of a world cycle. Therefore the refuse heaps are still full of them, all from the same mould. Their powerful, almost mathematically beautiful features end in a high, broad forehead. Once more you are reminded of Egypt.

But enough of temples—what of my murder?

The bus was full as usual—a magnificent setting for a murder. With great difficulty I had procured a seat next to the window, not on account of the view—for outside the darkness had swallowed up fields, hedges and houses—but so that I could at least have a little protection on one side from the press of the crowd. A young man flung himself down beside me, leaving the third seat on the bench to a young girl who had got in with him. But the couple was not alone. A second girl hurried after them. She was fair-haired and did not look in the least Mexican. I could not take my eyes off her: actually I could not understand why the young man at my side preferred the broad clumsy features of his present girl friend to this slender, almost fragile face.

It was easy to see how things stood: the blonde was the deserted bride who was now pursuing her faithless lover with the idea of revenge. She flung herself upon him and dug her nails into his face, trying to drag him from his seat. The young man defended himself against the fury. He even struck her, and this is something Spanish chivalry itself does not condone even when the *caballero* is in the right. The whole bus was now on the side of the fair-haired girl. The ticket collector pushed his way between the antagonists and upbraided the young man for his brutality. And then the tragedy happened—the murder.

The fair-haired girl, separated from her hated lover, felt in her pocket as though looking for a handkerchief to wipe her tears, and suddenly I saw the barrel of a revolver just under my nose.

For some curious reason this did not surprise me. We civilized
Europeans have become so unaccustomed to using weapons in
our daily lives that the idea never crossed my mind that the thing
could be loaded, until I saw a flash and smelt a whiff of powder.
Everything happened so swiftly that the whole bus was taken
unawares, including my neighbour, who continued to sit in his
seat for a moment in amazement without realizing that the bullet
had entered his chest. The next move followed with the same
lightning rapidity. "If you please," murmured the fury, "Excuse
me, please." Pushing the passengers aside with a *"Permiso,"* she
was soon on the way to the door. She opened it and got out as if
nothing had happened. Not a soul dreamed of detaining her. No,
everyone courteously allowed her to pass, for after all a murder
is a purely private affair. By the time the young man at my side
let his head fall with a groan into his girl friend's lap the blonde
had disappeared in the darkness.

The incident which had begun so fantastically continued in the
same vein.

What would an intelligent driver in a civilized country have
done? He would have put his foot down hard on the accelerator
and taken the dying man to the nearest first-aid post, but here
nothing of the kind happened. The bus remained stationary. The
ticket-collector got out. It was his duty to see where the blonde
girl had disappeared to. The man next to me was bleeding from
his chest and back. Slowly two red patches began to stain his shirt.
The shot had obviously missed his heart and only pierced a lung.
In such an event one dies slowly, or one does not die at all, provided
medical attention is at hand, but the bus never moved. The dying
man stood up, a prey to a deathly anxiety with the red harlequin
patches on his chest and back. He too wanted to get out and
follow the murderess he had once loved, but his knees began to
quake and he sank back once more, groaning, with his head in
his companion's lap. I stood up and gave him my seat so that he
could lie down. No sign of the bus starting. The passengers had
turned round in their seats and were watching the scene, their
arms folded beneath their bright-coloured ponchos; they merely
stared with indifference, without displaying a trace of terror or

excitement. A man was dying. Many men died, so what did it matter? Death is a private affair. The ticket-collector returned about a quarter of an hour later. He had learned nothing and merely shook his head. "Let's get going now, for God's sake," he said to me. But now the curtain rose on the final act. A young friend who had accompanied the victim went over to the ticket-collector. "It's all your fault," he said to him. "You protected the woman." The ticket-collector looked grim and without saying a word gave him a left-hander on the chin. And now over the dying man a fight began in the middle of a loaded bus. The blows resounded as the two men hit each other, but no one stirred a finger to separate them. Everyone stared icily from beneath their enormous hats, with almost professional interest. Two men were fighting. What else was there to it? Suddenly the friend fell on top of the victim and at last the bus drove off.

As was only right, the driver made for the nearest hospital. The shot man was put on a stretcher and carried inside. Well, now he's saved, I thought with relief. There was no sign of the bus moving. Through the window I saw the ticket-collector talking to the hospital porter and gesticulating. I got out and joined them. "I tell you," screamed the porter, "there's no doctor here." The young man on the ground was even paler than before. The woman had started to weep again and supported his tortured body, which refused to lie down. She looked like a weeping Madonna with a crucified Jesus in her lap.

When we arrived in Mexico City late that evening there were big headlines in the papers. The local elections had taken their bloody toll. A few trucks filled with supporters of the opposition candidate had been stopped on their way to the polling booths by a band of government supporters accompanied by armed police. There had been an exchange of insults and suddenly revolvers went off on their own. The result: seven dead including a child. With touching objectivity the press printed statements from both sides in which it was proved that a member of the opposite side had shot first, thus soiling with bloodshed a friendly political difference of opinion. The topic was news for the next few days and then the incident was as good as forgotten. The Aztecs are

Taxco, Mexico: Colonial street scene
below: Juchitán, Mexico: a merry prison

Chiapas, Mexico: New Year's Day in a Chamula Church

The meeting of old and new: a drunken Indian asleep outside a beauty parlour

supposed to have slaughtered 20,000 prisoners in one orgy to their gods: in comparison, the few dead at an election seem very modest.

All the newspapers devote a page to crime and they never lack for material. And they certainly go to town. The evening newspapers immortalize the criminal by publishing his portrait together with a poem. In the case of our murder it ran something like this:

> *Abandoned by her lover*
> *In grief that they should part,*
> *She fired her gun with deadly aim*
> *And shot him through the heart.*

Sometimes of course you can read articles where even the poet foregoes his rhyme and only horror remains. For example, there was the case of a man who murdered a neighbour who not only had done him no harm but had no money which might have aroused the envious greed of the wretch. The man committed the murder because he wanted to assure himself of his own virility. He murdered in order to feel that he was a hero.

That is *machismo*, the terrifying streak of brutality in the Mexican character. *Machismo* is the over-estimation of sex. The root is always the same: fear of harbouring any trace of femininity in the male breast.

Guitars, girls and funeral wreaths

ANYONE who failed to recognize in the raw Mexican soul its other, tender side, which can be detected even in the most gruesome manifestations, would be guilty of partiality. In Mexico City I lived in a very strange hotel. It was central, not a stone's throw from the Alameda where the expensive luxury hotels for the American tourists lie, but on the other side of the square. Here the popular quarter begins. It would be more honest to say the quarter of thieves, girls and funeral wreaths. Two old baroque churches with crimped towers look down upon a small *playa* where a most remarkable sight can be witnessed every day. Roses, carnations and lilies, every flower that the rich soil of Mexico produces in profusion, are displayed here on silvered leaves, making a coloured symphony for the dead. Mountains of wreaths are made each day from this floral wealth, and nearly all of them find a buyer.

Behind these wreaths, however, in front of their house, which is proudly called the *Hotel de las Flores*, sit the prostitutes, sunning their wasted bodies. "*Ven, bonito,*" or "Come, Sweetheart," they call with a leer as you pass. They are there at every hour of the day, for love here is not confined to the night. Innumerable *casitas* open on to the street with their short swing doors like those through which the hero always swaggers in cowboy films. The juke boxes blare: they are everywhere and they are never silent. Throughout the whole of Mexico, wherever civilization has passed, the same melodies and the same singers go the rounds.

My hotel lay behind the flower stalls and the brothels. It was quite new and almost modern, with a bath and a telephone in each room. At night the green-and-red neon lights played on my ceiling. Despite the sordid neighbourhood it was a respectable hotel. Its permanent residents were artists from a nearby music hall. For weeks, a saw which belonged to a magician, who used it for sawing women in two, stood in the porter's lodge. Obviously he could not pay his bill and had to leave the tool behind as a pledge. I did my best to find out how he did the trick, for it was a real solid circular saw without any secret device.

The hotel proprietor was a very genial man, one of the most genial I have ever met. He sat the whole day in his office looking at magazines with pictures of naked women. Below them some camouflaged caption such as "How to draw nudes" gave an artistic touch to these particular portraits. My friend was not an artist. He merely looked at the pictures as if it were the most natural thing in the world to do. His little slitted Indian eyes betrayed no trace of excitement: he might have been studying a handbook of entomology—exactly as the people had looked at the dying man. Sometimes I looked beyond the funeral wreaths at the men on their way to visit the prostitutes. There was no dallying, no ceremony. They stood on the opposite side of the street and stared at them, like crocodiles watching their prey. Suddenly they would scream, grab a girl by the arm without a word, and drag her off as though they would have liked to devour her.

The following is a good example of the hotel proprietor's good nature. The doors in this worthy house were so ingeniously built that when you went out they closed of their own accord and you could not get in again without a key. Unfortunately I am rather absent-minded and usually leave my key in my room. This meant that I was constantly running to the office for help. In normal conditions the problem would have been quite an easy one to solve with a master key, but my friend had lost his many months before. Naturally he should have had another one cut, but being a true Mexican he had done nothing of the sort. When, locked out of my room, I stood before him helpless two or three times a week, he laid down his naked women on the desk with a sigh and collected several keys which the other guests had left on the board. Then he accompanied me upstairs. With the patience of an angel he tried all the keys to see if they would fit my door. If he could not find one he took a chisel, stuck it in the jamb and broke open the lock. It was of no importance: he merely nailed it on again afterwards. I was not even charged with the damage. The hotel, as I have already said, was almost new and yet it was practically a ruin. But it was a most romantic place to live in.

One night I woke up and could not believe my ears. Music was coming up from the street below, although it was 3 o'clock in the morning. I hurried over to the window and saw four young men standing in the street. They were wearing the usual gigantic Mexican hats and heavily embroidered jackets which betrayed them at once as the professional musicians known as *mariachis*. It is an ancient guild and only the name is modern. In the middle of the nineteenth century when the French seized the country under the Habsburg Kaiser Maximilian, these musicians were employed at their weddings, and thus a corruption of the French word *mariage* has stuck to them ever since.

One of the young men below the window was plucking a guitar while another played a flute. The other two were singing a love song. *La vida sin el amor no es una vida,* wailed the tenor. His song sounded incredibly sad, as though for years he had been deprived of all feminine consolation and was burnt up with irreparable longing. But even when fulfilment beckons there is no gaiety. Love is always melancholy: pain becomes ecstasy and ecstasy pain. I closed my eyes. Was the singer endowed with a woman's vocal chords? He seemed to be intoxicated by his own trills. Somehow this music was familiar. Of course. It was the dreamy *flamenco* floating over the Andalusian hills, the *fado* from the Portuguese harbours and the same melody which the Arabs sing in far-off Africa. The troubadour's song from the Middle Ages had left its heritage here. *La vida sin el amor no es una vida.* . . . Below me a window was flung open and a girl's head looked out. "Thank you," she cried in a melodious voice. "Sing it again, please." I suppose this will go on until morning, I thought angrily. Are there no police here to stop such noises in the night? But I immediately banished such thoughts, for they issued from the barbarity of a civilized world. I left the window open, lay on my bed and listened to those soft, lilting feminine voices.

The dangers of Mexico

EVEN the dogs in this country despise death. A host of stray curs scamper about the streets with such contempt for danger that the bumpers of passing cars reap a golden harvest. A sickening thud and a corpse lies in the gutter. No one bothers to remove it. The kites are soon on the spot squabbling round the corpse, their beaks burrowing into the soft flesh. Nothing scares them away. They must know that no one can bear their gruesome presence and that they fill people with loathing; they are as common here as they are in India. When an animal has died somewhere in the fields the whirling cloud of these birds of prey soon betrays the spot. They are a perpetual reminder of life's transitoriness.

By and large the motorists who run over the dogs are not much better than their victims. They drive like lunatics along the

city avenues at fifty miles an hour. The Mexicans would appear to
be constantly in a hurry, to have adopted the motto "Time is
Money" from their northern neighbours. But in fact this is
quite untrue: they waste hours on end. No, this love of speed has
quite different roots and it has nothing to do with time. Here the
car has become a transcendental object, a man-eating monster
like the earlier gods of this race.

At least twelve men are knocked down every day in Mexico
City. There are plenty of policemen to control the traffic and one
can often see half a dozen of them at a single street crossing, but
it is not infrequent that the officers themselves are run down, and
their occupation is as dangerous as that of a lion tamer. No one
will stop you driving on the right instead of on the left. Corners
are invariably cut. In a traffic jam you simply forge ahead on the
wrong side of the column and eventually get entangled with
another car. The most dangerous vehicles are those belonging to
the generals and the politicians. This new aristocracy is rich
enough to be able to afford smashing up a car or two and powerful enough to be immune from fines. Take care, as an ordinary
civilian motorist, not to be run into by a general. You may be
completely innocent. It will not help. Generals are very important
figures in Latin America and they are above all the laws.

In the daily presence of death everything becomes unreal and
life is turned into a macabre game. The whole of the Mexican
existence springs from this root. With death, time comes to a
stop, so why should time have any meaning at all? One day, as I
accompanied a Mexican friend to the air-line company, a man
suddenly rushed out of a café. "*Ah, mi amigo,*" he cried excitedly
to my friend. "How are you? I haven't seen you for a very long
time." I saw the two men embrace and bang each other on the
back. I have never cared for these *abrazos*: they have always
seemed to me highly suspicious as though the other man were
seeking out the spot in which to plunge his dagger. My friend
displayed no more pleasure than I had done at this unexpected
meeting. "Where can we meet?" the stranger went on un-
perturbed. "Where can we have a nice peaceful chat? What
about tomorrow at 4 o'clock?" "O.K. *Hasta mañana.*"

The two of us continued on our way to the air office. "But aren't you leaving by plane tomorrow morning?" I asked my friend. "Of course," he replied. "But what about the date you have just made for tomorrow afternoon?" "Heavens," he said "do you imagine the other fellow will turn up?" It is a curious custom, not only in Mexico but in all the Latin American countries, to make the most friendly dates and then simply not turn up. But how disagreeable and impolite it would be to dismiss the other person with a brusque refusal. One accepts and nothing happens. That is politeness. "Of course, tomorrow at 4 o'clock," my friend had replied, although he knew perfectly well that he was leaving by plane the following morning. "But supposing he turned up?" I insisted. "Who is he by the way?" My friend stood still for a moment and thought. "To tell you the truth," he said at last, "I have no idea."

This is the disagreeable aspect of this Latin charm: there is nothing solid about it, no foundations on which to build. It is the despair of all Europeans and Americans who come for the first time to this continent. They waste considerable time and overtax their nerves until finally they too adopt the same fashion. When, for example, you do not turn up for an appointment or turn up an hour late, you can be sure that the other person will behave in exactly the same way. One finally knows by instinct whether to turn up or not.

In Mexico even the food is mortally dangerous. When you arrive, well-meaning compatriots are careful to paint these dangers for you in grim colours; the dangers your bowels run in this barbarous land. You should never eat unpeeled fruit or salad unless you take anti-enteric tablets. You must drink only mineral water and clean your teeth in water that has been boiled. You must be careful about meat: there is always a risk of trichinosis. In short, during the first few days you are terrified to take a bite, for in this country hideous creatures called amœbæ thrive in the stomach. Should you ever meet a deathly pale man suffering from diarrhœa and depression you will know at once that the poor man is a martyr to the amœbæ. You swallow them by scores in any raw titbit which you are told you should have heroically refused to eat.

It is possible that you are a fatalist like myself. Why, I reason, should I preserve myself for the atom bomb when I can bring some pleasure into the lives of these small amœbæ? Consequently I ate everything without a qualm. I sat in small Mexico City popular cafés and tried all the native dishes. They are marvellous. You know nothing about Mexico until you have eaten their *tortillas*, which take the place of bread. Every peasant house has its millstone where they grind the maize, make it into dough and bake it into brown spotted pancakes as their ancestors did. Mincemeat stews in the pot: the cook takes it out of the oven, tips it out into a *tortilla* and the favourite national dish is ready. Or he wraps meat covered with paste in a maize leaf and lets it simmer: these are *tamales*. Crouching women can be seen making them in their smoking pans at every bus stop. But above all I love the chillis with which the Mexicans season nearly all their dishes. They are very similar to *peperoni* and paprika and are as hot as fire in the mouth. They must be swallowed down when fresh. One gets to like them so quickly that today I hanker after them as I would for an old friend. From the hygienic point of view they are invaluable. The chilli not only contains an enormous quantity of vitamins, but its pungent content destroys all the dangerous parasites, whether they are called amœbæ or by some other name. Had I paid attention to hygiene, with all the things I slung in a heathenish manner into my stomach I should have been in my grave or at least in a hospital bed instead of sitting here at my typewriter. Although I have an excellent digestion, I am inclined to attribute my health to the enormous quantity of chillis or *ajis*, as they are called in the Andes, which I have enjoyed.

Anyone who does not possess this fatalism will share the fate of the poor Americans. I have never encountered such pathetic tourists as these worshippers of the great god Asepsis. Have the vegetables been washed with permanganate? Has the butter been pasteurized? They live in a perpetual state of hunger and end their convalescence or their holiday trips with a loss of at least 20 lb. in weight—or a terrible dysentery. Think of the devil and he is bound to appear!

A town is sinking

THE Aztecs, according to the legend, when looking for a safe place to found their city, came across a rock in the middle of a lake in the Valley of Mexico, upon which an eagle was devouring a snake. According to their augurs, this was looked upon as a propitious omen. The shallow lake bottom was drained, and from it grew a lagoon city like Venice. Dams connected Tenochtitlan to the mainland and within the city boats glided on canals from palace to palace. The snake-eating eagle is still today the heraldic beast of the country.

Plaited osiers swaying in the water bore the first soil; from these swimming platforms young trees put out their roots and finally came to anchor in the depths. Today they have long since become solid ground. Every Sunday the canals are full of life: boats decorated with flowers glide up and down them. Each of them bears a pretty girl's name worked in a horseshoe of blossoms: Lolita, Juanita, Lupita. . . . A gondolier stands in the bows and poles his canoe through the waters which, with their green swaying reeds, have been transformed into a sunken garden. Under the flowered arches sit a couple in close embrace, completely undismayed by the glances of the merrymakers on the banks. Or else children lie and play in the boat looking at their reflections in the dark water and paddling their hands in it while their elders and relations enjoy the highlights of Mexican cooking at a table. Naturally the hawkers and traders do their best to destroy the peace of this idyll. Full orchestras of *mariachis* arrive like corsairs in their own boats and deafen the ear with their incidental music. Salesmen harry the American tourists and spread out their carpets. Even the photographers have mounted their cameras in boats and dart like sharks through the crowd in quest of clients. There is a shrieking, a clamouring, a tooting and a whimpering and only the flower sellers, buried beneath a weight of blossoms as in a coffin—the youngest with eager, morello cherry eyes—really fit into the bucolic picture.

Ancient Mexico must have been very like this. What evil spirit impelled the Spanish conquistadores to destroy this marvel and to build a city on European lines? Even though one deplores their ruthless vandalism, one must admit one thing: they built with taste. The land offered priceless material—red porous tufa, spewed from its volcanoes, snugly decks the façades of their palaces and churches.

Mexico City, Spanish in its roots and today American, is one of the most enchanting cities in the world. Skyscrapers tower above spacious palaces, gleaming limousines speed along the broad avenues past rustling cypress groves, and fountains play behind crumbling gateways. Amorphous, hastily-flung-together suburbs cluster around a pitch-black baroque church. Without tradition, not a stone's throw from each other, the two faces of the capital can be seen: the rich quarter and the slums jostling each other. The latter are disappearing gradually, destined to wander ever further away, for the price of land is rising at a giddy rate. The smart *Paseo de la Reforma,* an avenue in the west of the city not unlike the Champs Elysées in Paris, has already become too short for the superfluous millions that have been poured into these palaces of steel and crystal. Soon they will push eastwards into the poorer quarters. The new strongholds of capitalism rise from the crumbling walls of poverty. All this denotes the urge for the superlative that reigns in this city. Its cathedral is the largest on the American Continent; the *playa* before it, the Zócalo, is the second largest in the world, surpassed only by the Red Square in Moscow. At the turn of the century the largest American theatre, the largest bull ring and one of the broadest triumphal arches in the world appeared.

And yet it seems as though the land were hostile to the city, as though decay were already gnawing at its splendour. Enter the gigantic cathedral and you will be met with a smell of decay. Earthquakes have shaken the vaulting and left huge cracks in it. What was right and proper on the firm soil of Spain was by no means suited to this treacherous volcanic foundation. It smells of dust and mortar, not of incense. The only part that stands fast was built on the good pagan foundations of Huitzilopochtli's temple, which the conquerors razed to the ground. The cathedral apse built on the uncertain soil of filled-in canals is sinking, and although great pains are taken to preserve its foundations it threatens to break up and collapse. The same applies to everything the Spanish built: façades decay, towers lean and whole churches become lopsided. This is the long-delayed revenge of the Aztecs for the destruction of their lagoon city.

For it is an illusion to believe that one is living on firm ground. Not only the churches totter, the whole town is sinking. The more new buildings that rise in the centre, the faster it sinks. Mexico City is built on sand, virtually on sand.

As long as this sand remained heavy with water from the filled-in lake it could bear the weight of this new Babel. But thousands of hot springs began to absorb the ground water: the dry soil shrank and treacherous dust clouds were whirled by the wind from the new dust bowls, darkening the air in the dry season. Until a few years ago people irresponsibly shrugged their shoulders. The town sank almost a foot annually. Then this suddenly increased to a foot and a half. Panic! Two feet in a year. The heavy residential palaces of steel and greasy Italian marble, the pride of the 1900s, have sunk even more rapidly. The stairs leading to the streets break because the surrounding soils lags behind, until the city has jestingly been called "The underground station." The worst feature is the drains. Since the centre sinks most rapidly, the sewage no longer flows away. In summer during the rainy season pumps are working in the middle of the streets, diverting the evil-smelling waters into the higher lying channels. This expedient has lasted for years and it is appalling. When the rain is heavy in the summer the streets are turned into lakes. A remedy was urgently needed, but how could they build canals when the subsidence has no end? "There is only one consolation, we still lie 2,200 metres above sea level!" say the Mexicans laughingly.

Then an ingenious architect hit upon a good idea. He cheerfully built his skyscraper on sandy soil. It stood firm. The joke was that its foundations had to be sprayed constantly with water. This would have been a great solution had the growing town not suffered from a chronic lack of water. To sink or to thirst were the alternatives. The administration has devised a $100,000,000 plan. No more ground water must be brought from the depths unless it is replaced by the same quantity of casual water, and buildings of more than ten storeys are forbidden in the future. This is the only way in which Mexico City can be saved. In some way or another the lake, the mother of ancient Tenochtitlan, must return to its own soil. By means of a gigantic plan, some river which oozes not far off must somehow be linked to the foundations of the town. Otherwise the terror will have no end.

Quite a number of experts consider this plan to be impossible. Alberto Arai, one of the foremost engineers in the country, proposed a radical solution—the progressive clearing of the city and its re-erection in another and safer spot. The streets and avenues in the old dying town must then be torn down and planted with trees to bring back some moisture to the earth. In this way at least historic Mexico City, its cathedrals and palaces, could be preserved as a national monument. Perhaps at some future date, in a night club built in the penthouse of the highest forty-two-storey skyscraper, tourists will be able to lean over the balustrade and enjoy the view of a phantom city.

It sinks and sinks, and yet gold and men pour into it without cease. Today there are 3,000,000—tomorrow there will be 4,000,000. The arteries of the city are beginning to be clogged and nature forbids new ones to be opened. The sandy soil will not allow an underground railway. Whether you go on foot, by bus or in your own car, it takes you hours to get home. It becomes ever more difficult to live in Mexico City, which has exceeded its own proportions. Despite all this, I still maintain that it is one of the most enchanting cities in the world.

One afternoon I drove with a friend through the southern exit. Ten minutes after leaving the precincts of the city we came to a mighty wilderness: a green sea of stunted bushes dominated by curiously shaped black sandbanks dotted here and there with wild flowers. It stretched to our right as far as a hill, towards the edge of a crater, while to our left it became lost in the immensity of the Mexico valley. This wilderness, according to the geologists, is 6,000 years old. At that period burning lava flowed from the volcano Xitle. In its fiery path over the countryside it buried for ever the culture which earlier races had created.

Suddenly we came to a left-hand turn. A stocky hill rose out of the wilderness. It had withstood the stream of lava as a break-water halts the raging tide. Archæologists have laid bare the buried foundations. It is the Temple of Cuicuilco, the oldest monument on the American Continent. Five-fold, broken by terraces, the ringed walls rise to a cone. On its summit, according to scholars, the holy flame burnt long before the gruesome divinities of the later arrivals penetrated this valley. Who were these fire worshippers of 6,000 years ago? What trace remains of them?

A remarkable sight made us stop. In Copilco, not far away, the lava suddenly broke off short as if it had been smashed by some giant's hammer. It had grown thicker below the surface from the increasing pressure of the molten blanket. An artificial cave yawned in the depths of the carbonized soil: it was lit up with electric light. Below lay men who had breathed long before Adam and Eve were thought of. They were entombed here long before the active volcano destroyed their living brothers and thus, protected by a cover of earth and lava, they had endured for centuries. Who were they? Giants, dwarfs, pre-human ape-like beings? No, they were exactly like ourselves. They lie there at peace, their faces buried in their arms as though dazzled by the daylight, with clay figures and vessels for company in their last resting-place.

If only these lava corpses could speak! A hundred questions arise. Were they an autochthonous American race? Were they the descendants of later tribes who crossed the ice bridge of the Bering Strait from their Asiatic home, chasing the wild game to another continent? No one knows the answer.

Out into the light. Back to the present. In the immediate neighbourhood of these, the oldest men in the world, and of the fire temple, the building machinery rattled and the cranes swayed. Here, founded on the lava cliff, a new, more secure Mexico City, the modern city, is being built.

Until a few years ago no one had ever thought of migrating

to the lava wilderness of Pedregal. No one could walk a few steps
here before without tearing his clothes and shoes on the jagged
porous rock, until one day a brilliant young man bought the
desert. He bought it for a song. What did this lunatic want with
it? Luis Barragán was a modern landscape gardener who designed
artificial grottos and crazy pavement for very rich men. One day
as he visited Pedregal he began to scratch his head: why should
one build artificially in a place where nature had already laid out
the most beautiful garden of all? Only one thing was needed: to
build roads, to smooth out paths through the rocks, and the most
magnificent building site was ready. His vision became reality.
Go-ahead young architects joined up with the landscape gardener.
Dream houses began to rise from the lava rocks. There were no
bounds here to creative fantasy.

Today Pedregal has become fashionable. Artists, film stars,
authors, anyone with a name or who wishes to make a splash in
society, buys his plot of ground. Each buyer must agree to one
clause in his contract—the building must be modern. The solitude
of the Temple of Cuicuilco will soon be a thing of the past. As
far as the eye can see white boards denote the sites of future
buildings and workmen are erecting ghostly scaffolding in the
uninhabited wilderness. Down below, however, where the
lava field vanishes in the plain, one of the mightiest works of
modern architecture has risen. The University City was built
in a couple of years at a cost of some $50,000,000. No less
than 156 architects under the supervision of 38-year-old Carlos
Lazo gave free rein to their artistic whims. Their creative extravagance has produced the most fabulous blossoms: a library
without windows; a façade entirely covered with a giant mosaic
of Indian motifs; a fairy-like pavilion on sheer concrete supports
with rounded triangular gables serving as a cosmic ray research
institute. In a lecture hall the stairs curve into the façade in open
ornament like melodies rising into the air. But most wonderful of
all is an Olympic stadium to hold 100,000 spectators, built of *adobe*
and faced with the same volcanic tufa with which the Aztecs decorated their buildings. This was not entirely a deliberate stylized
return to the old tradition. Lazo took pride in telling me that this

age-old individual method of construction, used for hundreds of years by the Indians who had carried earth and stone in slings, had cost only a quarter of what a reinforced concrete building would have done. Obviously the marvel of the University City has not prevented certain people from being sceptical. In the old dispersed institutes in the centre of the city, the most eminent scholars, for the sake of prestige, had given free lectures to their students. Now that this gigantic institution has been built on the outskirts of the city, taking several hours to reach, the old cheap and homely methods of teaching have been jeopardised. The upkeep of the university alone threatens to burden the budget with $3,000,000 yearly. Can the country afford this for any length of time, this Mexican lack of proportion once more risen to a point of *hubris*, which is bound to end in disaster? Is it idle to ask whether it was pure mania at work or whether it is the enduring realization of a dream?

The virtuous president

MEXICO CITY is a haven of modern civilization in a world with which it has nothing else in common. Hardly anywhere else on earth will you find so many contrasts. On the Avenue Juárez you will see simple peasants in *ponchos* with their noses glued to the shop windows behind which a television set offers all its wonders. They waddle beneath sky-scrapers, in which the office calculating machines wrestle with millions, and wonder what they can buy at the next fair in exchange for their home-made pottery. The observer whose imagination is fired by statistics will learn to his indignation that half the 26,000,000 Mexicans do not possess a pair of shoes; that half the 12,000,000 children are undernourished, the majority being in danger of starvation. He will shake his head when he thinks that in a town which shelters 500 dollar-millionaires, not to mention a million men, half the population vegetates in appalling slums, and that in the suburb of Ixtcalco half the children die before they are twelve months old. But indignation over the social conditions does not touch the root of the problem: it lies in the fact that the highest and the lowest in the land no longer have any point of contact, because centuries of development lie between them.

That Mexico has become an eldorado for foreign capital is by no means due to the wisdom of a liberal economic and trade policy and a free convertible currency, but to a far greater extent to its position. Although it lies very near the United States it has every prospect of remaining far removed from any conflict and utter destruction on the outbreak of war. The branch establishments of the large American companies spring up like mushrooms out of the ground, in particular of all the leading car and tyre manufacturers as well as Westinghouse, General Electric, Dpuont, Kellogg, etc.

No visitor to the country will for one moment forget the presence of Coca-Cola and Pepsi-Cola. Down to the last *cantina* where only a wooden table stands they plaster their red advertisement posters on the walls of houses and telegraph poles. In many of these new undertakings Mexican capital has been invested; the days are over when business and exchange lay in the hands of foreigners because they alone were supposed to possess the blessing of the "go-getting" spirit. A law compels businesses, irrespective of whether they are foreign or native, to recruit at least 80 per cent of their staff from local sources. Between the "have-nots" and the "haves" a middle class is gradually growing up. That this new capitalism has come into being in Mexico today sounds like a paradox, because fifteen years ago this capitalistic paradise was ruled by a President who, although not an accredited communist, adopted all the basic communist methods.

Lázaro Cárdenas lives today on the best possible terms with his capitalist successors. He has retired to his property in the State of Michoacan. He is a good example of what curious destinies political ideologies and systems have in this world and how quickly they become tainted and transformed. So quickly that words fail. The newspapers today are still full of revolutionary articles and the orators on their platforms storm against the capitalists, although the stream is already flowing in another direction. The term "revolutionary" throughout the whole of Latin America has assumed a rather decorative character. A new party which does not incorporate this word is quite unthinkable, and when it crops up in its shortened form of R everyone knows what it means from Mexico's State Party PRI (Partido Revolucionario Institucional) to Bolivia's MNR (Movimiento Nacional Revolucionario). Revolution here is condemned to permanency because it represents *no* change or only a very slight change. Thus the atmosphere resembles a constant storm threat: an occasional flash of lightning gleams, but the beneficent rain is never released. "Revolution" here is merely a promise and very seldom a fulfilment, and that also is why Lázaro Cárdenas' "communism" has after a decade gone the earthly way of all revolutionary ideas. Mexico's first revolution, the fight for freedom, petered out and was a failure. As soon as freedom was achieved, practically nothing changed. The domination of the Spanish crown was swept away, but the land continued to belong to the noble families of Spanish and mixed blood and their ally the Church. The revolution subsided with the restoration.

At the turn of the century modernity knocked at the door of Mexico. Porfirio Díaz, a dictator, was President. He opened the country to the foreign businessmen who built harbours, railways and telegraph lines and began to exploit the wealth of the soil. But it was the old predatory capitalism. Equivocal laws took away from the Indians those lands which still remained to them and handed them over to ruthless profiteers. There were only masters and slaves. Then in 1911 the second revolution broke out and the great Civil War. Its ramifications are slightly confusing, but the main lines were once more the same—the struggle of the dispossessed peasant for land which he considered to be his own. The year 1917 promised them a new deal and, at least in theory, an agrarian reform. This promise remained theory for at least twenty years until the arrival of Cárdenas, a legacy from the revolution who now brought it to fulfilment. He restricted the possession of land to 300 hectares and distributed the rest—but not to individuals. For what could a wretched Indio do with this unexpected windfall? Dealers in "hooch" and usurers would

Chiapas, Mexico: Chamula village school

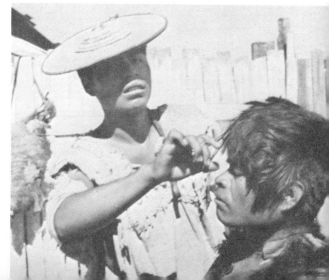

Chiapas, Mexico: hairdresser in Huistan

destroy him. Thus the old tradition of the pre-Spanish age was revived: the land was vested in the village community known as "Ejido". It was ploughed and sown communally and the harvest was sold for the benefit of the community. Cárdenas did not only think of the sickle but also of the hammer. A young professor and barrister, Vicente Lombardo Toledano, created from the chaos of warring syndicates a huge single union, the CTM. In 1938 the President signed a decree expropriating the British and American oil companies on Mexican soil and for a short time it seemed as if they were to be given over to the workers to manage. This was certainly a new spirit, and although Cárdenas subscribed to no International he made no bones about his spiritual relationship with the Soviet Union. No counter-revolution has destroyed the work of Cárdenas. The same party which brought him to power is still there and elects its own Presidents—Presidents whose policies are constantly changing. What then actually is the ideology of the PRI? This party is less an ideological association than a kind of inheritance, namely the inheritance of the revolution, and the most heterogeneous elements from anarchists to bourgeois shopkeepers are to be found in its ranks. Every six years they choose a new candidate for the presidency and this election already means victory. For it is the party which manipulates the peasant organizations, the great unions and the middle-class organizations like puppets. No member dares to be a thorn in its side even when one of the opposition candidates shows the most outstanding qualities. Thus each election, whether for the presidency or a simple governor's post, is a sham in which the defeated man is branded for the future. Opposition candidates have only three possibilities. Either they are ideological Don Quixotes who wish to publicize their convictions, whether these may be on the side of clerical catholicism or of the extreme Left. Or it is a question of a megalomaniac who believes that he has been specially "called" and that the country has been waiting for him. Or the opposition candidate will, as evil tongues maintain, be put forward and paid by the government party so that the astonished world can witness a real election and an overpowering victory.

Chichen Itza, Mexico: the pyramid of Kukulkan
below: Copan, Honduras: "The astronomical conference"

While, to outward appearances, one sees a firmly installed party dictatorship in Mexico, it would be a mistake to deny its democratic character. The will of the people must follow its unchallenged path. A typical example of this type of democracy was the election of the present President, Ruíz Cortines.

His predecessor Miguel Alemán, who was elected to high office in 1948, will go down in history as a controversial figure. Previously the Presidency had been the prerogative of the generals—not of generals from the military academy but rather group leaders of the Civil War who had risen in their command by genius and push. Alemán, however, had never smelt a whiff of gunpowder: he was a *licenciado*, a doctor of law who had chicaned rather than won his prestige in the ante-chambers.

Veracruz, the most important Mexican port, produces quite a different type of men from the highlands: gay, sly and easily approachable as a result of familiarity with foreigners. They are infinitely more worldly than the obtuse, melancholy Indians from the mountains. The liberators and revolutionaries bled and died in the highlands, but peace gave this son of the coast his chance. It was the civilian Alemán who opened the doors to foreign capital and plunged the country into a whirlpool of industrialization and modernization. The price paid was inflation, as a result of which even the higher wages sank to a point of inadequacy. On the other hand, good roads and railways were built in remote mountain valleys which formerly could only be reached on mules through the jungle, previously the abode of shy wild beasts. He flung $75,000,000 into a plan comparable with that of the Tennessee Valley. For centuries the floods of the river Papaloápam had inundated this fertile valley in the rainy season and carried away the inhabitants and their harvests. Now the dams for a power station were built which, on their completion in 1956 were to produce current capable of driving the pumps in the parched land and the machines in the new towns and villages. For the great struggle was not being waged over industry but far more over agricultural production. The distribution of the land had solved the social question but not the question of food. Mexico, where two-thirds of the inhabitants are peasants, is by no means self-supporting. The soil is poor on the mountainside and only 8 per cent of it yields a harvest: the remainder is wilderness or desert. Tractors, better sowing and farming methods, artificial irrigation: only the most rigid organization could solve Mexico's most urgent problem and provide not only work but food for its increasing population.

No one can deny that Alemán was a genius as an economist, but the people did not love him. Moreover, in his time, if you asked a peasant his opinion of the government, he would shrug his shoulders and utter a single word—*ladrones* (thieves).

Financial corruption is a refrain the traveller constantly hears repeated in Latin America. It may ring louder in some places than others, but it is ubiquitous. Possibly it is wrong to use such a hateful word as "corruption". If one compares the so-called honest and so-called corrupt governments throughout the world, the latter will be in the majority—the whole of Asia, the Middle East and parts of the Mediterranean belong in this category. But since the majority represents the norm it is perhaps unjust to make an exception in this case and to condemn it with political puritanism. It is far more essential to develop a special morality for corrupt governments and to measure them by their own yardstick. Once when I was in India and was warned against a politician, and I suggested to the critic that he should look to the mote in his own eye, I received the following answer: "He takes more than 10 per cent."

That was already a recognized international norm. Another viewpoint is that of the effect on the public good. In this category we find a productive and an unproductive corruption. If a Minister builds roads and irrigation canals with public money and uses the opportunity to speculate in land, his illegal gains are a stimulus to the permanent creations from which the country profits. Unproductive, on the other hand, is corruption when the funds provided for public contracts trickle into the Minister's pocket, are wasted by crooked contractors, and the work remains uncompleted. In practice it is obviously difficult to separate these two types since, as a general rule, they are closely correlated. Thus in President Alemán's works genius and graft went hand in hand. There is no question that, together with a host of friends, he amassed millions of dollars from his gigantic plans—a later estimate mentions 800 million, 100 million of which disappeared into the President's own pocket. However, one cannot dismiss the effect of the fillip he gave to the whole Mexican economy. More dubious perhaps was his inclination, like some medieval prince, to present his cronies with monopolies which lay like a malignant cancer between the producers and the consumers. The ordinary man's daily bread; maize and black beans, sugar, rice, fish, petrol, a taxi or a bus, were all monopolies, which lowered purchase prices, swelled selling prices and financed the most fabulous luxury with inflation and blood-sucking poverty. How quickly the revolution was forgotten! Admittedly the old families, the descendants of the Conquistadores, were now no longer the oppressors and the exploiters. No overseer now lashed the Indians' backs with his whip. An anonymous group now quietly drained the country's life blood, and finally the leaders of the revolution itself, the generals, ruled the hungering masses, built palaces in the Paseo de la Reforma with their blood money, spent their week-ends in luxurious *haciendas* (no land reform laws limited their expansion), or settled down with glamorous film stars in the fashionable coast resort of Acapulco. Could the country ever rid itself from the curse of the betrayed revolution? Must the liberators always follow in the footsteps of the dispossessed, and must this land live perpetually in riotous extravagance and immeasurable poverty?

As Alemán's presidency drew to a close, while the robbers once more exhausted themselves in a last riot of pillaged wealth, an event occurred which confirms the theory I have mentioned above, according to which even under a dictatorship a State Party can conjure with democratic strength: the next candidate for the Presidency was a virtuous man.

This self-healing of the Mexican régime was quite miraculous. Naturally the clique surrounding the former President had no wish to give up their lucrative gains, and it appeared that Alemán's six years' rule "by the unanimous wish of the people" would be prolonged. But Mexico had learned to its cost during the thirty years' dictatorship of Porfirio Díaz how firmly a strong President can cling to his seat, and since then each President without exception has been forced to give up his post after six years. Official departments now ended their correspondence with the warning slogan "Effective suffrage—no re-election" instead of "Very truly yours," so that the last inhabitant should be clear as to this highly important law of the Republic which had become a principle. No exception was made even in the case of the people's hero Cárdenas: after six years his presidency came to an end and even the possibility, which exists in other Latin American countries, of standing again after the lapse of a few years was forbidden him. He was one of the grand old men of Mexican politics whose personal influence endured behind the scenes. He became a popular legend like Villa and Zapata who, according to the superstitious peasants, gallop over the plains on stormy nights among the immortals. They are still inclined to say with reverence of anything good that issues from a new government: "Cárdenas proposed that. . . ."

When the Party looked around in their choice of a new presidential candidate it was fully aware that he must be a man of integrity. The people's horror of the robbery which had taken place during the term of the outgoing President had reached a point where there was a general longing for a worthy successor. This in actual fact brought about the miracle of a complete change of course. In Alemán's Cabinet was a modest middle-aged man, the Minister for the Interior, who had stood aloof from the general chase for wealth. His ascetic cadaverous face had earned Ruíz Cortines a nickname among the people, *Cara de Calabera*, which means skullface, and his candidature was even more welcome since he was already over sixty. In a northern country this age may denote a fruitful time for a politician who has blended the wise experience of age with an undiminished vitality. In Latin America, however, this age is tantamount to peaceful senility, and the man who was now extolled to the people in a gigantic campaign as a marvel of honesty seemed to Alemán's clique as a not particularly dangerous potential reformer. "Skullface" was elected according to all the rules of the modern plebiscite.

But when he took office in December, 1952, something very strange occurred. The man who had been looked upon as one who would play the part of a man of straw and who, during the campaign, had shown himself particularly Laodicean, seems to have drawn unsuspected strength from his presidential chair. A flood of reforms streamed over the country. In the first few weeks Alemán's friends were flung out of their parasitical key positions. The multi-millionaire Jorge Pasqual had to return the "rake-off" he had extorted from five independent oil firms only a few months earlier. The price of comestibles fell 10 per cent in a few weeks. A big building contractor whose 75-mile-long road appeared like a Potemkin village on the maps but which in reality was still covered with thick jungle had to pay treble the sum appropriated in the form of a fine. The cleaning-up campaign continued down to the ticket boys who held the public up to ransom for theatre seats. The President made everyone else follow his good example. He published a list of his possessions—despite his many years' service they had remained very modest, a total of $34,000—and demanded similar details from his 250,000 civil servants, from the highest to the lowest. Everyone at the end of his term would have to furnish new accounts, and woe betide anyone who showed a suspicious increase of wealth.

But was corruption and bribery rooted out in this way? An American importer to whom I put this question shrugged his shoulders with a smile. "It's become more expensive," he said curtly, "because the risks are greater. They will never be rid of it as long as Mexico is ruled by Mexicans. As in Spain, it is too deeply rooted in the people. Today we are going through a very unpleasant transition period. In the old days it was very simple. When you wanted something from a government department you paid the official in question the usual sum for such a service and everything was in order. Today, under the slogan of probity, it has become very difficult. You risk not getting what you want if you omit to pay a man who expects a *mordida* from you. On the other hand, you risk messing up things if you offer a bribe to one of the honest ones. It is a great art today to discover who can be, who must and who must not be paid. Formerly it was much easier and everything functioned much better too, because everyone was interested in being active because activity alone brought in *mordidas*. Honest officials here are indolent. Not half so much business is done since the government turned honest and things are dull. To be perfectly frank, we long for the bad old times to return."

But it was not only the ideal of integrity that stood behind the intentions of Ruíz Cortines' government. It was also a very sober social concept. The crazy industrialization threatened to go too fast for the country. Two-thirds of the inhabitants still lived as simple peasants in poverty. The anti-social mentality of the former President had to a great extent diverted the profits of industrialization into the deep pockets of the contractors and had not benefited the workers. This accounted for the rising difference between extravagant luxury and great poverty I have already mentioned. Every national economist—and the President was one himself—must have realized that it would not be long before the highly developed industrial head could not live while the consumer body below was wasting away. In addition to this, under Alemán's giddy expansion drive, works had been left uncompleted or been abandoned, as a child gets bored with a game. The pedantic man of honour had to put all this in order, and it was not a very enviable task.

The paradox lies in the fact that this urge for social reform did not revert to the old ideals of the revolution, but on the contrary to the innate conservative instincts of the people. The reintroduction of the collective *Ejidos* in Cárdenas' time was hailed with great enthusiasm as a return to the true Mexican way of life. But results have always shown that the socialist tinge of the *Ejido* does not entirely suit the simple upland peasant. He did not want the community land redistributed, did not want it to be farmed on co-operative lines, but to *possess it* with all the tenacity with which a smallholder clings to his plot of ground. Collectivization entails a new premise as regards the land. It is no longer individual property but only a method of production: the man labours and sells his product like a shirt or a watch. This rational relationship to the soil has never caught on in Latin America. The landowner still sits on his property like a king in his own kingdom, even when he leaves enormous expanses untilled, and agrarian reform is to a certain extent a social declaration of war. Cárdenas' successor had already given the peasant certificates guaranteeing him and his heirs the enjoyment of their piece of land in perpetuity, only when he left his land for two years without farming it did it revert to the *Ejido* for redistribution. That is as good as possession. Under Ruíz Cortines the tendency has been to disband the *Ejidos* and to return the land as freehold once more to the Indios.

An even more important retrogression took place in the nationalized oil industry. A few months after its nationalization, Cárdenas himself realized that it would be useless leaving the workers' councils in charge, because the good folk with their ideas of possession demanded little work and princely wages. When the administration of the oil wells was finally transferred to the State company of *Petroleos Mexicanos* (Pemex), the latter had to deal with strikes and discontent on the same scale as the British and American companies. These internal difficulties were similar to those which have recently taken place in Persia. The dispossessed companies took refuge in a boycott. Mexico could obtain no boring materials and could buy no more pipelines, for the factories were controlled by the trusts. No tanker loaded the Mexican product and no customer would buy black market oil. England went so far as to break off diplomatic relations, and the reason that the United States did not follow its old custom of sending troops to protect the interests of its nationals was because Franklin D. Roosevelt had decided upon a new type of relationship with Latin America, the so-called "Good Neighbour policy". For a while the Mexican oil industry did not look too rosy. Foreign engineers had left the country and had been replaced by young men straight from the university. The world press waited cynically for the capitulation of the industry. And then the miracle occurred. Mexico managed to get together the necessary material, and to make things easier the Axis powers, Germany and Italy, entered the field as buyers. The Red President sold his oil to the Fascists. The luck held. At the end of the Second World War the cold war with the communists broke out and the Americans began to look with other eyes on Mexican oil. The Arabian wells are far away and even Venezuela and Peru are separated from the United States by the sea. The same grounds that attracted so much American capital to Mexico—the strategical position—increased the value of Mexican oil. In 1948 President Truman sent a commission to see whether there was any possibility of doubling production. There was only one fly in the ointment. The required credits were to be furnished by the American oil companies, which naturally required some sort of reciprocity. It is said that President Alemán wanted to conclude the deal and was only prevented by the great man in the background, ex-President Cárdenas. The Mexicans still remembered the past like a nightmare, that period when the Oil Trusts invaded their soil as though they were the lords and masters, using their gold to meddle in politics and steer them in any direction they pleased. Thus nothing came of the business. Mexico preferred to jog along alone rather than expand with foreign help. Whereas in the twenties the annual production was over 190 million barrels, bringing her into second place in world production (of which she delivered one-quarter), today with her 80 million barrels she has slipped back to seventh place and has been superseded by Venezuela.

Even so Mexico has not succumbed to foreign aid. For twenty years fabulous sums had been lavished on the oilfields of Poza Rica at Tampico in the Gulf of Veracruz. The cracking towers rose like trees in a forest, turning the neighbourhood into a garden straight out of the Arabian Nights. But now the experts are beginning to doubt the span of life of this splendour, and above all to blame the intensive exploitation which has been to the detriment of the oil-fields. In the meantime, through industrialization and the construction of a network of roads the home consumption of petrol has greatly increased. The diesel engines, pumps and tractors all eat up crude oil. Moreover the Oil Trusts, laughing up their sleeves, were ready to accept a sum in dollars for compensation, and Mexico has made it a point of honour to pay this debt promptly to the last penny. As a result she must also export oil.

Thus new fields had to be found, and since *Pemex* did not

possess a sufficiently expert technical staff they were compelled to make a new deal with the Americans. A contract with the Texas oil man Edwin W. Pauley promised the latter, in the case of a strike, half the output until his costs were covered and later 15 to 18 per cent.

In spite of everything all oil beneath the soil of Mexico belongs to the State, and this knowledge of being master of her own wealth is of great psychological value, even if the production cannot be compared with that of the foreign oil companies in Venezuela. In actual fact the State of Mexico is founded on her mines and oilfields. More than half the revenue comes from these, and should they dry up, agriculture and industry would have to shoulder the burden and so they must be built up in the meantime. The feeling that they must allow foreigners to dictate their economy is hard for any people to tolerate, and most of them would cheerfully accept a fall in output so long as they can feel proud that they are masters in their own house. On these grounds the success of the Mexican oil experiment has been highly significant, firstly for the oil companies, who should be able to read the writing on the wall, and secondly for other lands where huge royalties can dampen the government's ardour for nationalization. This above all holds good for the Latin American peoples. In Mexico they have proved that the exploitation of their own riches is possible with their own strength. The example of Mexico has kindled the imagination of revolutionaries and has become a spur to individual daring. Thus President Cárdenas' decision in 1938 was far more than of mere national importance—it was the first successful stand taken against economic colonialization, and even if today foreign co-operation has once more become necessary, this time the foreigners are merely guests and the laws lie in the hands of the nation.

Art for the people

PERALVILLO is no better and no worse than any other suburb of Mexico City: dilapidated huts hastily erected for the proletariat with the plaster on the walls full of hideous cracks; mean stalls in the streets along which rattling old-fashioned trams raise clouds of dust and refuse. The unavoidable melancholy aroused by a stroll through these streets will suddenly be broken by an astonishing sight. Among these hovels can be seen a wide, gay entrance—the entrance to a picture gallery. A beggar raises his hand to you as you cross the threshold; on the other side an old woman is selling nuts. But your eyes have not deceived you; neon lights cast their gleams on the walls and gradually you begin to take stock. Yes, that's a Rivera and there's a Siqueiros . . . and over there an exhibition of modern Mexican painting. On my first visit I sat down on the round sofa in the centre of this gallery. Before looking at the pictures I examined the visitors. An Indian in a gaudy poncho came in cautiously, looking suspicious as though expecting to be kicked out of such an elegant establishment. His wife slouched obediently behind him. The man stopped for a moment before Rivera's picture of President Juárez with Kaiser Maximilian lying dead in the background after being shot by a firing squad. The Indio knew the story: spoke eagerly to his wife and pointed to the scene. Behind him a workman in blue overalls stood in front of Siqueiros' self-portrait. By the use of slick exaggerated perspective the passionate painter brandishes his fist at the visitor as if he wants to strike him. The workman smiled, shook his head and went on his way. That is the kind of public you will find in the Peralvillo art gallery—an appreciative public, the custodian told me. It has hundreds of visitors each day. Admittedly the entrance is free, but even so it is astonishing to find so much interest among the proletariat for such demanding art.

Later I visited Susanne Gamboa, the Rumanian-born wife of the director of the semi-official Institute of Fine Art. I met her in another gallery which she runs in the centre of the business quarter. Both exhibitions, the popular and the exclusive, were arranged by the Art Institute, the former to give the simple people some idea of the importance of Mexican paintings and to inspire some latent talent, and the latter to give young unknown painters an opportunity of showing their work to the public without any financial burden. Susanne's gallery sells their pictures without deducting a centavo commission. The Institute is even generous enough to grant loans to promising young artists which they allow them to pay off in pictures. The go-ahead policy of the Art Institute has already allowed its influence to be felt. Mexican collectors have begun to buy the canvases of their own countrymen, thus allowing them to persevere with their art without starving to death.

I nodded my head enthusiastically at all Susanne's explanations, not of course without making some mental reservations to offset her proud optimism. One only had to wander round the impressive show in the Peralvillo gallery to admire unreservedly the old school: Diego Rivera who in the twenties on his return from Paris led the new renaissance in painting; the deceased José Clemente Orosco, whom most of the critics hailed as the greatest; David Alfaro Siqueiros, who returned a few years ago from Venice after winning international repute and a prize. With this great triumvirate can be compared Rufino Tamayo, a sensitive artist who became a cosmopolitan in Paris without renouncing the warm brilliant colours and the mythical forms of his own country. In my own opinion this international painter was the one who had remained most deeply rooted to his Mexican way of life. And what of the newcomers? Naturally these youngsters were not lacking in talent. Obviously they were trying in all honesty to remain Mexican like their forerunners, but there was no denying that the chaos of style, the sick headache of spiritual lack of direction which has mutilated the art life of the whole world today, has not stopped at the Mexican frontier.

The three great painters knew exactly what they wanted. They were perhaps less important as painters than as ideologists, as the glorifiers of the mighty social revolution which burst over Mexico in the second and third decade of this century. All three of them were and are communists, each in his own manner, and each has painted his beliefs in over life-size on the walls of public buildings. The artists go on painting unswervingly, but their works fade with the ideas that gave them birth. In the National Secondary School the students scratch their initials and foolish remarks about the sinister ladies of the capitalist bourgeoisie whom Orosco painted trampling proletarian bodies underfoot on their way to church, and no harm is done. It would almost appear as though the genius of Orosco strove to debase him to the level of a pamphleteer. In his great moments he soars above this political credo to a tragic view of a tortured, possessed humanity and when he spits on society it is an accusation against life itself. On the same wall, only one storey higher (this too has not been spared by vandal hands), one is arrested by an immortal picture: three men carrying their guns on bowed shoulders as though they were infinitely weary, striding out to battle; at their heels come two frail women with their children strapped to their backs. It is the unpolitical heroic song of the people's war, dumb and tragic as the soul of the Mexican people.

That is the root of it all: silence. Whenever a painter shouts, preaches and interprets, he ceases to be a real painter. Siqueiros is the greatest Stentor of the three. His frescoes and pictures are so poignant that you feel tempted to close your ears to them. At times too he exchanged his brush for other instruments of his ideology—for the propagandist microphone and the tommy gun, for example, with which in 1939 he made an attempt on the life of Trotsky, who was then an exile in Mexico. The latter escaped the painter's bullets because he had been prudent enough to crawl under the bed.

If you were to accuse Diego Rivera of being a communist to his face he would probably protest most energetically; nevertheless he is one. He is also one of the happiest, most enchanting and good-natured men in Mexico today, a man who would not harm a fly. It was he who arranged an asylum in Mexico for Trotsky because he did not consider him to be an enemy of the Party, but merely a persecuted man who had incurred the wrath of the Kremlin. This did not prevent him as communist No. 1

from marching in the ranks of the Red demonstrators and painting the victory of the hammer and sickle on the walls. Only someone who has been fortunate enough to know Diego personally can understand the colossal political charlatanry that lies behind his communism.

He may invite you to his beautiful old country house in Coyoacán. You will wait in a drawing room where the walls are covered with pious votive tablets up to the ceiling. You will see the Holy Virgin miraculously rescuing an unfortunate man from the horns of a bull; flinging herself in the path of runaway horses while a man in the cart lifts his hands imploringly to the sky; healing a dying man in hospital. Even more remarkable, the Mother of God also takes the trouble to free prisoners from their gaol, to cut down a hanged man from the branch of a tree during the revolution, or to protect a thief caught red-handed from his pursuers. This Virgin is patient with human weaknesses. She knows that man is fettered with original sin and therefore turns a compassionate eye upon her supplicants.

The mighty corpulent figure of Rivera appears in the doorway; he is carrying a hideous cur in his arms, stroking it and calling it Señor. It is one of the very rare descendants of the Aztec *techiche* dog, the only pets, apart from the turkey, the ancient Indians looked upon as friends and also liked to eat. The small beast is hairless, with black smooth skin like an elephant, and is obsessed with a pathological self-hatred. How else can it be explained that the bitches of this disappearing race turn away in rage from one of their own males and kill the young from other matings if they in any way resemble the mother.

Rivera let his huge frame sink on to the sofa with a sigh. "Excuse me for having kept you waiting," he said. "I was eating. Food has become very dull since the revolution. It's terribly difficult to get hold of human flesh and almost impossible to obtain young girls' livers, a delicacy I am particularly fond of."

I looked at the master somewhat taken aback, hoping to see some trace of irony in his features. I was disappointed. He was deadly serious. And then he began to talk like a book, or rather his words poured out like a torrent. When Rivera succumbs to his mania for story telling and philosophizing he forgets time and space. He developed for me his favourite biological theory of the origins of the white races. He has even imortalized it on the Lerma dam and at the same time crowned with his genius a mighty engineering feat which leads water through gigantic pipes from a nearby valley to the thirsty capital. His huge fresco "The Birth of Mankind from the Water" cannot only be seen on the walls but even below the water level, where he has continued painting in indelible colours. In the Darwinian mode the whole of creation is portrayed in a genealogical tree from the infusoria to the apes. The white man, however, is shown as a product of the mating of the primitive Mongolian and negro races.

Rivera explained to me that the latest Russian research has discovered that in the ninth generation an albino variety was produced. The Mongolian Eskimos inhabited Germany when Hannibal's negro armies arrived and thus brought about the historical meeting of the two basic races. As a result the whole of European culture was saturated with the Judaic spirit. Even an anti-Semitic movement like National Socialism was not an original German thought but of Old Testament origin. Baron Edmund de Rothschild had told him personally that Hitler's father was a Jew whom he had employed in his banking house, that Goebbels came from a Chilean and Göring from a Brazilian family. The triumphant rule of the Oriental-European spirit has lasted for thousands of years, but now it is at an end. In thousands of years Europe had not made a single discovery which would serve to spare it from its own destruction. The legacy of science would now pass to those races who knew how to use it without allowing it to destroy them—in America. The technical culture of the USA and the spiritual tradition of Latin America would one day become united to their mutual benefit and profit. Naturally only after capitalism had been destroyed, the Red Prophet went on, as I stared at him in amazement.

During the whole of this speech he had been just as serious as when he had mentioned his cannibalistic tendencies. Obviously he believed implicitly in what he said. The fantasy of the artist in his case has developed into mythomania, where the boundaries between dream and reality have become strangely entangled. In this twilight, this curious fellow sees himself enhanced in the most flattering manner. The more astounded his audience appears, the greater and bolder the heights to which he feels bound to rise. *Epater le bourgeois, épater soi-même:* Rivera's communism can be reduced to this basic formula. He knows that the American tourists pay higher prices for his pictures as long as they can shiver at the thought of their dangerous creator. The fact that in the twenties the Party drove him out for his heretical nonconformity is only a mild threat of what awaits this amiable gossip should humourless communism ever really take root in his country. How could they spare the life of such a disrespectful comrade who announces to his friends that Stalin was not the son of a human father but of a wild pig, and that his abysmal intelligence was the result of such a parentage. I did not hesitate to tax the painter with these unorthodox thoughts and later on he confirmed them. "You're right," he said rather sadly. "Fundamentally I belong just as much to the old collapsing world as you do." This was perhaps the only moment during our political discussion when he was not posing and when the true man was revealed.

He stood up. We walked up and down the room which looked out on to a courtyard; then we visited the sick bed of Frieda Kahlo, his young wife, who damaged her back in a motor accident and has been bedridden for several years. By her features I immediately recognized her unmistakable Hungarian origin; the old artist has painted her on countless frescoes as an absolutely genuine Aztec. The young woman, herself a very talented painter, has tried to free herself from her invalid's bonds. She has arranged a mirror on the ceiling and paints self-portraits from her bed. On the wall, however, hangs an enormous photograph of Stalin. She too prays to the swine-begotten God of her husband.

Rivera has amassed untold treasures in his house. He is the greatest collector of pre-Colombian art, and the money he earns from his canvases for the most part goes into the pockets of excavators who know exactly where to get the most generous prices for their treasures. He has presented some magnificent objects to the National Museum. In Pedregal he has built his own private museum and the cupboards and drawers in his house are full of treasures. In Frieda's studio bright-coloured bogeys with red horns hang on the wall. They are Jews. The Indians burn similar images during Passion Week. Below these bogeys as a strange contrast hangs a cubist composition painted in Rivera's youth when his Parisian colleagues baptized him *l'Exotique*. "In those days," the master commented when I looked at it, "I was still imbued with a colonial inferiority complex. I thought that I ought to look for my form in Europe and that as far as possible I must renounce my Indian heritage. Only when I turned my back on Paris and felt my own soil under my feet once more did I begin to feel the true significance of my art. The older I grow the more I try to please the people, the noble Indian people whose ancestors created similar work." He pointed to a small clay group from Colima which made one of the deepest impressions I retain of Mexico. A couple sit side by side staring into space, with apparently nothing in common. But the woman with unnaturally long almost handle-like arms raises a vessel to the man's lips and gives him to drink without deviating from her hieratic loneliness, and this bridge epitomizes the whole shy, tender significance of man and wife. "Can you tell me any modern who could have created anything like it?" Rivera asked. "Or mention one of the old masters, including the Renaissance, whose work would not seem clumsy beside such delicacy. No one can deny it: on this Mexican soil the very highest was achieved—what today the most refined artistic intelligence is searching for, the return from nature to super nature. Here it was realized centuries ago. The ceramics of Picasso or the sculptures of Henry Moore appeal only to a small élite of æsthetes who set enormous store by them, but these clay figures stood on some peasant's hearth. The children played with them and broke them. Each day new masterpieces are dug up. This art belonged to the people and we must go back to it. That is what I'm trying to do. Come and see me tomorrow in the Palacio National. I'm working there again on a new cycle. The critics frown and find that I'm slipping. They miss the classicist varnish of my earlier frescoes; they find the figures ugly, the composition ingenuous and the colours crude, but the Indios who whisper behind my back like them."

Dog-nosed Cortes

NO one would even glance at the roomy Palacio National in the Zócalo had not Rivera adorned the three walls of the staircase well with episodes from Mexican history from the beginning to the present. Something of the calm nobility of Piero della Francesca lives in the first fresco to the right, where Quetzalcoatl is shown teaching the wisdom of a civilized existence to the savages. Into the centre bursts the savage *Conquistá*. An armoured horseman on his white stallion falls a victim to Aztec nobles arrayed in their wild animal skins. Their puny weapons are of no avail: soon the foundations are laid for the Christian cathedral. Under the fanatical eye of the Bishop of Zumarraga, fire destroys the manuscripts containing the religious and scientific wisdom of the vanquished; Franciscan monks baptize the Indios, and their great friend Bartolomé de las Casas with raised crucifix protects them from the greed of worldly feudal rulers. But his example is not followed. The fires of the Inquisition consume the heretics: Slaves are driven into the mines. The whole of the modern history of Mexico is compressed in the upper part of the picture, where statesmen with legal parchments, generals, and the animated peasant faces of Villa and Zapata mingle like skulls in an ossuary.

Twenty years have passed since the master finished his historical fresco. Now his scaffolding has been erected on the other side of the gallery. He is continuing his work and the subject is the same: the landing of the Spaniards in Veracruz. As soon as Rivera saw me he called to me to climb up and once more he began to talk like a book. The devil knows how he managed to gossip and at the same time to put the last touches to one of the most terrifying figures his brush has ever created. But the music of his own words seemed to excite him, and I learned an astonishing new story, the story of this monster, for this is no anonymous figure of fantasy. It is a portrait of Cortés.

Obviously twenty years ago it was quite a different story. In those days Rivera had used contemporary pictures of the Conquistador. They showed a brilliant youth in the prime of his manhood and the conscientious painter had portrayed him thus in his historical panorama. In the meantime a find of the greatest importance had come to light. Hernán Cortés, history tells us, died in the year 1547 as a forgotten man in Spain after losing royal favour. The honour which had been denied to him when alive was bestowed upon his corpse. It should remain in the soil he had conquered through strength and incredible cunning. But his bones enjoyed no lasting peace. When Mexico threw off the Spanish yoke and the rebellious mob threatened to desecrate his remains, his descendants transferred them secretly from the crypt and hid them in an unknown spot. Cortés' corpse vanished for more than a hundred years. Then a yellowing document turned up one day in the archives of the Spanish Embassy, where it had been deposited by the above-mentioned heirs. It denoted with great accuracy the church and the chapel where the Conquistador's remains lay. A search was made and the skeleton came to light. There was enormous enthusiasm on the part of all Spaniards and Hispanophiles, but the anthropologists who examined the bones shook their heads. Was this really Cortés? This man had a small head with a birdlike face, an extraordinarily low forehead and a pug nose. His skeleton is twisted, with bone tumours on the legs, a hump back and a withered arm. Nothing therefore in the nature of the ideal Knight about it. "Physiologically senile, an effeminate type," proclaimed the scholarly discoverer of the treasure. So that was Cortés the conqueror of Mexico!

The twilight of the gods! Eulalia Guzmán, an intelligent historian of Indian origin, wrote a book proving that all the existing portraits of Cortés were false and the mere flattery of courtiers. The real portrait of the conqueror must now be painted for the first time. Rivera did not wait to be asked twice. He settled down, studied phrenology, physionomy and anatomy. He clothed the shameful skeleton with flesh and there stood the monster, Cortés, with his pug nose, rheumy eyes and apelike forehead, a hunch-backed dotard, his body twisted with gout. His sword waves feebly over an Indian who is bringing him gold. Behind his back hecatombs of Indians hang on the trees like fruits. The crucifix in the hands of a priest becomes a knout for the slaves. Nothing remains of the objectivity the painter had at thirty. The Spaniards are no longer noble conquerors but a robber band led by a freak.

"No, that's not good enough," I protested. "You cannot deny the fact that Spain is a great nation or at least was a great nation."

"She was a great destroyer," replied Rivera thoughtfully, "so great, in fact, that she destroyed herself. Examine the historical facts without European prejudice. Why did they conquer us? Merely because their weapons and their instruments of destruction were better and we were the less experienced. In every other respect our civilization was higher than the European. In an age when in Europe Galileo was made to recant the truth at the stake, our priests knew how to forecast with superb accuracy the path of the planets. I have already spoken enough of our art: the conquerors replaced it with their baroque decadence. It is always tragic to live under the yoke of foreigners. Nothing could be more appalling than to fall into the hands of the Spaniards. The pioneers who populated North America were puritans, and quakers, the revolutionary left wing of their age. Their colonies were founded on progressive thought and the revolution went out from her towards Europe. But what came here from Spain? The feudal *hidalgo*, a class which in Europe was doomed to extinction. In its dying throes, after this leap to the New World it came to life again and with it came the priests for whom protestantism had begun to make things hot in Europe. Nothing except retrogression. What else could bloom from rottenness? The quakers worked like ants on their soil, but the *hidalgo* let slaves work for him. That is the double tragedy of Latin America— not only were our cultures rooted out ruthlessly but we became the last bastion of feudalism. The gold and silver of our earth nourished the anti-bourgeois resistance even in Europe. On us lies the curse of putting back the historical clock, of impotence and retrogression. Do you understand now why I hate the Spaniards and why many other Mexicans do the same? History gave us a raw deal; otherwise the English would have landed on our coasts instead of Cortés."

The old man had finished his work. He stood back and looked contentedly at Cortés' pug nose and wiped his brush. We climbed down from the scaffolding. As we made our way down the broad steps I looked once more at the features of the noble cavalier on the white stallion. How conventional and false they now appeared to me. A magician walked at my side, a double-headed Janus full of fantasy and deep insight, madness and wisdom, the most admirable liar in the world.

Bones in search of a hero

I HAD already noticed the girl without her features making any particular impression upon me. On the contrary, she displayed the same rather foolish dreaminess that could be seen on the faces of her school comrades—that animal thoughtless indifference common to most Mexican women. Wearing the ancestral feathered headdress on her small head, she had walked through the village in a procession behind the flags of the combined Latin American nations and the United States. She entered the homely old church with its coarse decoration which betrayed the inexperienced hands of native masons. Now, still wearing her Indian costume, she stood at the microphone on the platform in front of all the strangers. Suddenly she seemed to undergo a transformation as she recited

"*Cuauhtemoc you are not dead,*
And you will crush the tyrants still,
A bulwark in our hour of need
An image of your country's will."

Her coarse face was suddenly animated to passion; the verses made her voice rise to a pathetic chant. Among the spectators stood her happy smiling father Professor Romero, a schoolteacher from nearby Taxco, a poet and the author of the lines she was declaiming. Armed militiamen stood in front of the shrine which held the skeleton of the hero, Cuauhtemoc, the last King of the Aztecs. They all had the insolent marble faces which already in Spanish times had earned the mountains of Southwest Mexico the warlike name of Guerrero. Above them gleamed an enormous star of yellow marigolds and the whole apse was decorated with wreaths and flowers as though a saint were being revered.

In this way the remote village of Ichcateopán celebrated on October 12th "The day of the Latin-American people", the anniversary of the discovery of the new world by Colombus. This *fiesta* celebrates the common Spanish heritage which unites all the peoples of Latin America in the same language and culture. Originally it was a gesture of gratitude and the manifestation of a bond with the Spanish homeland which by the discovery and the Conquest had borne the seeds of occidental thought to this continent. This at least is what people thought when they inaugurated this birthday celebration in the year 1916. Today the meaning of this ceremony has obviously undergone a radical change. From the whole region schoolchildren had come to the grave of the man who had put up a last desperate struggle against the conqueror Cortés after the death of the faint-hearted collaborator Montezuma. Not only the schoolchildren but even the students had arrived with their standards. Now the schoolmaster from Taxco mounted the platform from which his little daughter had recited her hymn and made a speech in glorification of the "race"—no longer the race of the Spanish barbarian conqueror but of their own subjugated hero folk the Aztecs.

The whole feast in Ichcateopán church was not lacking a certain comic element. It was by no means certain that the skull which grinned from a glass casket and the half-carbonized bones really belonged to the national hero who was being honoured. Historical skeletons in Mexico seem to lie under a curse. The much maligned Cortés has at least one satisfaction: the scandal of his remains was to be surpassed a year later by the adventurous story which devolved round the bones of his opponent.

One day Don Salvador, a medical quack from Ichcateopán village, went to the priest and confessed that he could no longer keep a very grave secret: in accordance with an old family tradition the remains of the last Aztec King Cuauhtemoc were buried under the high altar of the church. Since this revelation could only bring kudos to the priest, he immediately revealed the secret from his pulpit *ad maiorem gloriam Dei*. The nation lent an ear. People turned expectantly to the scholarly heads of the Institute for Anthropology and History, but these good men shook their heads. It was a swindle, they said. Every child knew that Cuauhtemoc had suffered a lengthy martyrdom. To begin with Cortés, in order to extort from him the hiding-place of the Aztec royal treasure, had his feet roasted over a fire, then took the unhappy sufferer with him on his expedition to Honduras, and finally had him hanged from a tree in the Province of Tabasco on the threadbare pretext that he had participated in a treacherous conspiracy. How could his corpse ever have reached this Guerrero mountain stronghold all the way from the tropical jungle? In order to check Don Salvador's supposed documentary proofs the scholars sent Eulalia Guzmán—who had already made a name for herself by unmasking Cortés—to Ichcateopán. She discovered that it was presumably a question of late and inaccurate copies of lost originals which proved nothing although they could not actually be refuted. This intelligent historian, however, pursued her researches and found that in the village the story of the king's tomb had been handed down for centuries from mouth to mouth. Thus there must be some grain of truth in it.

The experts still shook their heads, but now a new factor came into play—politics. The Governor of Guerrero was only too keen to have his national hero. "Let us excavate," he said, and of course a general's wish is law. But the archæologists were unwilling to stake their reputation on such a humbug. "Even if that ingenuous female Eulalia believes it," they said, "as far as we're concerned she can go and grub about after the bones but she won't find anything." The ingenuous female began to excavate amid general laughter and scorn. The ground was hard and progress was slow. Day after day nothing, and then all of a sudden heavy blocks of marble, and an oxydised copper plate bearing the inscription: "King Cuauhtemoc" and the date 1692. Below, a small crypt, hacked out of the natural rock, and in it, lo and behold!—a skull and some charred bones. Eulalia had won the day. The experts had shaken their heads so long that they could not change their opinion now. "Rubbish," they said. "The lady is not a qualified archæologist. The excavation is a work of an amateur. The most important proofs which would give the age and the genuineness are lacking. The whole thing is a fake." A commission of ten was called in to give a verdict on the discovery. An analysis of the bones, it declared, showed that they belonged to a number of different individuals and that the skull was that of a woman. The writing on the copper plate was not in the style of the period, and so on and so on. Since they were very great experts their verdict was recognized officially: Don Salvador's grandfather had been a smooth rogue. He had wanted his village, which was infested with scorpions and tarantulas, to become a national centre of pilgrimage and had somehow buried these bones under the altar at the turn of the century.

But Eulalia Guzmán was by no means disconcerted. She found supporters. Doctor Quiroz-Carón, the Director of the forgery department at the Government bank, started an investigation on his own account; proved beyond doubt the age of the oxydized plate—400 years out of contact with the air—and disproved point for point all the findings of the commission. A marvellously romantic theory was born. The followers of the unhappy King had secretly cut down their Sovereign's corpse from the tree in the remote jungle, had embalmed it with herbs and salves against corruption and brought it back on an endless march to his own home, the Guerrero mountains. Spanish rule and with it the Christian religion had hardly penetrated here. Although Cuauhtemoc had adopted the new faith and had died after receiving the last rites, his corpse was burnt in accordance with ancient custom together with a few sacrificed slaves: hence the alien bones among those of the King. A few years later a propagator of the Christian doctrine arrived in this remote spot, not as a pathfinder for the Spanish rule, but very much to the contrary. The Franciscan

Father Motolina had aroused the hostility of the wordly powers in the capital because of his friendship for the Indians and had been obliged to flee. He arriven in Guerrero land as a friend and in search of asylum. When the Indians told him of the King's tomb he had quickly seized this opportunity of enrolling them more fervidly in the new religion. Had not Cuauhtemoc died in the same way as Christ? Therefore he merited a Christian burial under the altar of the newly built church.

That was the story. Don Salvador was able to corroborate it from an old Codex which had been in the possession of his grandfather—one of those wonderful old picture books in which the Aztecs perpetuated historical events. It contained pictures of the whole wearisome journey from the jungle to the mountains. Unfortunately the valuable document disappeared in the chaos of the revolution and he was now making every effort to trace it.

Until it turns up the secret of the King's tomb will remain a mystery, an insoluble problem. Prominent experts on both sides have thrown their judgments and opinions into the scales. The arguments more or less balance each other. What is the next step? Let us imagine that in another land a similar find came to light—for argument's sake, the bones of Jeanne d'Arc in France or of Arminius the Teuton hero, in Germany. The public would not rest until a decision had been reached as to their genuineness and all the scholars of the world would be mobilized. In Mexico, however, a ticklish problem like this is solved in a far more simple manner: they have left the apse and the kingly grave exactly as it was before the excavation, full of dust and mortar; the bones have been enclosed in an officially sealed glass shrine where no one can touch them or cause a disturbance by any further unwise assertions. Time will do its work. The true or bogus remains of Cuauhtemoc will slowly disintegrate into dust from the action of the air. And Mexico will be left in peace again. . .

Or perhaps this will not be the case. Was not this pilgrimage to the questionable tomb proof enough that beyond the historical and archæological wrangling the myth has already taken possession of this spot of earth—a myth admittedly not yet recognized but nevertheless a vehicle in the heart of popular sentiment which certain shrewd people know only too well how to exploit? The good Governor of Guerrero fell into a trap with his national hero, but politics should not cease to arouse enthusiasm for the unhappy skeleton on this account. Who were the tyrants of whom the poetic schoolmaster spoke in his hymn? There was no shadow of doubt as to the meaning of his speech. He was not referring to the Spaniards; they only served as an historical scaffolding; they had long been out of the game, but the new oppressors and imperialists were therefore all the more dangerous. They had attacked the freedom-loving peoples of Korea. Their capital was once more likely to enslave Mexico. The Yankees! Cortés has gradually assumed the features of the powerful Wall Street tycoon. I smiled a little sadly. Poor Cuauhtemoc. So ultimately you will join the communists! In actual fact the Mexican public has abandoned the entire question with an indifferent shrug of the shoulders. Since they did not want to be accused once more of ingenuous superstition or of being lacking in patriotism, they merely remained silent. Only the Reds seized upon the kingly bones as a symbol of their conflict. The poor exploited Indios against the imperialists of all shades and colours! The propaganda sheet of the Soviet Embassy, *Cultura Sovietica,* published in addition to all the old wive's tales of their workers' paradise deeply serious scholars' opinions as to the genuineness of the skeleton. The position now became highly dangerous. Whoever attributed these much discussed bones to the King laid himself open to being suspected of communist sympathies. This was a double reason for keeping your mouth shut.

Grumbling communism

BUT even this identification with the revival of the Aztec cult, even the transformation of the Spanish conquerors into Yankee imperialists, cannot camouflage the decline of the communist party in Mexico. To be accurate, one cannot even speak of such a party because the law demands 75,000 signatures for the official recognition of a party, and the few intellectuals and artists who are self-admitted Reds cannot muster even a fraction of this figure. Even Vicente Lombardo Toledano, who backed President Cárdenas in his great reforms, considered it more judicious to call his own party The People's Party and his available newspaper in the capital *El Popular*. This newspaper is unique throughout the world. Although it appears in a free country and has all the international news at its disposal it refrains in the main from using the great American or European news agencies, preferring the *Agencia Latina* which, thanks to its Argentinian origin, had, at least for some time, an anti-imperialist slant. However, since this agency has no correspondents in Europe the gaps in *El Popular* are filled in from Soviet and Polish sources. As a result there are invariably a considerable number of omissions. Thus the readers only learned of Stalin's death two days after the event, and the news of the Korean armistice only appeared after a long delay via Budapest. The Mexican *Pravda*, faithful to the Soviet, published the whole of the Kremlin propaganda. What difference is there then between The People's Party and the communists? The editor to whom I put this question bridled as though caught in a pair of dialectic tweezers. "That is a question," he replied, "that I can only explain to you in great detail. How about meeting tomorrow afternoon at 4 o'clock?" I called on him next day, although I knew beforehand exactly what to expect: true to the Latin American custom, the man did not turn up.

I therefore visited a youth demonstration which Vicente Lombardo Toledano had staged in a hall of the big stadium. Large flags bearing instead of the hammer and sickle the diving falcon, the symbol of Cuauhtemoc, draped the speakers' platform from which Lombardo spoke to a host of rather sophisticated-looking youths behind whom yawned row after row of unlit empty benches. "I'm no communist," he said, "but I'm a Marxist." He proceeded to outline a very vague general programme which demanded a better distribution of wealth, a departure from the one party system, and increased economic independence from the USA through home industrialization. Any other patriotic man with a social conscience could have said as much. I saw at once—and I corroborated this later on in other Latin American countries on several occasions—how difficult it would be for communism to take root here. Lombardo Toledano was a communist and denied it, Rivera maintained that he was one and it was untrue. What a crazy position. I could not help feeling slightly sorry for Lombardo. This highly educated man with several doctorates and degrees in law and philosophy to his credit had in the most irresponsible manner wasted the power he had acquired as creator of the unified trades union when, after 1939, he relinquished his independence to follow Moscow's directives. Rebellion in the union ranks split it into groups: it began with the electricians, followed by the railway and oil workers, until ultimately, in 1948, he retired from the ranks of the MTM and remained the leader of a very insignificant group. Since then his role in Mexico has become almost meaningless and today, as a mere general secretary of the CTAL (Confederation of Latin American workers), he plays more an intellectual than a practical continental role. When in 1952 he dared to oppose Ruíz Cortines for the Presidency he only obtained 2 per cent of all votes. The youth meeting I attended had something tragically comic about it. Young boys sprang up in the empty hall and shouted a few enthusiastic phrases about "our great leader Lombardo Toledano". When a handful of other youths applauded loudly, this lonely man, standing before them with a mixture of disappointment and disillusioned conceit, bowed to the empty benches.

The Yankees, envied and unloved

I FOUND the chap unsympathetic at first sight. He had wormed his way into the market place of Toluca among the buyers and sellers who hurried past with heavily laden donkeys. He spread out in front of him an anatomical chart on which all the human organs were painted in bright colours and began to draw a crowd of simple-minded Indios. In their bright ponchos they squatted or stood round him, motionless, with rapt expres-

sions on their faces as though he were a teller of fairy tales. "Do
you ever wake up tired in the mornings?" he asked. "Has your
wife ever been unable to suckle her child for lack of milk? Does
your father suffer from rheumatism? Does . . ." The fellow
understood how to suggest all the maladies which could overtake
the peasant in his adobe hut. All these maladies he maintained
came from one single source—the kidneys, which did not
sufficiently cleanse the blood. Every man from time to time must
cleanse them to prevent such dangerous attacks on his health.
Then he held up a small bottle of white salt. A pious priest had
mixed the medicine and given it his blessing. Even in the best
chemists nothing like it could be found except at an exorbitant
price, but the holy man wanted to help the people, genuinely
wanted to help them, and therefore this young man had been sent
to distribute it to them for a mere trifle, one peso. to anyone who
needed it. Whoever wanted to profit by this great opportunity. . .
The Indios who had sold their fruit or their homespuns pressed
with great confidence round this quack. He would have needed
several pairs of hands to distribute the bottles quickly enough to
the outstretched hands and to cash in the peso notes. I opened my
camera and was about to take a snapshot when the "barker"
became aware of it, let everything drop and rushed over to me in
a fury.

"You bloody Gringo," he shouted. "Get to hell out of here
with your camera. You shan't go home and laugh with your
friends at the poor Indios." His eyes glittered and I thought he
was going to attack me. Obviously he had not reckoned with my
being able to speak Spanish. "Poor Indios," I jeered, "whose hard-
earned gold you entice out of their pockets with your swindle.
Let me tell you, I'm a doctor and I know that bottle contains mere
rubbish." This unsuspected damaging propaganda aroused him to
the utmost fury and he raised his fists in order to silence me.
Suddenly a tall middle-aged man came between us. The quack
was disconcerted for a moment. "Come with me," said the giant
quietly, leading me away into a side street, "and don't get mixed
up with this ruffian." "He hates you," he said, "because you're a
foreigner. He's an idiot. I know better. I know America," and

with a broad laugh he brought a few dollar vouchers out of his pocket and flourished them under my nose. They came from Chicago. I looked at them with interest and was told the story of his adventures. My friend had been to the United States three times, always illegally, and on each occasion had worked for several months in factories in the north. He had saved his money and on his return home had bought a small property which he increased after each trip. At the moment it comprised 80 hectares. During the coming winter the man intended to wade once more across the Rio Grande and to leave his property in the care of his brother.

A curious idea, I thought later. I had met that afternoon two diametrically opposed and yet typical representatives of Mexico— one who had felt offended by a sharp look and a camera lens, and the second a "wetback" who with natural peasant cunning had recognized the higher civilizing benefits of America and had known how to profit by them to his own advantage. Which of the two represented the typical Mexican? How easy it would have been to have made a quick generalization about each of them, about the anti-Americanism of the one and the pro-Americanism of the other. The former has become a byword not only in the case of Mexico but throughout the whole of Latin America (although the problem grows more acute the nearer the country lies to the rich neighbour). And yet here too generalizations are dangerous. Obviously in a certain sense the Gringo has taken the place of the colonial *gachupines* as the Spanish colonial rulers were called, but just as the latter in their dominating role aroused the duality of native feelings—hate and envious admiration—so the Creole feelings towards the Yankee are difficult to bring into a common denominator.

"Poor Mexico," the dictator Porfirio Díaz is supposed to have said with a sigh. "So far from the good Lord and so near to the United States." Neighbourhood, in the relations between races, invariably means a memory of unhappy frictions, territorial pillage and assaults. Even the good neighbour policy of President Roosevelt has not been able to extinguish the memory of the Mexican war in the middle of the last century. "How can I disguise from my pupils that Texas belongs to us, that Los Angeles and San Francisco, Colorado and Nevada, are Spanish names?" argued the school teacher Romero one day when I tackled him on this subject after his lecture. In our discussion I think we put our finger on the sore spot of Mexican and Creole anti-Americanism: it is far less prevalent among the *peones* than among the educated and above all the half-educated, among teachers and journalists, down to my recent acquaintance the quack from Toluca. They have read their history books; they are filled with ambitious dreams of their own greatness and with the nagging knowledge that there is no way which could lead to their fulfilment. The unkindest cut is not that the Spanish name Los Angeles is pronounced in the American way, but that American California is a flourishing progressive land while the Mexican California Bay is only just being given roads, canals and other insignia of modern development. The inferiority complex before the camera is one of the surest yardsticks by which to measure colonial resentment. It is the fear of being stared at like some animal in the zoo, but with the mental perhaps selfish reserve that the picture will be looked upon later as a curiosity or used as an object of exploitation. Paradoxically enough this feeling has been increased rather than diminished by the positive achievements of American capital on Mexican soil and the active exchange of goods. Even as the percentage of import and export trade with their northern neighbour has risen since the last war to 80 per cent, so has the feeling of dependence only increased.

My "wetback" friend from Toluca had experiences in the United States which were not always rosy. Twice he suffered the fate of a million of his associates who stream yearly over the frontier to find work in the Texas cotton fields and the Californian orchards: an American frontier patrol seized him and sent him unceremoniously back to Mexico; but like the others he refused to be defeated and tried his luck once more. The problem of these legal and illegal harvesters invariably gives rise each year to an anti-American polemic in the Mexican newspapers with pictures of the inhuman treatment they have to suffer at the hands of the Texans. One newspaper published the story that a placard could be seen in a café in Miami which read: "Negroes, dogs and Mexicans not admitted". Another reported that Mexican workers were served with dogs' meat, marked "unfit for human consumption". The rumour only died when it was discovered that the tins came from Mexico containing magnificent meat and were only stamped in this way by a mistake on the part of the Customs authorities.

But here we must not forget that it is the intellectuals who make all this noise and not the "wetbacks" themselves, who, despite American inhumanity, still return to the north because they can earn fifteen to twenty times as much for their work as they can in their own country. I think that usually most of the reports which rail at poverty and social injustices suffer from the fact that the writer is too subjective. He reports on the fate of a coolie in Asia or an Indio in Texas as if he himself, the highly educated and well-brought-up Mr. X, had to drag a rickshaw or live in the overcrowded hut on a ranch. Admittedly among these simple men who have suffered in practice you will also find a dumb feeling of revolt. It is not however so dialectic or so ideologically concise as in the case of the intellectuals. When he possesses a natural intelligence such as my friend the "wetback" possessed he will rise above his unprivileged state and know how to avoid the repulsiveness of his companions. In short, whoever remains a victim usually has the resignation of the sacrificial beast which is always ready to rebel. but only when a clearer knowledge designates the goal—in other words, the anti-Americanism in Mexico and Latin America is by and large less a deep-rooted racial instinct—the suspicious hostility of the Indio who looks on *every* Gringo as a rogue even if he is the teacher or the grocer in his village—than a result of propaganda.

On the other hand, those people who are the most emphatic in decrying the Gringos are the most eager to absorb their way of life. Young girls walk about on the Zócalo in blue jeans and their admirers choose a baseball costume as the height of elegance. Everyone who wants to profit from the stream of American tourists must at least be able to babble a few words of broken English. This has become the leading foreign language and has

ousted French, which was introduced during the short and unhappy reign of Maximilian. Whether he be a shoeblack, a
mariachi or an engineer, English in all circumstances gives him the
greatest possibilities.

Americanization has spread so far that it has even corrupted
the Spanish language. You will eat in a *loncheria* for lunch, eat hot
dog, cake, *bisteque* and even *pay de manzana* (apple pie); drink a
coctel with friends; go to a night club in *trajés de high life* (evening
clothes) and continually reply O.K., not to mention the technical
words beginning with *troque* (truck) and *traque* (track) to "fair
play" towards your business partner. Admittedly in the spring of
1953 an attempted cleaning up of the national speech wrought a
change in the Anglo-Saxon shop signs, so that the barber's shop
is once more called *peluqueria*, the coffee shop *cafeteria* and the
dry cleaners *tintoreria*. But this too is a question of destiny which
takes a hand in everything here: one day this reform will be
forgotten and will be defeated by the more powerful natural
development.

Perhaps one can see in the outcome of Franco-Mexican
relations a kind of prophecy for the future of the Mexicano-
American relationship. France too at one time was an imperialist
arch-enemy to be driven from the land (incidentally with the
diplomatic aid of the Monroe doctrine-rattling USA). From the
cultural contact, however, which developed from this meeting of
races there is a tendency to sugar-coat even the past bitterness with
sentimentality. In this of course Paris has played an important
role, since it has become the spiritual home of the ruling classes
and a young man of good family is naturally sent to finish his
studies at the Sorbonne. In addition to this, France was the cradle
of the liberalism which in the nineteenth century under the banner
of freedom-loving humanism opposed the Spanish tradition and
with it the influence of the catholic church. Today all these functions have reverted to the United States. Europe will still be
visited and to a certain extent be regarded as a beautiful dream by
a Latin-American youth. But he will go for his studies to Harvard
and other American universities, and the popular subjects are no
longer art or literature but national economy, medicine and

science. Whether the amalgamation will take place as easily in this case as it did with the closely related artistic French tradition is a matter to be seen, particularly as the United States has never become a centre of an ideology which could arouse the enthusiasm of other races; for scientific "know-how" and progressive optimism no longer possess the slightest mystery.

Storm troops of civilization

THE little town of Patzcuaro in the heart of Michoacan State shows its preference for the conservative way of life in a curious manner. The road leading from the banks of the nearby lake to the capital is one of the most terrible on which my bones have ever been shaken. "We are anxious to preserve our colonial character," said my neighbour in the car. He seemed almost proud of this inhospitable characteristic which has a murderous effect on the visitor's tyres.

We were driving past a magnificent property and I caught a glimpse of a garden full of flowers. "That belongs to the former President Cárdenas," said my new friend as he caught my look of interest, " but he no longer lives in it. He gave the villa away and for six months it has housed a UNESCO school; teachers who will later struggle against illiteracy in their own lands are trained here from various Latin American countries. Under-nourishment and disease must be banished from the primitive populations. It is the first school of its kind in the world. The experience gained here will be put into effect in various similar centres in Asia and Africa."

I made a point of visiting La Erendira: Cárdenas called his property after the daughter of an ancient Tarasco chief. The international character of the undertaking was unmistakable. The Mexican director's secretary was an old Italian with a noble white mane, and when I asked for some information I was directed to an American lady. The deputy director, Gabriele Anzola Gómez, who finally took me round the school is a Colombian and the leading spirit of the place. He is responsible

for the education of the pupils. The Faculty is also composed of
Latin Americans. "What we strive for here," insisted Anzola, "is
of the greatest importance to our people. The same problem is to
be found from Mexico down to Bolivia—the Indians who form
the larger part of the people, and who in some States are in the
majority, live a life quite remote from modern civilization. In
the capitals you will find Ministers who have been to university
and have adopted enlightened ideas, but when they want to put
them into practice they come up against a wall of incomprehen-
sion against which their reforms come to grief. In other words,
no organized community has yet been created in any of these
countries where democratic forms could develop. This gulf
between the ruling élite and the unpolitical underlings must be
bridged if we wish to emerge from our chronic material poverty
and political tyranny."

"Wouldn't it have been a good idea," I asked, "to employ
European and American experts on your teaching staff?"

"No. It's been shown that only we Latin Americans can
accomplish fruitful work for our peoples," was the reply. "Nowhere can the difference between the mentality of the North
Americans and ourselves be seen so clearly as in an educational
task such as this. Fundamentally we have quite a different concept of happiness and, in consequence, of the aims of civilization.
We are more closely related to the Orientals, who see perfection
less in outer material progress than in spiritual formation. So, you
see, the book which has given us the greatest inspiration in our
work was written by an Oriental: *Bases for the Organization of the
Community* by the Chinese Yang Hsi-pan."

I contradicted him. "But isn't the idea to organize the un-
organized, to bring education and progress to the backward
primitives—an idea which was born intact from the active
American genius?"

"Not entirely. I can best explain by giving you an example.
When you visit the neighbouring villages you will sometimes
meet with the most appalling sanitary conditions. Most of the
inhabitants fetch their water from a spring around which the pigs
ferret in the damp earth, or they get it from the lake. Since few

of them boil it before drinking, epidemics break out every year, taking their roll of victims. Our American colleagues in such an event would study the problem seriously and eventually find the best technical solution. In this instance they would lay a pipeline at enormous cost. But we think otherwise. We build absolutely nothing unless the people themselves express a need for it, corresponding to their spiritual development. First we try to convince them that something is wrong with the water system, and then we consult with them what is the best to be done. We come to the joint conclusion that we must divert the spring or that we must dig it deeper and cover it with a well-head so that the pigs can no longer contaminate it. Do you understand? We do not wish to bring the people any progress they do not understand, and actually do not desire, except the basic amenities with which, by following our advice, they can better their lives. That is the difference between the North American and the Latin American mentality: the former strives for betterment through an external aid which is only too often inclined to be schematic and therefore threatens to be despised by those to whom it is brought because of their psychological incapacity to understand it. Our method, on the contrary, is more subjective and more organic."

During this conversation we had climbed the steps and watched the students reading their books and newspapers in the library. Next we visited the *Mirador*, a pavilion on the roof of the villa. From here my eye wandered through the glass walls over the countryside and the lake gleaming a tender blue among the light green of the meadows and the darker green of the forest. A few young art students were being taught by two painters to draw posters which had something to do with the work in the school— sanitary notices or invitations to a match with the local youth sports group.

"We have a very wide field to draw from here," said my companion. "Over there, in the middle of the lake, you can see Canicio Island with the colossal statute of the revolutionary Morelos. It is almost exclusively inhabited by fishermen, but you will also find purely agricultural communities, some primitive, some progressive. Elsewhere special handicrafts like hat-making have developed. In each village different problems arise and in each case we proceed in a different manner. We number fifty-two pupils and these are split into ten groups and distributed to certain villages. Each of the five members of such a group has a different task. The first specializes in problems of hygiene, the second in agriculture. Domestic science is usually in the hands of a female pupil, while the teaching of elementary knowledge and recreation is entrusted to students of both sexes."

The feast of the dead

ON the morning of October 31st we got up early at six o'clock and made our way to the landing stage. It was dark when we put to sea and we could see nothing for the mist. Our boatman was inexperienced and wandered aimlessly round in the grey fog. We had got up at this early hour because we did not want to miss the beginning of the famous duck shoot which takes place every year two days before the Feast of the Dead. We were afraid we should miss this experience. Our boat ran aground and we had to enter the ice-cold water to get her afloat again. After some delay a few Indian canoes loomed out of the mist to our right. The men rowed with their round paddles as peacefully and sure of their goal as if the brightest sun had been shining. Heaven knows how they managed to find their direction. I called out to them. Yes, they too were on their way to the duck shoot. We found it wiser to renounce the speed of our motor boat and to follow slowly in the wake of the fishermen.

Gradually the mist lifted and an astounding sight met our eyes. Canoes small and large hastened from all sides, making their way to the north-eastern end of the lake. As far as the eye could see they glided cautiously over the wide watery expanse. In front of us, where the shore was now visible, the water was black with myriads of wild duck. The flotilla of fishermen had slowly driven them into this bay. The circle gradually closed and suddenly the hunt was on. The first oarsman stood up in his canoe and seized a

four-pointed bamboo spear from the pile which lay in the bows.
He put it in his bow for better purchase and shot the spear with
all his might at the nearest wild·duck. In terror the bird rose un-
wounded into the air. It did not remain long aloft and fluttered
down slowly into a safer element, but of course there was no
security among this host of canoes. Wherever a duck settled the
paddles cleaved the water and the boatman reached for his spear.
The bird could seek salvation in the air or dive, but ultimately its
strength waned and its enemies were sure in their aim. Occasionally they managed to hit the bird in the air. Whoever had brought
it down rowed swiftly over to it and wrung its neck. With these
primitive bamboo spears the hunt took on the character of an
exciting natural spectacle, and the superiority of man had something of the guileless beauty of the beast of prey.

The massacre went on until midday. Not a single bird which
had been driven into the bay managed to escape. Mountains of
them lay piled up in the boats and some of the hunters could
boast of a bag of between forty and fifty wild duck. For once at
least the unassuming Indian bellies would be filled to bursting-
point with meat.

When we returned to the main square of Patzcuaro we found
that it had undergone a macabre transformation. Tables had been
laid under the arcades, decorated with strange and remarkable
figures. Friendly grinning skeletons of icing sugar stood in groups
apparently in regal conversation. The skulls, too, decorated with
names and mottoes, were utterly lacking in horror. Here and
there between baskets of flowers recurred a mysterious character.
I recognized her immediately as Coatlicue, the Aztec Ceres, the
spirit of the earth in which the dead repose. She leered in pagan
triumph on the Christian All Souls Day, but she did not manage
to disturb the pleasure of mothers and children who wandered
serenely between these images of death. Every Juan chose a skull
for himself with the appropriate name on it and every Elena
followed suit. Each idolized the image of his own transitoriness
both spiritually and physically, for since the death's head was
made of sugar it disappeared immediately into the living belly of
its owner. Even the mother of the gods could not protect herself

from the general gluttony. Life triumphed in an amazing fashion over all the insignia of death.

My professional duties obliged me to take photographs and to use a flashlight which had irritated many of my previous spectators. I hesitated each time before taking a picture and made my apologies. But now something very strange occurred. They did not find my intrusion in the least disturbing. On the contrary, I found myself immediately surrounded by small youngsters who waited for the flash like hungry birds and leaped upon the burnt-out bulbs. Or one of the mothers held out her hand imploringly because she would like one of the lamps for her children. I soon forgot my shyness. A spirit of boundless gaiety reigned which simply could not be broken. One spent a single night in the graveyard and there was nothing more to it.

The brown goddess

ANYONE who wishes to enjoy to the full the fiesta of the Holy Virgin of Guadalupe is well advised not to go to bed on the 11th of December. At midnight you take the bus to her basilica a few miles outside the town, or even better you follow the example of many pious Mexicans and make the pilgrimage on foot through the streets by night.

It is impossible to lose your way. A deafening din greets you on the church square. No prayers. Hundreds of electric organs are playing, but there is no choral singing. It is a real annual fair with entertainment booths of all kinds, with big wheels, great dippers, ghost railways and roundabouts. You make your way between the booths where you can buy every kind of sacred and profane object—rosaries, candles, pictures of the Mother of God, little arms, bones and eyeballs made of silver as gifts for the miracle workers, but also shirts, aprons, cooking utensils, chamber pots, etc. You can appease your hunger with a cake made in the shape of the Holy Virgin. And above all you must not forget to press close to the weakly lit façade which towers in front of you out of

the darkness. Unless you elbow your way through you cannot
reach it, so great is the crowd that comes from all parts of the
country to celebrate the *fiesta* of this national saint.

Who was she then? We can learn from a fabulous legend.
On Diego's historical murals we have already seen the fanatical
archbishop Zumarraga consigning the holy books of the Aztecs to
the flames. This vandal did the same to all the heathen images and
temples he could lay his hands on. But there were gods and
goddesses who proved themselves to be mightier than this praiseworthy upholder of the faith. On Tepeyac Hill outside the capital
stands the shrine of Tonantzin, a mild counterpart of the gruesome
Coatlicue. She was not the Earth Mother but the "Little Earth
Mother" in the form of the gentle Virgin Mary. Although her
outward resemblance to the Mother of God did not appease the
Archbishop, the touching analogy deeply impressed the spirit of
Juan Diego, the hero of the legend (the ingenious priest who
invented it). Three times in succession as he crossed the sacred hill
he received a heavenly vision of the Virgin, but she was a Madonna
such as the earth had never before seen. She wore the homely
features of the Earth Mother Tonantzin and had only changed her
superficial garb. It is easy to understand that the Archbishop would have nothing to do with such a diabolical idol. But
on December 12th, which is still today the Feast of Guadalupe,
occurred the miracle of the roses blooming from the naked rock.
The simple peasant took this as a welcome sign, that the Blessed
One had countenanced his downfall: even the grim Zumarraga
had to change his mind when Diego produced his flowers and the
wonderful image of the brown Indian goddess. A most dangerous
situation arose. The Indios had their "Little Earth Mother"
again and the missionaries, with a self-satisfied smirk, diverted the
pilgrims to holy Tepeyac to bring grist to their Christian mill.

At last the crowd entered the church. In front, on the high
altar, the Virgin gleamed in her almond-shaped glory, the tender
dreamy face bent slightly forward. The mob pressed forward to
the altar rails. The believers fell to their knees, but only for an
instant, for thousands pushed them from behind: a word, a single
syllable of the *Ave*, and the man with the Red Cross arm band

told them to get up and move on. Only a very few lucky people could kneel in peace at the rails, although they were perhaps the least deserving—the drunkards. Outside on the *playa* the alcohol flowed freely and bottles were smashed over many a pate. The Red Cross men are a pious guard who know the respect due to this holy spot. They bind up bloody heads with gauze, carry them into the church and dump them in a kneeling position in front of the altar rails. They are praying! It is a particularly brutal sight. It is also questionable if the men kneeling there are capable of any ardent piety. But it makes little difference: the man has knelt and the Red Cross men have done their duty.

It is five o'clock. Suddenly the human stream comes to a standstill and is frozen into a sea of expectation. Half a dozen men accompanied by musicians have reached the altar steps, and suddenly the violins and the flutes ring out and the men begin to sing.

Young men who in their daily lives are only ordinary *mariachis* and street singers wear a deep, ardent look on their faces. They sing as sweetly as angels. From beneath the mighty vaulting of the church the song echoes in the ears of thousands of simple Indios who live in adobe huts and till the land.

Hardly has the sun tinged with its bright colours the jewelled tiles of the chapel where the healing water from the Virgin's footprints bubbles than another pagan performance begins in the playa, the dance of the *Concheros*.

The Concheros are a kind of Indian freemasons, a strict organized body: membership is hereditary and often goes back to a vow. The ceremonial initiation is bound up with the acceptance of a strong moral code according to which the members promise mutual aid in sickness, death, or material misfortune, and furthermore respect for every stranger. Whoever fails in his duty is punished with the whip. The number of Concheros on the Altiplano is estimated at about 50,000. These are split into groups of between fifty and one hundred, making a so-called "Table". On the road they march in military formation and only the leader, disguised as a devil, whose duty it is to scare the gapers out of the way, can sport around them as he pleases.

The processional flags with pictures of Christ and all the saints waving above their feathered headdresses look magnificent here on the plaza. What a gay masquerade! Indians dressed as Indians .... Their costumes glitter in every colour with a preference for purple, and when they circle in their dance a host of ribbons flutter in the wind. Bells are attached to their feet which tinkle as they move, as though they were jesters. These dances are as simple as the men themselves and as ingenuous as their faith. The leader takes his lute, strikes the first chord, and all the others tune in with their instruments. The melody rings out in a single rhythmic unison alternately rising and falling. This dance has no other significance than the community, which finds expression in the ritual. Small hops with sidesteps, forwards and backwards, an occasional bending of the knees, a turn, a leap which ends on the toes—that is the dance of the Concheros. When the music reaches a crescendo the movements become more ecstatic. When no further speed and no louder fortissimo seems possible they suddenly fall silent to the drone of lutes and the feet seem to be nailed to the ground. The dance peters out, but after a few seconds it begins again as before without variations.

A modern dance group a little apart has some idea of choreography and a recognizable pattern: it draws a large crowd of spectators. This represents a circle of young townspeople who have taken upon themselves the task of instilling some new life into the ancient Aztec war dances. Their heroes appear dressed in extravagant costumes, attack each other with naked swords, and the dance ends with victory and defeat.

The sun rises to its zenith and beats down fiercely on the plaza. The dance goes on—monotonous, never-ending. Slowly, it growls like a distant thunderstorm and suddenly falls silent. The sweat pours down the faces of the dancers and of course invisibly beneath the glittering costumes. Never in my life have I smelt such an appalling stench as at the sweating feast into which this pious dance is transformed in the rising heat. I considered it prudent to take my nose somewhere else.

Christian paganism; pagan Christianity

I COULD not help smiling slightly to myself as I returned to the city. Something had gone very much amiss with the Christianity of this feast. Who had cheated whom? Had the missionaries hoodwinked the Indians or vice versa? Had not the good Dominicans and Franciscans of the Conquest irresponsibly garbed the old heathen gods and customs in a Christian robe in an effort to send home figures of the largest possible number of conversions? Following to a certain extent in the footsteps of the old magicians, they themselves became impregnated with these magic spirits whether they wished it or not. They believed that they were serving the heavenly Virgin and yet in the eyes of their flock and in fact—since ultimately the community determined the content and meaning of religion—they were the priests of the "Little Earth Mother". Could such a rift remain without consequences? Must not the cleric either have become involved in the pagan magistracy, generally ascribed to him, or have taken refuge in a dishonest mental reservation in which he alone protected the true ritual without bothering his head as to what particular interpretation his flock gave to it. On the other hand, it is unquestionable that the extraordinary strength the church has shown after a whole century of hostility and persecution can be traced back to the fact that it was deep-rooted in the ancient superstitions. Magic is the heart's blood of religion: the richer it throbs in the rites the more indestructible does it prove against the sharp sword of rational common sense. While the priests degenerated into magicians the intellectuals began to protest against clerical obscurantism. But this very characteristic made the Indians protect the priests when in the twenties President Calles tried to instigate a blood persecution. They protected their priest from the persecution of the police spies because they looked upon him as the servant of their gods. Catholicism had to a certain extent taken refuge in the garment of paganism and was thus able to resist the new European missionaries with their humanistic liberalism in the same way as the ancient Aztec belief once outwitted the zealous monks.

One of the most remarkable examples of the secret resistance of the catholic faith is the Convent of Santa Monica in Puebla. President Benito Juárez, who from a monastery novice became one of the great liberal figures of the world, did not rob the church with his reform laws of 1857, although it owned more than half the cultivated land. He merely dissolved the Orders and ordered their members to return into the world. With a radicalism which can only be justified by the danger of his opponents he banned street processions and forbade the priests to wear their *soutanes* in public. As I have already mentioned, this happened in 1857. In 1934, however, an anonymous denunciation fell into the hands of the Puebla police stating that for years a convent had continued to exist secretly and illegally at Calle 18 Poniente No. 103. The chief of police shook his head. Opposite the address stood the prison and its entrance swarmed with police. Had his men no eyes in their heads? He sent a squad of detectives to the house in question, arrested and interrogated an innocent family, the inhabitants of a perfectly harmless dwelling. They found nothing. Then one of the detectives accidentally knocked over a flower vase, which fell to the ground, spilling all the water. The culprit noticed a bell and pulled it, expecting to see a servant appear, when, lo and behold! a panel slid open in the niche which the flower vase had hidden, and the face of a nun peered out at the detective. He had unwittingly discovered one of the masked entrances to the convent. Today it has been transformed into a museum and is one of the great attractions of Puebla. Behind the secret entrance you enter the cell of the Mother Superior, who in person acted as a watch-dog at the door which led to worldliness. A statue of the pious Santo Domingo de Guzmán raises a conspiratorial finger to his lips: Be silent! Now you have to crawl on all fours through a kind of kennel in order to reach the chapel. Here on the walls hang the attributes of the martyred Christ beneath which the nuns sought to imitate his Passion: a cross on His shoulders, a rope round His neck and a crown of thorns in His hair. It is a harmless fragile crown of thorns hardly capable of tearing the flesh of the forehead. But anyone who thinks that this was merely a symbol of the will to suffer is mistaken. The visitor to the Mother Superior's cell will shudder at the sight of the heavy chains with which the tender nuns flagellated their flesh. As our party descended the dark steps to the cells a susceptible girl began to sob in terror. There in the darkness were hanging the straps with which the nuns had flogged the last vestiges of lust from their bodies. And opposite knelt the wax image of a nun on the day of taking the veil, a black hair shirt covering her naked body facing a crucified Christ and a pale skull. . . . This symbol of the transitory would in future be her constant companion: and Perfection at the end of the corridor beneath a coverlet of roses smiled down at her. Whoever entered this house never left it again. Even the corpses were buried in a cellar.

For almost eighty years this nunnery remained hidden and young novices disappeared into it in some mysterious fashion. Despite the secret door, it was an achievement that would be quite impossible in our gossip-loving Europe. But the art of silence is part of the Indians' inheritance.

Oaxaca, further to the south, is the fortress of anticlerical liberalism. Juárez and also the capitalist dictator Porfirio Díaz came from this part of the country. One must climb up to the ruins of Monte Alban to understand the existence of the Zapotecs who lived there. They built a city of palaces and temples, high above the plain, built it with such unfettered architectural obstinacy that they altered the natural shape of the mountain in order to have a superb view. The result is a spatial symphony the measured harmony of which can only be appreciated when one enjoys the infinity of the surrounding mountains.

I was talking to the editor of the local newspaper when a very well-dressed man came into the room. He wore a smartly cut suit of olive-green homespun and kept glancing at a magnificent gold wristwatch. Outside the window I could see a very expensive limousine. "I tell you," he said excitedly, "the Christmas gifts were simply magnificent—wonderful. The Governor's wife . . . quite delightful. How charming she was with the simple people. I tell you. . . ." I observed the visitor closely and wondered to what class he belonged. He must be a politician or a speculator, I thought. "Oh, I forgot to introduce you, gentlemen," said the editor. "This is Father Damian."

I met the Father next day in his office and found him to be a highly cultured man of the world. He laughed when I asked him the reason for his worldly appearance. This, I learned, was the style of the *avant-garde* of the priesthood. Their elders, who had suffered greatly from the persecution of the twenties tried to out-wit the ban of the *soutane* by wearing a kind of black clerical costume which made them look rather like North American missionaries. They continued to moan about the evils of the world and the persecution the church had suffered at the hands of politicians. But why fight with the politicians? Was it not better to make friends with them and gain influence in this way? Father Damian did precisely this. He was *persona grata* at the Governor's house and anti-clerical Oaxaca suffered the same experience as the rest of the country—the whole anti-clerical laws held good only on paper. No politician so far has dared to meddle with the sacred traditions of the reform and the revolution. But no one raises a bleat at the fact that seminaries continue to flourish in all the cities, that nuns tend the sick in their own hospitals—everything in fact that was forbidden. You must not expect logic from a Mexican. Did not the President himself that very same week donate 50,000 pesos for the building of a new masonic lodge and send his own daughter to be brought up in the Sacré Coeur Jesuit College in Quebec? Gradually the holy images have shown again their faces in the street processions. No, the whole anti-clerical legislation is a scrap of paper and the power of the church is constantly on the increase. Was not Father Damian a striking example of the successful illegality of church work? Not only did he console his flock: this very newspaper office was the headquarters of an educational and commercial school which he had founded and run since its inception. It gave forty pupils a two-years course of typing, book-keeping, English and other useful subjects for a ludicrous fee—the obligatory attendance at Mass and at Christian morality classes.

Nowhere in Latin America has the church suffered such ordeals as in Mexico and nowhere today is it so modern and so active.

The age-old law entailing ordeal and suffering has endured in its
finest form. Its return not only into social life but also into
politics was due to the Cardinal Archbishop, who was well
documented on all the questions at issue. He insisted upon
visiting the President in his ecclesiastical robes. When the new
President Cortines appointed Goméz Robleda, a notorious fellow
traveller, to be his Minister of Education, the Church after a
century of retirement became active once more in the political
arena, not merely on the defensive but militant. In the schools
pupils were still taught from books which had been written in the
spirit of the old anti-clerical and revolutionary ideals, describing
the landowners and the priests as enemies of society whose
liquidation was the order of the day. The struggle was short and
bitter, ending in a complete triumph for the Church. An ecclesiastical Commission read a number of textbooks and in December
1953 published a list of those which no longer conformed to the
spirit of the country. Goméz Robleda had previously been forced
to hand in his resignation.

The faithful prison

AT some stage in prehistoric times the mountain chain
which runs from the highlands of Mexico through the
whole of Central America as far as Nicaragua was torn
and smashed by some telluric upheaval. Thus today the road from
Oaxaca descends steeply into the depths through giant cactuses
which stand on the slopes like candles on a birthday cake, until it
emerges at sea level in the plain of the so-called Isthmus of
Tehuantepec. This isthmus is famous for two things. Firstly, the
most beautiful women in Mexico are supposed to live there; and
secondly, for a long time the rulers were absorbed in a plan for
trying to open up communications between the Atlantic and the
Pacific. From Cortés to the Regent Bucareli and Alexander von
Humboldt, great men's lust for enterprise has always conceived
new projects. In 1869, when the Suez Canal dream became reality,
these new ideas sprouted like weeds. A canal, a tunnel, a three-

track railway capable of carrying steamships—nothing remained undiscussed. But since any idea of a canal was out of the question on account of lack of water, towards the end of the last century an English firm was given the contract to build a railway. It was constructed in 1907 and functioned perfectly until 1914, when the Panama Canal was opened. From this moment it drifted slowly towards bankruptcy and was impounded by the State under Cárdenas in 1937. Since then it has reached the peak of efficiency. When you enquire at a station the time the train leaves for the Guatemalan frontier the official will shrug his shoulders. Theoretically at such and such an hour, but in practice no man can say. The train may be one hour, six hours or even ten hours late. The only thing to do is to follow the example of the Indians; to sit on your rump and wait until the monster comes puffing along. It is possible of course that one of these trains by some miracle arrives dead on time—in this case it is exactly twenty-four hours late!

As regard the beautiful women, plumpness is the ideal here. One day I was being served in a small restaurant in Juchitán by the very pretty and graceful daughter of the house who one day had caught sight of my correspondence which bore the title of Doctor. She came over to me shyly with an ampoule in her hand. Since I was a doctor would I give her an injection? I did not mention that my title was Doctor of Philosophy and not of Medicine, and asked with curiosity why should such a healthy pretty girl be in need of an injection. She sighed. Her *novio*, she declared, would not marry her until she had put on weight. Everyone had told her that to be as slim as she was was a symptom of ill health, and so, on the advice of a girl friend, she had bought this ampoule although she did not quite know the effect of its contents. I sent for the *novio*, put on my sternest expression and gave him my diagnosis. The best possible remedy for putting on weight in the case of women was marriage. He should not therefore delay any longer. The boy was obviously impressed and I hope that he took my advice.

Incidentally it is not particularly easy to catch a glimpse of these famous beauties. The whole day long a hideous wind blows across the isthmus, and hardly have you spotted a peach than the sand gets in your eyes. It is a great deterrent, and most visitors who have dreamed of spending a few pleasant hours with a black-haired Tehuana soon abandon the idea. This anti-erotic climate is even more unfortunate since the women of the isthmus rather fancy foreigners. Innumerable races have passed through here on military expeditions and by rail—Spaniards, Frenchmen, Americans, Irishmen, Arabs, Chinese and Russians, not to mention negroes: all of them have left behind certain biological traces. The Tehuana is a very independent creature who knows exactly what she wants. She is incredibly vain and spends a fortune on clothes. This has one happy result: these women, in order to gratify their whims, have to work. In all the cities of the isthmus you see the same sight: women, nothing but women in their embroidered blouses with the geometrical patterns. They deal in pottery, fruit, hens, brooms, anything that the country produces. They are very experienced traders and their men work and sweat in the fields. In the evening at dusk they return home slowly in their creaking carts, with a goad in their hands to drive their oxen. Then the Tehuana returns to the marital yoke and the market-place is deserted.

In Juchitán I landed quite unexpectedly in gaol, fortunately of my own free will, but all the same unexpectedly. As I wandered round the market-place looking at the bright-coloured scene I suddenly noticed a beautifully dressed girl. Her blouse was embroidered with gay roses and her features, framed in a broad lace collar, were those of a great lady straight out of the Renaissance. She appeared with two girl friends who were equally beautiful and made her way through the crowd like a vision from some other world. Out of curiosity I tried to pick her up, but she suddenly disappeared into a dark doorway. I followed her boldly. But what was this? A guard stood there with a loaded rifle and behind him a door with iron bars. With an embarrassed greeting I slipped past the cerberus without being molested. A broad staircase led to an upper arcaded gallery where a host of men were sitting and standing. The beautiful girl had disappeared into a room above whose door I could read the words Registrar's Office. I could only see her through the half-opened door and

fortunately ran into her bridegroom who had turned up a little
late. Yes, he was getting married in the modern way, he told me
proudly. What did he mean by the modern way? The traditional
courtship is a highly complicated and burdensome affair which
costs a great deal of money and often ends with a refusal on the
part of the girl's strict parents. This was bound up with the painful custom of the girl having to show proof of her virginity to
the guests present on her marriage night. Taking into account the
passionate ardour of the Tehuanas, the girl could usually cheat by
making her nose bleed. Now the young people had opted for a
much cheaper and more simple method of marriage. You eloped
with the bride—of course only if she agreed. A man disappeared
quite simply for a while with her and then presented the parents
with a *fait accompli*. Thus the Renaissance lady behind the door
had been his wife for some weeks and the ceremony was just
about to take place.

While we gossiped together we leant over the balustrade of the
gallery and my eyes fell on the courtyard below. It was an idyllic
picture. Scores of men were lying at rest in the shade. Some of
them were busy weaving straw into bright-coloured mats or
baskets; others played with excitable children or embraced their
wives who had come through the iron-barred door with full
market baskets. That was the prison, the bridegroom told me.

I found it delightful that the gaol should be in the vicinity of
the Registry Office. In this way the poor rogues had a constant
view of happy respectable people. The latter on the threshold of
so important an event in their lives were thereby warned not to
stray along dangerous paths.

The prison did not look in the least terrifying. I asked the grim
warder through the Judas grille to let me in, and he agreed with
the greatest cordiality. A foreign visitor to the prison! It was a
sensation for the inmates. They let fall their work and I was soon
surrounded by a crowd of murderers. They were nearly all
murderers and only here and there, when I began to chat and ask
questions, did I find an occasional unfortunate thief among this
noble company. I have never in my life seen such amiable
murderers: most of them looked as though they would not have

harmed a fly. Actually my pleasant impression was fully corroborated by the men themselves. They were all innocent and they were only in custody thanks to the malice of their neighbours. One little railroad worker with the face of a cat had been sitting peacefully drinking his beer when a false friend rushed at him with a loaded revolver and informed him that the Government had ordered him to kill him. The threatened man had knelt down before him and begged for mercy in the name of their friendship. When the other man remained deaf to his entreaties was it so surprising that his own knife was quicker than the revolver? Now he was inside for thirteen years. The railway had granted him ten years' leave hoping that by then he would be released for good behaviour. A pale, haggard young man over there had been involved in a cheerful brawl in which one of his drinking companions had been left dead in the road. He had been arrested with all the others. The real murderers bribed the judge with 2,000 pesos and were released. The poor devil was now serving a twelve-year sentence. He was an extraordinarily striking figure. He had built a roof over his head of straw and slats which allowed him to work even in the midday heat. His nervous movements betrayed an inner tension as if he were determined to hide and suppress a bitter memory. I could tell a dozen stories of these hair-raising injustices. The prison of Juchitán was a world turned topsy-turvy: the pleasantest and most honest people sat here behind bars while outside the real rogues ran around at liberty or sat in high office.

Naturally my credulity began to wane. So many miscarriages of justice were hardly possible even had the judge been the devil personified. One of the men whose story I learned from the bridegroom in the upper gallery was really innocent and had been confined here for interrogation for many years by his political enemies. The mills of Mexican justice grind slowly. Actually Don Adolfo caught my eye at once on account of his respectable appearance and perfect manners. He owned a large farm and was the President of the Sugar Planters' Union. One day the Alcalde, with whom he was on bad terms, died from the bullet of a murderer who was duly shot while being chased by the police.

He was shot deliberately in order to conceal the truth, Don Adolfo told me. He himself was then accused by his enemies of inciting the other man to the crime, because his pistol was discovered on the dead man.

The dubious case of Don Adolfo was now taken by all the miscreants in the courtyard of Juchitán as a proof of the corruption of Mexican justice. They were all innocent lambs like him, the victims of some dark enemy conspiracy. Were they lying? During these interminable days and nights of confinement had they invented a story which they themselves now really believed? Almost all of them had committed their crimes in a state of drunkenness. Alcohol was the terrible power which had laid its hand on these unhappy creatures.

Now they were imprisoned in the picturesque arcades of this beautiful old house. The courtyard was to be their home for ten, twenty or thirty years. That was all the State gave them—living space and a jug of water daily. They had to earn their keep or, as in the case of Don Adolfo, let their families look after them. Their meals were put through a hole in the wall by the market women from the square. The work too was privately organized. A murderer serving a sentence of thirty years—the only one who seemed to me to bear the sign of Cain on his forehead—acted as a capitalist. He provided his fellow prisoners with coloured straw, found a market for their wares, taking half the proceeds of the sale. He was a vital, busy man who should obviously have been working at some handicraft. He kept walking up and down like a panther and calling to the brides through the door. As soon as I entered he rushed up to me to relieve his boredom and offered himself as guide. He took me into the dormitory, a shady room at the back of the pound. A little lamp burned faintly before an altar. Above it was painted the tariff newcomers had to pay for lodging, in accordance with the seriousness of the crime: a murderer fifteen pesos, a cheat ten pesos, a drunkard only eight pesos. I did not stay long in the room. It was visiting day for the wives, and in Mexican prisons this did not merely mean platonic conversation. At the foot of the altar a couple were making love in the half light: I did not want to disturb them. A straw puppet

which the prisoners had made for the New Year's celebrations
grinned down discreetly on their activities.

New Year's Eve in Chiapas

THE morning sun was beginning to tinge the hilltops as
we hurried forward on horseback through the mist. Our
hands and feet were frozen and our breath steamed.
Gertrude spurred her horse forward and I followed close behind
her, when suddenly the road curved and automatically we came
to a stop. I turned to an American colleague who had ridden up
and said: "Don't you feel that at any moment Cecil B. de Mille
will take up his megaphone and shout 'Ready, take'?"
The scene could have been a shot from a gigantic Hollywood
historical film and yet it was reality without a trace of theatre.
Before us lay a grassy plain, snow-white beneath the hoar frost.
An enormous crowd dressed in short white trousers, black ponchos
and huge flat hats with thick red fringes had gathered on this
meadow. They had tied their sticks up in bundles and were now
seated round the crosses which served as markers. They did not
seem to feel the cold, which made us shiver, although their legs
were bare. Their feet were encased in leather sandals of exactly
the same type I had seen on the carvings of Palenque. Nothing
betrayed the fact that we were in the twentieth century. We
seemed to have gone back centuries in time.
For months Gertrude Duby had implored me to leave tourist-
haunted Central Mexico and to visit her in San Cristóbal de las
Casas. When not exploring the primeval forest for buried Maya
cities with her husband, the Danish scholar Franz Blom, she lived
on the outskirts of the city in a beautful old house, the Casa del
Jaguar, which she had turned into a museum for their treasures.
Chiapas, the southernmost and almost forgotten State of Mexico,
had become a real home for this astonishing woman who, despite
her grey hair, could still sit in the saddle for twenty hours at a
stretch without getting tired, and who for weeks on end, far from
all civilization, would hack her way through the jungle with a

knife. Here she found everything she loved so passionately and on its account had cheerfully given up all the comforts of Europe. Even the Conquest left no traces on these Indians, and modern civilization is only just beginning to build roads through this lonely mountainous region. The Tzotzil and Tzeltal Indians still live dispersed in their hamlets on pine-covered hills; they are ruled by their own authorities and are only in contact with the central official departments through a white *ladino* who acts as community secretary. These *autoridades* are replaced every year and we were to witness this performance on New Year's Eve.

A path suddenly opened in the teeming mob and a troop of young boys ran in. They advanced about ten paces, suddenly turned about and knelt down in two ranks with their staffs out-stretched. A few dignified men strode gravely behind them and the kneeling youths began to cry in chorus. I could not understand a word of their speech, but their cry was translated for me: "Come Little Father, come Little Mother. The day has come for us to elect the new officials. God has been clement to us during the past year since no ill luck has befallen us. Now we will hand over the staff and take the oath." Hardly had their speech ended than they sprang up, advanced another ten paces and repeated their cry on their knees. As soon as the worthy men reached the door of the church, its white walls bathed in the morning sun, then they turned their heads in the direction of the altar. Helpers at their sides removed their hats—for the gravity of the moment forbade these new wielders of the power to make such a profane gesture—and they lowered their faces for a moment in prayer. Then there was more running, kneeling, crying and leaping up until they reached the homely open space where the retiring officials waited for them, took their oath and handed over the silver inlaid staffs of power. The Chamula community totals seventy-six hamlets: seventy-six times the performance of reception and the oath-taking in the community house was repeated. No stranger was allowed to enter and watch the ceremonial business. No white man could even enter the church. When in ignorance I stepped forward over the odorous pine needles towards the devout men kneeling in the half light before the pictures of the Saint and the lighted candles on the ground, the sacristan came up to me and in a friendly tone requested me to leave the church. The reason for this exclusivity lies in the long tradition of exploitation and cheating which these Indians have suffered at the hands of the white man. Even today the hucksters try to take advantage of San Cristóbal's ingenuousness in order to cheat them. This unfortunate experience has left a deep distrust almost approaching hostility in the minds of these brown men. They have difficulty in overcoming it. The Chamulas therefore greet with suspicion everything which comes from the *ladinos*—even the well-meaning attempt on the part of the government to present them with a road, a hospital and schools. And yet things are developing here exactly as on Lake Patzcuaro: today, where the Pan American highway has opened the region to international traffic, no idyllic and isolated existence is possible. If these unaffected races are to participate not only in the vices but in the virtues of civilization, the benefits of the modern age must be brought to them when necessary with kid gloves. In 1948 in Mexico City a native Institute was created under the direction of the well-known anthropologist Alfonso Caso: it has only recently opened its first practical centre in Chiapas.

On the following day I rode once more with Tapas, a young Yucateco who works at the new branch, among the straw-roofed Chamula hamlets—this time to visit a school. The Institute has begun its work with great intelligence. Adopting the premise that it should accept the Indian mistrust for the white men, it found an original solution to get round this most dangerous resistance. A young man from the most important family was enticed from each village to San Cristóbal, where he was given a course in reading and writing, certain elementary knowledge of agriculture, and taught the rudiments of medicine. Then the new expert was sent back to his village as a government employee: his first pupils soon assembled in his hut. In the curriculum, too, caution had been learnt from earlier experiences. Young brains had been overtaxed by making them learn the alphabet from a Spanish grammar, thus making an unfamiliar language doubly difficult. An American philologist who had studied the native dialects for many years produced grammars in the Tzotzil and Tzeltal tongues. When Tapas and I dismounted in the first village we could hear small Indian voices chanting the alphabet. A modern pedagogue would have found his hair standing on end had he seen the cramming that went on here, but the enthusiasm with which the young folk kept repeating the same syllables could not help arousing the sympathy of the visitor. "It is a common error," Tapas said to me on the ride home, "to believe that the Indio has fallen into a state of abject passivity and cannot lead a modern existence. If he is treated in the right way he is exceedingly keen on acquiring knowledge."

On the return journey our horses shied at a yawning grave in the red soil which presumably had been washed open during the last rainy season. "That is another problem we must look into," said Tapas, "the loss of our soil. Although there is a law forbidding the cutting down of living trees, the Indios ignore it. When they require a new maize field they simply set light to the forest as they have done for hundreds of years, and when they want to sell firewood they cut them down. As a result of this crime you see these red wounds everywhere in the green of the landscape. The remote Institute in the State of Michoacan is already concentrating on another project. There you found mighty forests which are being irresponsibly exploited by the local Indians. Untold wealth is lost in this way. To retrieve the wood we are thinking of building a paper mill in that district with foreign workers at first, but with the idea of eventually teaching the Indians. Before this happens there is a great deal of educational ground to be broken. Otherwise there is a danger that the inexperienced and uneducated people like those in the oil centres will spend their very high wages in the *cantinas* and the brothels. The third great plan of the native Institute is the transfer of no less than 300,000 Indians from the State of Oaxaca. Here the barren mountains are very thickly populated by unhappy, constantly famished men who earn a needy living from weaving, while below on the coast the most magnificent land is almost uninhabited and overgrown with jungle. This could easily be cleared and scoured of dangerous diseases and those who are dying of hunger today could become prosperous peasants. All that is required is money and more money. You can imagine what all that would cost. The displacement of 300,000 men."

The Institute has also successfully begun to halt the decline in traditional folk art. The artistic sense instead of being diverted into mass-produced goods is, on the contrary, to be carried to civilized centres to embellish the existence of the town dwellers. In this way it is hoped to achieve a unity of race consciousness of which Anzola spoke to me at Patzcuaro: on the one hand through a civilization of the Indians and on the other hand through the Indianizing of the town-born half-breed. The Institute has opened a showroom on one of the largest business streets in the centre of Mexico City, the *Artes Populares y Industriales,* where Indian handiwork is on sale at modest prices not only for foreign tourists but also for the natives. Many an Indio who in the old days only made his works of art to while away his leisure hours after working on the land now sees the possibility of earning extra money from his hobby. On the other hand, the *Artes Populares* flourishes so that dangerous influences and breaches of taste may be eliminated. The native workers are encouraged to give up using aniline dyes which had already found a ready market among them and to return to their old mineral and vegetable extracts. Admittedly this has made their wares more expensive, but even if the cheap industrial goods were threatened it served to create an amateur market for artistic folk-lore objects. Obviously the old conditions are gone when the people created beautiful things without knowing that they were works of art. But after they were turned out of this paradise the museum and commercial trusteeship was the best solution against degeneration of their art.

GUATEMALA

The good old times are dying

NO, I did not care for his face at all. What cold eyes.
How hateful and gruesome he was even to himself.
So this was Pedro de Alvarado, Cortés' boon-companion,
the eternal restless spirit. Through luck and treachery he was
victorious in Guatemala and was rewarded by his King with the
rulership of the Gran Capitania which stretched southwards as
far as Honduras. But this did not satisfy him. His restlessness drove
him to Ecuador, in order to contest the fruitless pursuit of Inca
gold with Pizarro. How could Guatemala satisfy such an adventurer? Pedro Alvarado never achieved the position which could
have gratified his greed. He died an almost necessary death on a
new expedition.

I stood in the Casa del Capuchino in the ancient capital,
Antigua—a ruined city. How tragic is the history of this country!
These walls were not even standing when Pedro's wife, Beatrice
de la Cueva, became mistress of the impoverished land. In those
days the capital—the original capital—stood on the slopes of the
Agua volcano which still hangs like a threat over the city. But
one day the mountain began to spew. A crater lake burst
through a chasm in the depths and drowned the capital together
with the Conquistador's widow. From the ruins rose a second
Antigua, more magnificent than any other capital in the world.
The rulers proud men, scions of the Andalusian aristocracy who
enjoyed a patriarchal life. Even greedier robbers, the Basques
and Catalans, flung themselves on the gold and silver of Mexico,
but Guatemala became a feudal domain. The art of living and
refinement ruled there.

Then came the second catastrophe. An earthquake in 1783
reduced the city to ashes. Madrid ordered that it should be abandoned. A third capital was built, the present-day Guatemala City

which lies apparently outside the earthquake belt. But the tragic soil preserved its own people; the noble familes remained in Antigua. The splendour of the churches was never restored and the visitor today is astonished by their ruins. Under the broken arches of proud Jesuit churches the Indians, more brightly dressed than in any other country, crouch, selling their market produce in the open market. Antigua still lives in a forgotten dream, but it lives on.

In Antigua I was the guest of Don Eduardo, the descendant of an old house dating from the Conquistadores. He was one of the largest coffee planters in the neighbourhood. His plantation covered the whole mountain and, as is customary here, lay in the shade of a wood. The trees were tall and stately. We strolled over the slopes and watched how the women pulled down the slender branches and tore off their scarlet berries. Behind his exquisite colonial house a vast sea of coffee beans had been laid out on a cement floor to dry after they had been stripped of their red flesh and left for a time to ferment. After dinner we drank a cup of his own brand which should have put us in a good mood. But Don Eduardo was gloomy. He had been eaten up with worry and anxieties for some months, worry about the political danger which threatened his country, or to be more precise himself.

Formerly things had gone very well for this settled class of landowners. Neighbouring Mexico had just survived a bloody civil war, but in this tiny country until a few years ago they had enjoyed their privileges and their freehold estates. Guatemala has remained the most Indian of all the countries of Latin America —75 per cent of the 3,000,000 inhabitants are pure Indians and the remaining 25 per cent are divided into *mestizos* and a very thin white crust. The original owners of the land have bowed their backs under the foreign yoke. They borrowed money from the rich, pledged themselves to serve as debtors, and since they never had enough money to repay the loans, nor even the interest, a type of slavery arose. Even the native Carrera who at the head of an Indian army assumed the presidency at the beginning of Guatemala's independence, never dreamed of staking the claims of his own race, but let himself be hustled like a good dog by the clergy and the aristocracy. Thus even today Guatemala remains a conservative land of lords and serfs with 70 per cent of the arable land in the hands of 2 per cent of landowners, and on the other hand 76 per cent of the latter sharing 10 per cent of the holdings. By and large the widely divergent classes have one thing in common—they plant coffee, the stand-by not only of Guatemala but of the whole of Central America as far south as Colombia. Coffee comprises more than three-quarters and bananas 8 per cent of Guatemala's exports, and nearly the whole harvest goes to the United States.

The aristocratic régime was so firmly ensconced in Guatemala that for a Latin American country she had had an almost peaceful history. Her dictators were very long lived and their imposing ranks reached a peak in the thirties with the picturesque figure of Iorge Ubico—and came to a close. Ubico was a thorough tyrant. He shrank from nothing when it was a question of shedding the blood of an opponent. But when Don Eduardo spoke to me about him over a cup of coffee his face was a mixture of admiration and melancholy. Under Ubico everything was in order. Admittedly in 1936 he abolished the debtor slavery. Basically that was only right and proper, but he introduced another system to compel the Indians to work—compulsory labour. Each Guatemalan was given a labour card on which all working days when he had been usefully employed had to be entered. Anyone who had not worked at least 150 days during the year was compulsorily put to work on the rail-road. Permanent ways were Jorge Ubico's great passion. He built roads that reached to the farthest corners of the country, and moreover he used them, for he was a passionate racing motorist. Some official would be idling in the sun in some god-forsaken post thinking that nothing could happen, when suddenly there was a cloud of dust and the dictator got out of his car and began to storm.

This Ubico was a crazy fellow. He created such an efficient police force that crime in Guatemala became a disease as antiquated as the pest or cholera. Ministers and officials were honesty itself. The land flourished magnificently under his despotism, but it is quite easy to understand that he remained alone and that even his friends became his enemies. In 1944 the students from the university revolted and three young army officers brought their *putsch* to a successful close. Ubico was exiled to New Orleans and died shortly afterwards.

Hardly a tear was shed for him in his own country and the old gentleman's whims had even got on the nerves of Don Eduardo and his friends. They did not know that the devil they had driven out had been replaced by a far more unpleasant Beelzebub—at least from their standpoint.

The three army officers who had led the revolt were to outward appearances well-disposed progressive men with good intentions towards the democracy. They did not keep the power in their own hands, but allowed the people in an honest election to choose a professor to be their President. Juan José Arévalo, however, refused to bend the knee to the aristocrats. He was determined to bring about a long-needed social revolution. Thanks to new laws the workers found themselves protected from the duress of their bosses and in receipt of regulation minimum wages. Unions which had been suppressed during the dictatorship were organized. A democratic spring had blossomed in Guatemala, a true rule of the people. Was there any need for Don Eduardo to sigh?

Well, he was a dyed-in-the-wool reactionary, like so many of his colleagues, who kicked against these modest reforms with all his might. He had taken it amiss that agrarian reform law laid down that unused land should be abstracted from the *haciendas* and given over to the peasants to farm. Was it not only just that the wasters should have their surplus taken and put under cultivation? He had successfully protected himself against such expropriation as quickly as possible by ploughing up a few idle *caballerias* on his property and sowing them. Thus to a certain extent the government unwittingly made money for him. No, one could come to terms with the reforms, but, *C'est le ton qui fait la musique.* The accompanying music to this redistribution of the land rang shrilly in the ear.

"We are not communists, long live Christ the King." This slogan could be seen pasted up on countless doors not only in the capital but also in Antigua, and it expressed a genuine alarm. The democratization of the country had degenerated into a dangerous demagogy.

All this had arisen quite stealthily from a hopeful start. Among the politicians surrounding Professor Arévalo were also to be found communists. Extremely well-mannered and idealistic colleagues—at least in appearance—they won Arévalo's confidence and even more the confidence of his successor, Colonel Jacobo Arbenz, one of the three army officers who had brought about the revolution. These gentlemen, Fortuny, Gutierrez and Pellecer, from time to time visited Moscow and attended the peace conferences. Good, but were they dangerous on this account? They had hardly any following. Only four of the fifty-six deputies of parliament were communists. Why should one not use good brains? If they turned out to be really dangerous one could easily get rid of them. But these "brainy boys" were more cunning than the President. They let their collaboration be paid with various posts—key positions in the Union, on the agrarian reform committee, in the editorial department of the government press, in the State-run broadcasting; it was the old tactic of infiltration by means of which a determined minority secretly manages to seize power, even against the will of the people. Communists brought the news to the landless Indios that they could take possession of their master's uncultivated land. Even before the government could carry through the expropriation on a legal footing, the communist-led mobs took the law into their own hands. A wave of lawlessness and unrest spread through the land, and everywhere insubordination triumphed it bore the communist insignia. But it was not only among the illiterate masses that a handful of communists sought and found a following. Since for their ultimate goal they took the ideals of a democratic social revolution, they found steadily growing support among the deputies of the other parties. This went so far that one day the President of the most important government party, the PAR (Party of Revolutionary Action), described the communist party in Congress as the only true one and the other parties as merely temporary magic lantern shows. When Stalin died the Guatemalan Congress mourned him with a demonstration of silence.

During my stay in Guatemala, shortly before the fall of the Arbenz régime in the spring of 1954, I felt something familiar in the mood which reminded me of Hungary in 1948. There, too, I met a whole host of intelligent people who informed me that they were basically in sympathy with the reforms which the communist-inspired government had brought about, but—and this "but" could be seen in a look of desperation on their faces— they would under no circumstances approve the most recent development, the further radicalization which they saw taking place with the helpless passiveness of a mouse hypnotized by a snake.

But the development finally took another course. In Guatemala there were strong anti-communist forces, particularly in the cities, where a politically conscious bourgeoisie recognized the dangerous movement and ultimately had sufficient power to bring about a counter-revolution under Castillo Armas.

We drove for hours across the Tiquisate plain, through the lowlands on the Pacific coast of Guatemala, and everywhere the same picture met the eye: banana palm after banana palm. A sharp wind made the broad leaves sway to and fro, tearing them into thin fringes. Here and there we came across a cloud of smoke rising from the dry stalks. A rain of ash darkened the sun and suffocated us. From time to time a flame rose from a banana palm and consumed it. "What's going on?" I asked my companion. Pérez Asturias shrugged his shoulders. "It's a fire, as you can see." "What caused it," I insisted—"self-combustion?" My friend gave a wry smile. "Bananas don't go up in flames on their own. That is the result of a human hand." I did not understand. "I suppose you mean sabotage?" Pérez stopped the car. "You must realize," he said, turning to me with a note of bitter irony in his voice, "we're crossing a kind of battlefield here. A war is being waged, a war between the democratic nationalists and the American imperialists."

The plantation I was visiting belonged to the American

United Fruit Company, which plays a similar role in Central America to that played by the big oil companies in Mexico before their nationalization. It set foot on this soil for the first time some fifty years ago. The company bought land in unhealthy tropical regions which had been almost depopulated by malaria. Naturally it had a plan in mind. It began a bitter struggle against these diseases and won the battle. Banana plantations grew up where previously only sterile jungle had luxuriated; and among them workers' settlements, schools, hospitals and railroads. "Our company," boasted Pérez, "has shovelled more earth in cleaning up this country than they did when they built the Panama Canal, but it was worth the trouble." Americans at home grew more and more used to the new fortifying banana fruit with its high vitamin content. The company flourished, expanded, and today has almost a monopoly of the banana trade in the United States. It became a little power of its own, a power which waxed as a result of a series of unstable Central American potentates and in several cases decided upon their success or their failure. When they required a new concession they did not have to wait long for an answer: the dictator bowed to their representative rather than the reverse. They only had to raise their little finger and they obtained all the privileges they required.

Here in Guatemala, for example, the United Fruit Company signed a contract in 1936 with the dictator Ubico, giving it freedom from duty on the import of all materials required for its plantation in addition to extraordinary tax remissions. It controls the only railway in the country, which runs from the Pacific Coast to the Atlantic, and while independent banana growers, including the government itself, have to pay from between $200 to $250 freight to Puerto Barrios, the United Fruit has to pay only $90. Privileges brought wealth, wealth brought power and power demanded new privileges. American business ability and organizing efficiency became involved in a vicious circle. Was it immoral to obtain tax remissions and cheaper freights? What intelligent man, were he in the same position, would act otherwise? But one had only to read the government press to learn that this denoted the crime of imperialism. The

Guatemala: a water carrier

Chichicastenango, Guatemala:
pagan sacrifices on the steps of
a church

Chichicastenango, Guatemala:
women at the market

whole hatred of the nationalist inferiority complex was directed against the all-powerful fruit company, and it was obvious that it was determined to cause as much damage as possible to this power in the land and perhaps even to drive it off Guatemalan soil.

The chicaneries began with higher wage demands for the 13,000 workers. In the first few moments after a visitor enters the administration buildings of Tiquisate he is given an impressive picture of the tremendous social benefits which the company has bestowed on its employees. Well-dressed children tumble about the meadow in front of a roomy school and disappear in good order when the teacher blows his whistle. A hospital with every modern equipment cares for the sick, the shops of the company sell food at a fraction of its value. In addition to all these achievements the United Fruit Co. pays its workers three times more money than the peon used to earn in Guatemala in the old days, and fundamentally the unions should be grateful that they have forced up wages to this level. But this was no question of justice, merely a political struggle. At the crucial moment a great storm laid waste a great part of the plantation. Since the new plantings had swallowed $10 million, the company flirted with the idea of liquidation and dismissed 3,700 of the workers: as a result of the wages conflict they remained out of work. The government declared this dismissal illegal and threatened the whole board of the company with requisitioning and enforced sale to the highest bidder. At this dramatic moment a compromise was made on both sides. The United Fruit Co. promised to reinstate the dismissed workers with back pay to the sum of half a million dollars. The plantation should not only be replanted, but enlarged: in return for this the union bound itself to keep the peace for three years. The agrarian reform which was actually directed against absentee landlords became an anti-imperialist weapon in the hands of the government against the most active economic power in the land, the United Fruit Company.

Pérez stopped the car in a plantation where the tops of the bananas already showed traces of the drought and led me among the trees. He stuck his knife in one of them and cut a thick lump from it. Inside it was rotten. "It's the Panama disease," he explained. "All these plants are affected. They rot from inside and wither at the top. A fungus is the cause of it and in a few years it has spread from Panama over the whole of Central America. No antidote has yet been found, except on the Atlantic coast of Honduras, where they succeeded in destroying it by flooding. Here there is not enough water and the soil is composed of porous volcano ash. Nothing remains except to leave the infected soil fallow or abandon it."

I noticed that this had already been done in certain places and that the area had been planted with American oil plants. I now saw wherein lay the vulnerability of the United Fruit Company, which the régime knows how to exploit. In order to allow this land to remain fallow long enough it must possess enormous land reserves, but even these reserves have now been expropriated by the terms of the new land laws for a mere fraction of their value. Pérez reckoned that in five years the company might have to pull out, since they no longer possessed any healthy banana country. That meant a loss of some $20 million of the shareholders' money, but for the country it meant a yearly loss of $15 million in wages and a sixth of its income from foreign exchange.

Once more our car stopped in front of a row of wooden huts which served as workers' dwellings. They were built on wooden piles with a clearance below for the men to store their maize and other provisions. Sometimes they slung their hammocks there or played draughts with bottles of beer for draughtsmen. "Don't they do any work?" I asked.

"By rights they should," said Pérez. "But now we are not even masters in our own house. Some of these boys have left our service, but a paragraph of the famous law allows them to go on living in our workers' settlement all the same. Most of them are politically active, even though only a few of them can read and write. They are waiting to get their share of our confiscated land."

Even more astonishing was the case of the squatters, whose straw-roofed huts we met with everywhere on the plantation. These fortunate house owners had in actual fact no right to sun themselves so proudly before their doors. Years ago they left the company's employ of their own free will, settled down at some crossroads and began to plant their maize. Since it was mostly a question of fungus-tainted land the company had tolerated this in silence, but in accordance with the new law these parasites had now also become owners in the middle of the plantation. The walls of their huts were decorated with huge pictures of President Arbenz, and when I spoke to them they looked up gratefully at the picture of their benefactor. Incidentally it was not only mistrust that made them monosyllabic in front of a foreign visitor. They were mostly good-natured but not particularly bright youths who did anything the communists whispered in their ears with no heed for the possible results.

"Democracy!" said Pérez mockingly as we drove off.

I had now seen for myself the material of which the revolutionary following was composed. An irresponsible mob.

"One's only got to chuck about a dozen men out of the country," sighed Pérez, "a mere dozen men and there wouldn't be a single communist left in Guatemala. Many of them are not even Guatemalans but Red Spaniards. They have no real following, they merely rant and rave. If their mouths were shut the whole bogey would vanish. Here the politicians form public opinion, not the other way round. That is what so many Europeans and North Americans don't understand."

Pérez underestimated his northern neighbours. How could he possibly have known that in Washington plans were afoot for a liberation? The communist influence in Guatemala had become a very thorny problem. A Soviet régime in Central America in the immediate neighbourhood of the Panama Canal could not be tolerated on purely strategic grounds, let alone economic and political theories that called for the expulsion of a rival, trod on American toes, and might stir up revolutions in the neighbouring countries. On the other hand, American military intervention in Latin America has always aroused such a storm of protest that, since President Roosevelt's Good Neighbour Policy, the idea of sending marines was unthinkable. But what was to stop them from conforming to the old Central American tradition whereby the

potentates of these dwarf republics mutually watch the political
pot and spit in it when the need arises? Next door in Honduras an
exiled Colonel, Carlos Castillo Armas, had collected around him
a troop of anti-communist refugees and at his leisure planned the
liberation of his native land. The opportunity arose when a
British ship arrived at Puerto Barrios with a cargo of weapons
from Poland. Guatemala was once more in the historical lime-
light. It turned out later that the weapons in question were merely
obsolete captured German war material. If the Kremlin really
intended opening a bridgehead in Central America, the attempt
was made with the most suicidal and inadequate means. In any
case the ship from Poland was a godsend to the States. No one
was entitled to call the overthrow of a public disturber of the
peace intolerable interference. When Castillo Armas invaded
Guatemala he met with little resistance. The few antiquated aircraft which dropped bombs and leaflets on the capital met with
no enemy fighters. The war was decided to all intents and purposes in the Officers' Club. The army sphinx had emerged from
its twilight and opted for the anti-communist cause. Arbenz and
his gang had to go. A few communists tried from pure obstinacy
to carry on the struggle by rousing the Indians to make a descent
on the capital. Things turned out as Pérez had prophecied;
"Throw a dozen people out of the country and the communist
bogey would vanish from Guatemala."

Obviously democracy could not have a long life in this unhappy land. What did democracy mean to this mob which would
follow blindly any leader, whether from the Right or the Left?
What these folk needed after so much demagogic "boloney" was
an iron authority of the Ubico type, and Armas, the haggard
fanatic, was ready to give it to them. Did a liberator of his kidney
need a secret ballot. Ridiculous! The Indio merely had to go to
the hustings and give an uncompromising "Yes" or "No" in the
choice of his President. With his triumph order was restored and
Don Eduardo could heave a sigh of relief. For many a citizen
of Guatemala sees with anguish in the haggard face of Castillo
Armas the image of the old dictator Ubico. There is much to
remind them of him: the law which imposes up to three years

imprisonment for any criticism of the regime; the outlawing of the Labour unions; and even the fact that the old police chief is back at his desk—together with his old methods of torture. In Latin America it is always the same old story. Arbenz, the communist, enriched himself personally just as the worst jackals of the *ancien regime* had done; and the friends of the new anti-communist President profiteer by speculating with the nation's food.

Alcohol

CHICHICASTENANGO is a town, but a town without inhabitants, or, to avoid being accused of exaggeration, with about 1,000 *ladinos* in all. All the citizens of Chichicastenango live outside in their hamlets, dispersed like the Chamulas all over the country and separated by mountains and deep ravines. The Town Hall, which keeps the records of all these people, is usually empty.

I was beginning to get bored when suddenly an unusual procession appeared in the empty street. Half a dozen silent men dressed in black approached me. Their costume was peculiar and quite different from anything I had yet seen in the nature of Indian costumes. Their richly embroidered trousers reached to their knees and bellied out over the thighs; their jerkin-like jackets were also embroidered with red spirals and blue zigzag lines. To crown this they wore a magnificent red flower-like turban. The men carried silver monstrances on long poles with the name of Christ surrounded by gilt flames. Behind them a coffin wobbled on strong young shoulders. Next came a band of women just as fantastically dressed. Over a homely blue skirt fastened with a bright girdle they wore such richly embroidered blouses that they were positively dazzling. Huge black moons on a wine-dark background surrounded by white zigzags, purple flowers and dots. . . . I had been told that this ornamentation was symbolical; that the zigzags represented mountains, the stripes fields of maize and the crosses the sowing. So each of these women was garbed symbolically as the Earth Mother. In addition to this I could see a galaxy of gleaming silver bead necklaces in such profusion that they covered the throat and made the wearers look like harnessed horses. The *cortège* came to a halt. The most worthy and obviously the highest ranking man turned round. The bearers crouched while he uttered a formula with one hand raised. I could not understand it, but I thought it must be a kind of valediction. The women then laid a coin on the coffin, which was immediately picked up by one of the men. At the entrance to the cemetery the procession lost its dignified stiffness, for the pall-bearers suddenly began to spin wildly in circles. I had seen something similar in Bali and presumed that it was done with the same intention—to drive off the evil spirits who were trying to take possession of the corpse.

The grave was soon opened and the coffin sank into the depths. I was about to leave when an astonishing performance held me back. Three young men in an advanced state of intoxication staggered out of a side street and joined the procession. They were bare footed and their rags denoted the extreme poverty in which they lived. I imagined them to be good-for-nothings who in their drunkenness intended to importune the funeral guests. But suddenly the true status of these young drunkards was apparent. They were the sons of the dead man. As soon as the coffin had been lowered they began to wail loudly and to tear their hair. "*Mi padre, mi padre*," they wailed with a grief that was obviously assumed. They reached the side of the grave and began in unison to creep on all fours towards the hole in order to be buried with their father. It was the pleasant duty of their wives to seize them at the last moment and to pull them back with wails and protests. This farce, now tinged by the influence of alcohol, grew serious. It seemed as though the drunken misery of these youngsters really encouraged them to commit suicide. The resistance they put up to the gentle constraint of their wives developed into such a scuffle that other young people rushed to their aid and had to seize the fanatics by their hands and feet. Suddenly one of the raving creatures stood up and to my alarm made his way over to me. "I must tell you what's going on," he began with astounding clarity, although I could smell the fumes of the brandy. "The man we are burying here is my father. He got drunk for three days and three nights and never came out of his coma." I had no idea why the boy wanted to tell a foreigner and the whole crowd all these details. It seemed to me to be either a consolation or a kind of threat. So I pulled myself together and put on as big an act of hypocrisy as I could, although I was extremely sceptical about the whole affair. "Take an example from him, young man," I said pompously, "and leave the firewater alone." The boy came closer and nodded his head. His wife waddled up behind him with her child bound in her *rebozo*. "You have a wife and family," I went on. "Don't you feel any responsibility for them?" The man nodded. As we parted he stretched out his hand. "Give me a little money," he said. "Why should I?" "I haven't a *centavo* left," he crooned, "and I want to go home and go on drinking for the rest of the night."

"Why has drunkenness become such a dominating vice among all the Indians?" I asked an intelligent-looking young man who like myself had been watching the performance with a mixture of disgust and enjoyment. The *ladino*, who was a school teacher, shrugged his shoulders. "There are various grounds for it," he said. "Before the Spaniards arrived intoxication was an almost religious practice, a search for oblivion from the daily round and the overture to a trance. Therefore the Indians still drink today, particularly on festive occasions, for example at a funeral or at *fiestas*. The more drunk they become the greater favour they think they find with the saints. In addition to this origin one must not forget that their poverty cries out for intoxication."

"But it makes them even poorer," I suggested.

"Of course, but can you ever reason with a drunkard in any part of the world? And above all these Indians are so singularly lacking in any kind of rational household economy. There are young men who work conscientiously for months on a plantation and finally return home with a considerable sum of money saved. What do you think they do with it? They will spend it at the next *fiesta*. They buy gallons of *tequila* for the whole village until they have not only spent all their savings but have also run into debt. It does not bother them. The next time one of their friends will ruin himself by financing a similar "blind". In this way his sacrifice is so to speak evened out. With the jungle Indios you will find this curious trait even more pronounced. The community with the most disarming *naïveté* lays claim to the property of its individuals. This would not be so bad if this money was not wasted in so futile and so destructive a manner. How can these men manage to pile up wealth and invest it productively? The whole modern economic development here must first and foremost study their most primitive psychological foundations."

The sacred vitamin

ACTUALLY I wanted to visit the church of the Virgén de Augustías in the capital. Architecturally it is not very beautiful, but of great interest because it was built to the last stone by a pious man without any outside aid. The work took several years. Unwittingly I found myself more attracted by the building opposite, which bore the name *Incap*. This is one of the current abbreviations and means *Instituto de Nutrición de Centro America y Pánama*. This food institution founded by UNICEF and various American similar bodies is designed to give the peoples of Central America a better diet. I saw laboratories with bottles full of maize and beans; saw blood and urine tests in enormous ice boxes; and in order to get some idea of the institution's activities I was driven out to the village of Santa Magdalena on the slopes of the Agna volcano. Here the children serve as guinea-pigs for these dietetic experiments. School was over and the boys and girls were in the dining room which had been built to this effect. They were wearing bright costumes and singing a song in praise of vitamins.

> *Vitamins will make us strong,*
> *Soothe our nerves and build our bones;*
> *We must sing both loud and long,*
> *Vitamins give us new hormones.*

Upon this each one swallowed a vitamin B tablet: the soup contained vegetable proteins. Another group is given aureomycin instead of vitamins, and a third nothing but protein. It is a question of finding out which group makes the best progress—whether, in particular, the children who have been given aureomycin will emulate certain animals that have been treated with it and increase their weight by a third. In accordance with the results achieved even the village maize ears and the beans in the laboratory bottles will be enriched by this tonic.

I was very impressed until I read the report of an American dietician who has experimented with the most pathetic of the Mexican Indians, the Otomis in Mesquitaltal. The latter live, like all the Indios of Latin America, on maize, beans and chillis: they drink *pulqué* instead of water. The American expert in his report came to the astonishing conclusion that this diet, augmented by a few wild plants, represented a considerably more healthy and perfect food than that enjoyed by a middle-class Chicago family. And this in spite of all vitamin pills! Only the quantity was insufficient and this accounted for the undernourishment. . . . Why, I wondered, do the northeners bring their medicinal blessings into Central America instead of putting their own house in order?

I was invited by Bill, a young American farmer, to drive in his jeep to San Salvador. He came from Texas and intended to migrate to Nicaragua and to raise cattle on a large scale. We did not follow the main road, but made detours through the villages in a part of the country inhabited by a mixed population. We were just about to cross a bridge, the far end of which was invisible because of the arch, when suddenly both our front wheels sank in the mud. Bill got out and began to curse. Two planks had been taken out of the bridge. What was to be done? There was no need to worry. Some friendly villagers came up as though they had been waiting for us and were fully prepared to get us going again—for a trifling sum of $50. Two grinning youngsters soon appeared with a couple of planks, the very two which had been taken out of the bridge. Bill caught on. He was not for nothing from Texas. In a rage he took a revolver from his pocket and the company vanished like dust before the wind. We carried the planks over to the bridge and were soon on our way.

New troubles faced us at the frontier. An official in the capital had forgotten to sign a document Bill needed before his jeep could leave the country. Naturally the frontier official was prepared to turn a blind eye—for $30.

Bill hesitated. He preferred to return to Guatemala and get the missing signature. I drove in another car to San Salvador.

EL SALVADOR

A small state calls: "Help, I'm bursting"

WHEN you look at the map of Central America one dwarf State after the other lies before you. You cast an eye at the trade statistics: coffee and bananas, bananas and coffee. Everywhere they provide 90 per cent of the exports. The people mostly half-breeds—the picturesque Indian element has almost died out. In addition it is warm, in fact damned hot. You skid down from the heights into the *tierras calientes*. Is it worth while, you wonder? You are tempted to take an aeroplane and hop over all these dwarf countries as far as Panama. I advise you to do no such thing. It is not necessarily the size of a race which determines the greatness of its destiny. Central America too has its charm.

Among the republics the inexperienced traveller may dismiss scornfully from the map, the miniature domain of El Salvador looks the most insignificant. Overshadowed by its more expansive brothers Honduras and Nicaragua, which could swallow it up four times, it seems negligible, but, as often happens, this is only in appearance. This smallest of all the Central American republics is with its million population the largest numerically after Guatemala. This sea of humanity (245 inhabitants to the square mile) is continuously on the increase. When you walk through the streets of the capital and see all the young girls with children you say to yourself: where will it all end?

In countries like China or India over-population has led to a general impoverishment and to famine. El Salvador, however, is inhabited by a brave and able people who know how to ward off such a destiny by industriousness. While greater countries with plenty of soil at their disposal—so much that there are not enough men to till it—farm their land with antiquated methods, El Salvador has been forced to adopt an intensive agriculture. Despite the smaller acreage her coffee harvest is larger than that of

Guatemala. When you cross the frontier from this semi-feudal, semi-Indian country into El Salvador, it is like entering another world. You have left the dusty roads full of potholes which rattled you to pieces and you glide along magnificent macadamized roads as if you were in Abraham's bosom; stern mobile traffic police prevent you from pressing your foot too hard on the accelerator and running the danger of ending up in Paradise. You come quite quickly enough into the gay clean capital, which is mainly built of wood and tin on account of earthquakes. That of course is another danger. The cathedral, which is also built of these materials, caught fire two years ago and burnt to the ground in a few minutes.

Despite all their hard work the Salvadorans have remained just as poor as their neighbours in feudal Guatemala. Here too thirty families controlled two-thirds of the whole land and half the national revenue and, since conditions in this over-populated cauldron grew more acute, the social unrest in the thirties had already reached boiling-point. As is usual in such cases, a dictator held the destructive powers in check during the upheaval. This general, Hernández Martínez, was a very curious figure, a man who by his obstinacy put his picturesque Guatemalan colleague Ubico in the shade. Before coming to power he had been engrossed in theosophical studies and he put his theories into practice. The following was one of his most fatal principles: it is a greater crime to kill an ant than to kill a man, for by his death man suffers a reincarnation, whereas the ant is definitely annihilated. He was following this principle in 1932 when he crushed a communist-inspired peasant revolt with unexampled savagery that resulted in 20,000 deaths. When the capital was visited by an epidemic he caused the street lamps to be swathed in bright-coloured cellophane, he believed that such coloured magic would avert the evil spirits, and only when his own son died did he see the futility of such efforts.

However, in other respects Martínez was not quite mad. He tried to cure the social unrest by reform. A mortgage bank broke the power of usury. New labour laws gave the plantation workers an eight-hour day with paid holidays. His reforms, however, alienated the sympathies of the big plantation owners without attracting the workers to his side. One day the whole country rose in a general strike. Everyone struck without exception— doctors, lawyers, bakers, chauffeurs, clerks. Neither his theosophical wisdom nor his heavily armed guards were of any help to the dictator, and he had to go.

But the country achieved very little. More or less conservative and dictatorial generals jockeyed for his position until, in 1948, a military junta seized power. The instigator General Oscar Osorio still holds the presidency today. Physically this man is the complete opposite of his Guatemalan neighbour Arbenz, an intellectual small-limbed type. Osorio is an amiable type with a disarming hearty smile, a man with his two feet planted firmly on the ground, determined to allow no ideologies to throw him off his balance. We shall meet this type of officer several times on our trip through the Southern Hemisphere. They are not very brilliant men and certainly not idealists, but as realists they know that soldiers cannot fight on empty bellies and citizens even less; that certain social changes are preferable although they do not express any particularly exalted progressive feelings. El Salvador experienced a *petit-bourgeois* revolution. The year 1950 brought a new Constitution which, for the first time, permitted the workers to organize unions, with the important exception of the agricultural workers, who as a result might have taken the downward path. Another innovation brought wails from the landowners, as though they had already been beggared: minimum wages and income tax. A progressive income tax from 2 per cent on incomes over $2,400 increasing to 44 per cent at $60,000. "It's not an iota better here than in Guatemala," sighed one of these gentlemen whom I met at a party. They did not mention that their class still makes a net annual profit of between $12 to $15 million which they are careful to deposit in New York and Zürich banks. Obviously, despite everything, they were not to be pitied. But they were right according to their own lights: the good old days when you only needed to buy a ticket to be able to spend your holidays in a luxury hotel on the French Riviera are now a thing of the past. You can no longer fritter money away;

you have to calculate carefully as you have to do at home—even more carefully perhaps, because the human element is so unpredictable.

Only a radical change of the whole social and economic structure can rescue this over-populated land, and only industry can feed the extra mouths. So far a lack of electricity has hindered such a development, but now a mighty power station has been completed on the river Lempa and two Italian engineers are on the track of a second source of power. Why should it not be possible to make the spiteful gods who surge from the volcanos and lay the towns in ruins serve some useful purpose? In El Salvador two volcanos spew from open craters: the Izalco, which erupts such fiery scarlet flames that the sailors have christened it *The Lighthouse of the Pacific*. The two Italian engineers, however, chose the less spectacular Conchagua on the grounds of experience learnt from Vesuvius. In Chinameca, a small town which a few years ago was completely destroyed by an earthquake, gases rise from the earth which could easily be captured and turned into a thermal power station—no boring necessary, a pure gift of nature. It is reckoned that at a preliminary cost of about $3 million, 12,000 kw could be produced; this would correspond to half the power given by the Lempa station. All the other Central American States are following these attempts in El Salvador with the greatest interest, for all of them, with the exception of Honduras, possess a smoking crater which they could tap.

Because it is such a small country El Salvador is a natural laboratory for all such experiments and not for the taming of volcanoes alone. Every possible international organization has chosen her as an experimental field for plans in the field of health, agriculture, hygiene, etc. The most recent of these experiments was the recultivation of a whole valley to the north of the town within the framework of Point 4. The agricultural experts among other things introduced a type of maize which gave a four to five times larger harvest than all the previous species and a sugar beet immune from disease.

Despite the slow progress the country can expect from its President Osorio, the danger of revolution has still not been removed. The source of contagion, Guatemala, is not far away and propaganda is constantly being smuggled across the frontier. I did not take it amiss that the Salvador customs officials subjected my luggage as well as that of all the other passengers to a very thorough search. Government officials and trades union leaders constantly come in secret or openly from Guatemala. When in August 1952 a Pan American Airways Stratocruiser which, owing to a strike, was diverted from Guatemala landed at San Salvador with a team of delegates from the Peiping Peace Congress, the police found in their luggage no less than 150 lb. of communist literature and complete plans for loosing a revolution in the neighbouring country. Osorio did not remain idle. In September a state of emergency was declared during which seventy communists who were suspected of being in the plot were put under lock and key and a great quantity of weapons was confiscated. Peace returned to San Salvador. At least on the surface—for a communist-inspired student periodical, *Opinión estudiantil*, circulates in the university and communist influence is still active in the fifteen unions. General Osorio realizes that he must be constantly on his toes. He has enemies on both sides—the reactionaries on the right who would like to put back the clock and the impatient members of the left who would like to bring about an upheaval.

HONDURAS

Bananas and generals

THE smaller the country the greater its self-importance. Nowhere does this become more evident than on a journey through Central America. At the Honduran Consulate the official frowned. "My instructions are to enquire at Tegucigalpa before issuing a visa," he told me. That could take weeks. Not only are entrance visas required but also two stamps for the exit, one from the Foreign Ministry and the other from the Combined Services Ministry. Nicaragua in addition to all these dues both on arrival and departure demands a tourist tax of $1 per person. Never has my passport been so filled with stamps and my notecase so quickly emptied of money as in the official departments of the great powers of Central America.

Honduras has found a magnificent solution to all these complications. "Go and see the Ambassador," advised the Consul, "he has the right to give you a courtesy visa." The Honduran Embassy is a long way from the centre in the residential quarter on the outskirts of San Salvador. A luxurious car stood in front of it with a ghostly pair of legs hanging out of the window. They belonged to the chauffeur, who was snoring peacefully. I went over to the entrance and rang the bell. No one answered. The bell was out of order. I banged with my fist on the door. "Hi, don't make so much din," said a voice from inside, "I'm coming." The door opened and an elderly man in shirtsleeves stood before me. I could see his pants sticking out of his trousers. "I should like to speak to the Ambassador," I said. "I am the Ambassador," he replied. "Wait a minute." He was in the process of unpacking a case of stationery, but once he was ready he did not hesitate to stamp the necessary visa in my passport free of charge. He signed himself General. Honduras has no Military Academy, but it teems with Generals. In this land the title is equivalent to a Doctorate.

Antigua, Guatemala:
coffee harvest

Honduras : aircraft
and oxcart

Panama: melting-pot of races: negro and Chinese half-castes

Panama: street brawl in the negro quarter

I went by car to visit the famous Maya ruins of Copan beyond the frontier village of Ocotepeque north of San Salvador. "Has anyone anything to declare?" asked the chauffeur before we reached the frontier. A chemist pointed to a camera which he had bought at San Salvador. The chauffeur got out and hid it under the bonnet "so that we shan't have any difficulties," he said. But this precaution turned out to have been quite unnecessary. Never in my life have I experienced such an agreeable Customs. The inspector came up as we got out of the car and shook us all by the hand. "How are you?" he said amiably, and that was all. "Don't you want to look at my passport?" I asked before we drove off. "Quite unnecessary," he replied, "only respectable people use this road." Honduras is exceedingly broadminded!

The road came to an end in Ocotepeque. Honduras has practically no roads and this is the major problem of the whole country. In the course of its history it has made various attempts to link its capital with the coast by rail. The first attempt was made on the Pacific side towards the Gulf of Fonseca. Later, a contract was signed with the United Fruit Company. The latter was to expand towards the capital and to receive 600 hectares of land for every kilometre of track laid. Both plans came to grief. The contractors found it more profitable to let the railway meander in broad sweeps through the flat country than to embark upon the technical difficulties that would be met with on the shortest cut through mountains as far as Tegucigalpa. One day they merely stopped building, and thus the capital has a magnificent airfield but no railway station.

The same applies to each little settlement: it has an airfield but no road. People fly here instead of taking a taxi, and you keep landing on the most impossible airfields. I shall never forget the look of joy on our pilot's face as he got out of the cockpit after a quick halt in Santa Barbara. "You must all get out, gentlemen. The tyres have burst. We shall have to stay here." When I got out I saw the wreck of another plane and learnt that when it had tried to land a cow had wandered across the runway; in order to avoid it the pilot had banked sharply, turned, and crumpled one of his wings. Since the aircraft carry not only passengers but freight, you share the accommodation with sacks of coffee, bundles of tobacco, pigs, chickens, and occasionally with funeral wreaths.

We landed in Copan among the ruins. At the end of the airfield you enter a mythical world of courtyards and palaces. You climb the steps on which 2,500 hieroglyphics make a history book in stone. How wonderfully alive this world is. From every wall, faces intended to inspire terror look down upon you. An archæologist has named one of these most terrifying heads "the head of Venus", and yet nothing could be further removed from the æsthetic cult of the Greeks. An old man with toothless gums grins from beneath roots and withered leaves. The torch bearer on the spectator tribune is entwined by a snake, while another grows out of his mouth. Below, in a gigantic courtyard, stand the *stele*—priests and kings wearing exaggerated costumes as though the jungle had grown over them and had been turned to stone at the same time. Altars in the form of wild beasts tower in front of them: double-headed feathered dragons, terrible serpents, a gigantic tortoise. Everything lives and flourishes here in stone. In Uxmal you think of Greece, since everything there is so classical, but in Copan you are reminded of the Indians. It is the essence of tropical culture, where art and architecture have turned to the orgiastic, overloading the forms until they have become formless.

I remained a long time looking at the altar in the western courtyard. On each of its four sides four men carved in high relief are sitting, with their legs crossed. They are astronomers at a conference which, according to a dated inscription, must have taken place in the year 763 B.C. A hieroglyphic serves each one for chair. These presumably indicate the place from where they came, if only one could decipher them; for these stones are of the utmost importance. At this conference presumably a uniform calendar was drawn up based on the position of the sun in Copan. How far did the influence of this State extend—a State which must have been an Athens of pre-Colombian culture, a centre of the arts and sciences. The Aztec calendar, although it applied to a different latitude, was founded on the dates of this city. Since the calendar determined the life of the whole Maya belt, was Copan actually the cradle and the birthplace of the whole culture? If only one could find the key to these hieroglyphs!

In the capital Tegucigalpa, only the monuments are of interest, monuments which reflect the earnestness with which Honduras observes its international obligations. One of the two hills which dominate the city bears a UNO park very tastefully arranged with artistic ruins. The other is crowned with a statute of peace. ·The third and most remarkable of these monuments, however, poses a riddle to the visitor. It is a memorial to the great Honduran liberal Francisco Morazán who, immediately after the liberation from Spanish yoke, for some time ruled a Federation of Central American States until he was defeated by the reactionary Carrera from Guatemala and lost his life. This national hero wears a French Marshal's uniform dating from Napoleonic times. I found this suspicious, and quite rightly so. The Commission which travelled to France to order the statue succumbed to the temptations of the city so thoroughly that only a fraction of the funds available for this worthy object remained. As luck would have it, one of the French Provinces had ordered a statute of Marshal Ney which, for some reason, was rejected. The cheerful Ambassadors, who in no circumstance would return home empty-handed, seized this heaven-sent opportunity. Who in Honduras would bother about such trifles as a uniform and a lack of physical likeness? The name stood on the pillar and that was the main thing.

And what about the government, I can hear the reader ask? Well, Honduras is ruled by bananas. There is a reason why nobody is interested in building railways and interior roads. It does not pay. The fruitful regions lie on the coast where the bananas grow. Their export brings to the country half its revenue. The United Fruit Company owns the plantations and with them the whole country, naturally not directly, but in the traditional manner through one of the banana-conscious generals. That is not such a bad thing, for bananas are more appetizing than bayonets.

Since so far Honduras has been the most obedient of the

United Fruit Company's children, she received a great present ten years ago—the Pan American Agricultural School of Zamorano, to which a good road 26 miles long leads from the capital. It is an extraordinarily important school, possibly the national glory of Honduras. "Within twenty-five years," declared the American director, Doctor Wilson Popenoe, "many of our pupils will be in important posts in Latin America. I hope to see some former graduate from here in the position of Minister for Agriculture."

Students stream here from all the other South American countries because the fame of Zamorano as the most modern and best equipped centre for tropical agriculture attracts thousands of applicants yearly. The conditions are generous: the pupil must belong to some Spanish American country and must have received six years' schooling. In return for this he receives free a three years education with board and lodgings, clothes, and even pocket money for his holidays. The poorest students are accepted here and even preferred. Most of them are mere skeletons and riddled with vermin when they arrive, but after medical treatment they get as fat as pigs and fling themselves with the greatest zeal into their gardening, plantation farming and cattle breeding. It is a small island of perfection in this impoverished land: modern buildings with laboratories, a copious library, sports fields and cultivations which cover more than 1,400 hectares. The pupils have to learn English in order to understand the textbooks.

NICARAGUA

The dictator in the sugar factory

NICARAGUA is the hottest of all the Central American countries, hot in every respect, firstly because the mountain chain stretching from Mexico to Panama sinks here to a plain which is hardly above sea level. Secondly, Nicaragua is also too hot underground. The volcanoes stretch out as on a conveyor belt and a couple of them are constantly smoking. From the airfield you can see nearby Santiago smoking, and every citizen of Managua, the capital, will be able to tell you of the unhappy attempt of arrogant humans to flout the powers of the depths. When in 1929 Santiago began to darken the neighbouring coffee plantations with its exhaust, withering them with its poisonous breath, the inhabitants stopped up the crater by merely dynamiting the mouth. But volcanoes are no sucklings. In 1931 the suppressed energy was released in a terrible earthquake which laid the whole of Managua in ruins and the volcano began to smoke again.

One of the first things I was told in Managua was a joke about "Tacho"—"Tacho" or "Satanasio," according to the mood, is the nickname of a man whose real name is Anastasio Somoza and who for years has been the undisputed dictator of Nicaragua. One day, the story goes, one of his sons arrived home from confession out of breath and sweating profusely. He had admitted to the priest that he had behaved scurvily to his brother and had been given as a penance the order to run through the capital. Upon this Anastasio's wife turned to him anxiously and said, "Tacho, you mustn't go to confession any more or else the priest will make you chase all round the world."

It is almost legendary what people in Nicaragua find to relate about the President's affairs. You may be driving through the country and see a particularly beautiful *hacienda*. To whom does it belong? Somoza! Or again, you pass a particularly impressive factory. To whom does it belong? Somoza! And when he does not own it you may be quite sure that he takes a considerable proportion of the profits. Somoza has a monopoly of cattle export, one of the great sources of revenue. Why is there an embargo on lighters? Because Somoza owns a match factory. Why is sugar so dear? Because he owns a sugar factory. Where does the liquor come from which is sold illegally in travelling lorries? From Somoza's still. He is a fantastic man, a real genius in political business efficiency. When he came to power in 1936 as Commandant of the Guard he did not possess a single centavo, and today he is the greatest landowner in the country.

I was asked if I would like to meet him. "Naturally," I replied. The man who offered to introduce me to this powerful figure was a Swiss mechanic who had settled in Nicaragua after the war and in a few years had become a specialist in his own field and a wealthy business man. He could not lavish enough praise on the pleasures and possibilities this country offered to anyone who possessed real practical knowledge. The assembly of a diesel engine by native mechanics took as many years as it would take a European months, and any foreigner who cared to spend his time there was a made man in the shortest possible space of time. One of his grateful customers was Tacho himself, who had entrusted him with the installation and supervision of the countless electric plants on his properties. My Swiss friend had been summoned to a conference on the following day. Would I like to go with him? There was no ceremony and no protocol. We set off in the jeep, for the President seldom resides in the capital and is usually at his sugar plantation on the Pacific. The road led past a volcanic lake where the rich people of the country live in comparative coolness. It was only a few months since electric light and freshwater pipes had been laid to these heights and villa after villa had sprung up.

In the distance the road descended a picturesque slope towards the sea. It was a magnificent road, tarred throughout. There are none in Central America to compare with it. We entered a gateway which bore the inscription *Montelimar*. When we came to the private building, a guard sprang out with a loaded rifle. Where was the President? He must be somewhere on his property, but no one knew exactly where. We drove on to the sugar factory, a huge open installation where giant crushers pounded the crackling bundles of sugar cane while the sweet juice steamed to crystals in giant cauldrons. My companion irritated me. He was a terrible gossip. He shook every foreman by the hand and entered into a long rigmarole with him. I began to feel bored. I sat in the jeep and watched the guard who marched round and round the factory as though it were an atomic plant. Suddenly my companion put his head into the car. "I've found him," he said in triumph and switched on the engine. "This isn't the first time that Tacho has played 'possum.' His people always say they don't know where he is and you have to be a good psychologist to get the truth out of them. Nothing pays more here than courtesy and nothing is more despised than arrogance."

So we drove once more past the private residence, threw a jaundiced look at the row of waiting cars whose drivers had not been so shrewd as ourselves, and turned off towards the coast. Suddenly the secrecy surrounding the general was broken like a magic spell. All the workers we met gave us the information we wanted and finally we came to a shady palm hut on the beach built for the comfort of bathers. Here we found the President chatting to a friend. We might have been living in a robber tale: half a dozen *guardias*, rakish-looking fellows, prowled up and down with tommy-guns in their hands. The general noticed our arrival but pretended not to see us. As we waited we stared at the foamy breakers whipped up by the breeze. "Be patient," said my companion, "he always keeps his visitors waiting even when he is not busy himself, even when they are Ambassadors from the Great Powers."

At last a wave of the hands and we stood in front of "Tacho". My companion introduced me and by way of flattery said that I was anxious to meet the President of a country which had impressed me so much by its excellent running order.

Somoza accepted the compliment with obvious pleasure and began to embellish it with self-praise. "Certainly," he said, "everything runs well and the people are happy. The development of the land goes forward with great strides. We are twenty years ahead of the most optimistic prognostics." I compared this happy picture with the grim situation of Guatemala, where demagogy threatened to bring trade to a standstill, and asked the President how he dealt with his communists. "Quite simply," replied Somoza with a snigger. "We despatch them to see St. Peter." I was taken aback. What did he mean? I suddenly understood that he meant actual liquidation. I was speechless. I thought he had been joking, but he really had been perfectly serious.

Moreover, Somoza did not consider himself a tyrant but a real father of his country, because he had worked so unselfishly for his people and had nearly killed himself in the effort. When I questioned him on the origin of his own wealth he said, "Merely the result of business acumen." I must remember that he had originally been a business man who had taken a two years' commercial course in Boston and had been a motor-car salesman in his youth. Admittedly a great deal of business a dictator could quite safely undertake was full of risks for a private individual. But was it not of great service to the country when its leading citizen went in for business which other people would not entertain? Satanasio's powers of suggestion are quite remarkable. After five minutes I believed, at least temporarily, that his presidency was no sinecure but a constant self-sacrifice.

Somoza therefore has a clear conscience; it is so crystal clear that, as I have already mentioned, he speaks quite innocently of the death of a political opponent as a cat might talk of some unfortunate mouse. His profession did not seem to impress him a great deal. On the contrary. "Sometimes," he said, "I receive letters from American firms addressed to Señor Dictador Anastasio Somoza and other high-sounding titles. At first I thought I ought to get angry about this, but they are often enough quite serious business letters from firms who want to settle in Nicaragua and who have written to ask my advice. I gather that in the outside world the word 'Dictator' is no longer a particularly savoury title." He roared with laughter.

No. One could not really be angry with this Protean epitome

of integrity. He is a sprout from that absolutist age in which the slogan *L'état c'est moi* held good. Tacho recognized himself so lucidly even in the silences between his words that it would have been the height of tactlessness on my part to cast any aspersions on the virtues of his presidency. He has managed with certain clever dodges to outwit the constitutional ban on re-election— the last time in 1946, when he sought out a dotard to be his successor, removed him from his office twenty-six days later on account of senility, and completed the rest of his term as his representative. "Naturally I don't intend to bear the weight of power upon my ageing shoulders much longer," Somoza concluded with a sigh.

In the meantime his two sons have grown up. The elder, Luis, has already taken over command of the guard, which today, exactly as in the thirties, is the backbone of "Satanasio's" power. The younger, who is called after his father, is President of Congress, where naturally the supporters of the dynasty hold an overwhelming majority and where the opposition has just enough seats necessary to preserve a façade of democracy.

I allowed my companion to develop his plans for the building of a water tank. The general with his technical knowledge showed a remarkable tendency to be economical, but even during this conversation as a silent spectator I was struck by the complete isolation which issued from this man. His rather thick body slumped in his chair like an idol on its pedestal, he never looked his interlocutor in the eyes, but stared out at the waves while his hands played with a cigarette. He spoke slowly in order to compel the other person to pay attention, a picture of perfect egocentricity, and his companion was reduced to listening like a soldier taking orders.

Obviously after my interview I could not look upon "Tacho" as a bloodthirsty monster who every morning ate his political visitors for breakfast. In Managua there is no trace of that suppressed rebellion, of that anxiety caused by fear which you often find under European or Asiatic dictatorships. For those communists who are despatched "to see St. Peter" are very scarce in Nicaragua—in fact they hardly exist, and when such a misfortune occurs it is handled with great discretion. Nor is there a Gestapo or a GPU which fetches you at 5 o'clock in the morning and you are never seen again. At the worst you are taken to the frontier or exiled to the idyllic Corn Island in the Atlantic. A colleague who suffered this fate told me that he returned from there with a book of poems and a several pounds increase in weight.

No, it would be entirely false to dramatize "Satanasio" as a bloodhound. The people do not tremble before him. They laugh at him and they grin when he has been up to one of his pranks, for he cannot be accused of having no sense of humour. A wonderful example of this occurred in the year of the dictators' downfall, 1944, when Ubico in Guatemala and Martínez in El Salvador had to disappear. Somoza had already packed his bags for revolutions are catching. The Nicaraguan ladies organized a protest meeting. What would another Dictator have done? Called out the police, made arrests and ordered disagreeable interrogations. Somoza resorted to a far more elegant method. Instead of the guard he mobilized all the whores with whom tyrants are always on good terms, for the powers of both lie in human weakness. They broke into the meeting of the aristocratic ladies with finger nails, hairpins and loud yells. The latter broke up very quickly in the face of such vulgarity. The good cause was saved for ever.

The simple people look upon Tacho as a ruthless tyrant and in Latin America that is a sure guarantee of his popularity. "A crazy guy, our President," the people say with a smile.

Even if the good citizens of Nicaragua wanted to get rid of their "Satanasio" they could not manage it. The guard has the whip hand. Every officer who seizes power in Latin America invariably does one thing. He increases his officers' pay, gives them luxury cars and fine houses. Whoever commands armoured cars and aircraft gives the orders.

But few people in Nicaragua think about this. When Tacho boasts that he has helped his country he is not entirely wrong. It is a debatable point as to whether the rise of the country is thanks to him, but one cannot contradict the figures. Thirty per cent of the budget is devoted to economic development. In 1940 Nicaragua still exported goods to the value of $3.7 million and imported $7 million. In 1952 the exports rose to $42 million and the imports to $39 million. Agriculture, which previously was confined to coffee, has been expanded to include cotton, cattle, corn and sugar, and while previously the land hurried towards bankruptcy its credit is today impeccable. Somoza therefore tries by all available means to attract foreign capital: foreign experts, technicians and engineers are received by him with open arms. Such facts have silenced many democratic consciences, not to mention that of the American Ambassador. The mixture of feelings is really amazing. A potentate sits there who is a classical example of the Caudillo type—a cynical private despot—which has nearly disappeared from the Continent; and yet this potentate of all the rulers of the neighbouring countries is the most enthusiastic friend of the great democracy America. The proofs of his friendship are generous to the point of embarrassment and contain a certain comic element of parody. When in 1942 an American Air Force officer landed by special plane in Managua and asked Tacho's permission to build an air base—a complicated undertaking which he had estimated would take several weeks—he was immediately driven from the airfield to the government palace, and flew off two hours later with a signed blank contract leaving all the proportions and measurements to the Pentagon. In 1943 Nicaragua adopted the Atlantic Charter. Wherever, as is invariable at international conferences, the US seek support from the Southern Hemisphere they can count on the agreement of Nicaragua's representative. July 4th, the North American Independence Day, is also celebrated in Nicaragua. Should one dismiss so valuable a friendship because of a few undemocratic blemishes? And above all, when in face of the dangerous developments in Central America, a certain ally such as Nicaragua is beyond price?

For Nicaragua is not only a hot country climatically, it is also "hot" in international politics. A mighty navigable inland lake has its outlet through the San Juan river to the Atlantic. From lake Nicaragua to the Pacific is a mere jump over a small chain of hills.

With a pair of sluices an alternative canal could easily be built to lighten the burden of Panama. Thus Nicaragua is a strategic country far too prominent in the international field of tension to be left out of world trade. Therefore since the turn of the century its history has borne the imprint of constant North American intervention, which in 1912 and 1926 actually amounted to years of military occupation. Tacho began his career as an interpreter for the American Marines and his rise to Commandant of the Guard had a great deal to do with this; in short, he continues this rôle today to a certain extent; a continued occupation under a native general.

Nothing could better demonstrate what an important rôle the behaviour of the rulers plays in Latin America than the fact that the Nicaraguans who remember the American troops still demonstrate a great affection for the Yankees. The liberation hero Sandino, who for five years waged war with a handful of guerillas against the Marines until he was murdered after their departure (it is rumoured, on Somoza's orders), is honoured more in Guatemala and Costa Rica than in his own country as an anti-American symbol. I even came across a couple of young men here who are consciously trying to make a spiritual bridge with the USA. It was extraordinary in so dismal a spot as Managua to come across a window display, a shop filled with books of the deepest philosophical and religious content. I entered and met the two young owners, who belong to a leading circle of poets. It is quite the fashion for all educated young men of good family to write poems, and it is even more so in Nicaragua, where the statue of one of the greatest poets of the Spanish language, Reuben Darios, shakes its iron mane in the lake breeze on the shore of Managua. Ernesto Cardenal, one of the two writers, has admittedly completely broken with the French tradition of his great predecessors, seeks his inspiration in the modern North American living poets whom he knew in his student days, and tries to make them available in translation to the Spanish-speaking world from his own publishing house. The territorial alliance, he told me, is more important to him than the Latin-Anglo-Saxon separating line, and it was therefore illuminating

that Cardenal above all felt attracted by the bucolic poetry of the
United States from Walt Whitman and Emily Dickinson to
Robert Frost. The second young man, Renaldo Tefel, seems to me
worthy of mention because his presence throws a very interesting
light on Tacho's tyranny. Tefel, who in Europe came under the
influence of the great Catholic writer Jacques Maritain, on his
return home with youthful ardour joined the opposition and
knew both prison and exile. Actually his presence in his friend's
bookshop was illegal. He simply returned from San Salvador one
day without asking permission from the government, and after
a failure on the part of the police to arrest him, remained unmolested. Since then he has remained peaceful and that was all
that Tacho wanted, for, as I have said, he is a genial tyrant who
also at times writes poetry, or as an American acquaintance in
Managua said to me, "he is a silly old bastard, but a nice silly old
bastard."

COSTA RICA

Don Pepe and the citizens

LITTLE philosophizing is necessary to discover the spirit of the small country Costa Rica. As soon as I arrived in the high-lying capital San José and looked round for a few acquaintances I realized in a very strange way that this capital of 100,000 inhabitants has remained a small town. You look in the telephone directory for an address and find something like 7 The Avenue or 13 The Street. San José as a true colonial town is merely split into numbered blocks. Everything would be child's play if there happened to be any street number plates, but these are very rare. You can of course ask a passer-by, but he seldom knows what street he happens to be in. You then approach a landlord looking amiably out of a lower window of a house and you will find that he has to ask his wife. Had I entered a madhouse? Did people really exist who did not know their address?

There was a solution to the problem. The numbering of the avenues and streets is only on paper. The true Costa Rican gives his address in quite a different manner: 300 yards west of the flower market, turn left at the corner and then take the steps on the right. You have to keep this in your head, for no one (except the police, as I soon discovered) can help you when you only know the "mathematical" address. This city has not yet become an anonymous dwelling machine. An orderly friendly people live here, good workers with a lot of practical common sense and, what is rare in Latin America, with a talent for organization.

How did this happen? It is quite simple. The Conquistadores who crossed the seas in search of wealth had only one bogey— they hated work. They left such degrading activity to the Indians. Now, in this neighbourhood there were also Indians, their ears, noses and arms hung with wonderful ornaments, which encouraged them to call the country Costa Rica—the rich coast. This was a mistake, however, for the land was poor and the *peons* gathered in a harvest only as a result of very hard work. Thus in the future the only emigrants who came here were those who were not afraid of getting calloused hands, for the Indians died almost as if out of protest when the conquerors tried to put them to work. While in Guatemala and Mexico the aristocracy indulged in orgies and erected buildings of fabulous extravagance, Costa Rica became a branch of Spanish *petite-bourgeoisie* and peasantry without the inevitable class distinctions between feudal lords and hungering slaves to be found in the neighbouring countries. Moreover it was injected with a good dose of that old Spanish Catholic puritanism which had turned the preservation of virtue almost into a sport. However, coffee, which as a result of the rising demand was to become the chief source of revenue of this little country, brought in its wake a rich upper class without also bringing those extreme social tensions from which most of the other Latin American countries suffer. Although until a few years ago this upper class provided the Presidents and the leading figures, the social foundation of the State was provided by small property owners, and thus life was peaceful and quiet—an Arcadian existence.

While elsewhere the rulers extorted fabulous wealth from their peoples for the benefit of their own pockets, the integrity of the Costa Rican rulers was pushed almost to an absurdity. When in 1932 President Cleto Gonzalez Viquez retired—for here a ruler has never dared to prolong his stipulated term of office by means of dubious chicaneries—he had to sell his house because he had become so poor during his presidency. When Congress suggested a pension he waived it aside angrily, and his probity could only be appeased when a government post as an historical research worker was created for him so that he could earn his salary by honest work. This went on until 1940, when León Cortés, the first of a line of aristocratic Presidents to bring a popular tone into the palace, retired. A newspaper raised the terrible reproach that he had taken away a lamp with him. Cortés produced a receipt from the Minister of Commerce showing that he had duly paid for the object in question, but the poor ex-President was guilty with regard to a second accusation: he had, the paper discovered, during his period of office accepted a small pig from the State agricultural college. For weeks on end this pig made headlines in the press, and no one dreamed that a certain amount of moral indignation and hypocrisy lay behind this polemic—that under his successor a small pig would not be a bone of contention, but that the President's palace would become a veritable pigsty.

Doctor Rafael Angel Calderón was elected almost unanimously because he was a well-respected physician and a friend of humanity who very often forgot to send in his bills to needy patients. How could it happen that he showed himself so weak when it came to the temptations of power? The incredible took place. A Costa Rican President began to steal exactly as his colleagues did in the neighbouring countries. The whole of respectable society turned their backs on him in horror. Calderón grasped the only proffered hand—that of the communists who, as is the case in Guatemala today, soon had more to say than the President himself. A shameless mismanagement of the economy brought the land to the verge of ruin, and when in 1948 the resentment of the powerless nation had reached such proportions that even terror and roguery could not hinder the victory of a unanimous opposition, the votes were declared invalid by a complacent Congress. It looked as though the unhappy country would never get out of the clutches of the Red despots.

But quite unforeseen a saviour appeared, José Figueres, the son of a Catholic doctor, a young man who in 1928, without a cent, returned home from his engineering studies in the States and disappeared into a barren mountainous region. The name of the plantation was *La Lucha*, which in English means The Struggle; it still towers today above the steep slopes of sisal cactuses, with its well-built tracks leading to the remotest corner. This was the work of a resolute will and a powerful organizing genius. Figueres, when he entered politics, was a rich self-made man.

He had foreseen the new act of violence and did not remain idle. A band of young men who had joined his plantation attacked a nearby airfield and stole three planes. With the help of these they obtained weapons from abroad. A civil war started which has already become a myth in the minds of the people—a war of inexperienced fighters, students, employees and peasants against a regular army including communist shock troops. The miracle happened. After six weeks the dictatorship was broken beneath the courageous resistance of the whole country. Figueres as the victor became a national hero and entered San José as head of a provisional government, while the "old gang" with their followers went into voluntary exile, not because they had transgressed politically but because they had contravened the common law. With Figueres' revolution the old spirit of severe democratic probity returned to the land and everyone breathed anew. The plantation owners already dreamed once more of the golden patriarchal age and thought that things would be as they were before. But Figueres had not brought about the revolution in their name and the gentlemen of the Union Club were soon to recognize in terror that the communist devil they had driven out had been replaced by a no less radical Beelzebub.

Figueres told me the story of the eighteen months during which, as leader of the revolutionary junta, he took the fate of the country into his own hands and changed it. Not as a dictator; he had not started a civil war to that end. On the contrary, he intended to draw the teeth of the army for ever and to replace it by a police force. In November 1949 he handed over his office to the legally chosen President Otilio Ulate, a Conservative and an idealist, although not in the least in agreement with the revolutionary Figueres. The latter waited patiently until Ulate's term of office came to an end and in the summer of 1953 was elected to power with an overwhelming majority.

Now he could bring his work to perfection. He had not waged his struggle against Red despotism in the name of the old aristocrats. In his aims he probably stands nearer to the communists than to the latter, for he too wishes to help the people to a better way of life, but he has been involved in economics long enough to realize that one can only distribute when one has produced enough and instead of beginning with demagogy he endeavoured

at the outset to lay the necessary foundations. "Our plantation
owners hoped," he told me, "that I would repeal the communist
workers' code. If you happen to meet any of them they will
constantly complain that business with such burdens cannot pay;
that he will have to sell his property, etc., but that is all rubbish.
The gentlemen have become used to leading a soft life at the
expense of their workers—moreover, with the irrational methods
used by their fathers. Look, I'm a landowner myself and I have
done more for the workers on my property than the law compels
me to do and it still pays because I take the trouble. Well, the
others have got to do the same."

Thus during the year and a half that the fate of the country lay
in the hands of Figueres, a feverish activity reigned. He nationalized the banks to ensure that the capital was not used for
speculation but for agricultural development. He introduced a
10 per cent. property tax and created an office for raising production with the aim of freeing the country's economy from its one-
sided limitation of coffee. Formerly the population had huddled
together on a tiny plateau in great congestion. Now it was
necessary to make them settle in the hot coastal regions and to
make the latter fertile. A great deal was achieved in this short
space of time. Newly built silos were filled with supplies and
comestibles which formerly had to be imported could now be
exported at a good profit.

Pepe, as the people call him, is a short, almost insignificant man,
and often so sunk in his own thoughts that he appears insultingly
absentminded. But as soon as he begins to speak his sharply
chiselled features light up and his eyes glitter with an almost
youthful fire. I have seldom heard so impressive a political speech
as he made one Sunday at *La Lucha*. A host of students had come
to greet him on his birthday and amused themselves by singing
the old martial songs from the civil war. And then Pepe stood up
on a box on the platform of his plantation school and spoke to
them. Fundamentally it was a lecture in national economy, but
spoken with such passion and with such poignancy that even the
most sober members of his audience were deeply moved. Pepe
admitted in his speech to a socialism the roots of which do not

lie in Marxism. He has been too much influenced by American economic ideas not to appreciate private enterprise and political freedom. Only a few enterprises serving as public utilities did he consider should be nationalized—electricity and railways, both of which belonged to foreign companies. But in this too he did not entertain force but reasonable negotiation. Frank Buchmann's Moral Rearmament Movement has left a deep influence on his thoughts and he had even outlined the ideas of "the upright man" in a speech made a few days previously at a meeting of this movement in Miami. Private property, he also said to the students on his farm, only fulfils its true nature when it fulfils a social function. This could not be achieved through State decrees but only through an inner moral revival which led men to look upon themselves not as isolated individuals but as members of the community, not only as owners in the conventional sense of the word but as the administrators of a common property.

This appeal to idealism arouses the enthusiasm of these young men. They see in Pepe a magician who, through his own activities, creates possibilities for their capacities which the old-fashioned régime refused them. But it is also to a great extent pure self-sacrificing idealism which drives them towards him. The director of the State silo installation, a young engineer, spoke for example with a kind of mystical ecstasy about Pepe. He had just received an offer from Nicaragua which would have brought him a considerably higher salary, but he preferred to remain with Pepe. On the other hand, certain elderly enlightened people raise their hands on high at the mention of their President. "Figueres is a Don Quixote and his feet are not planted firmly on the ground. He is constantly dreaming about social justice." The facts show them to be partially correct inasmuch as enormous sums of money are wasted in irresponsible experiments—experiments Pepe's friends consider must be tried once and which, even if they prove fruitless, are more valuable than inactivity. One thing, however, is certain. This dynamic figure must not only reckon with the idealism of the students but also with the cautious mistrust of a great part of the people. They are afraid that his unbridled idealism will upset the *petit bourgeois* order of the land and that his urge for innovation will end in wild adventure. I could appreciate their feelings when Figueres drove me round the hair-pin bends on his farm. He cut them so fine that a pair of steps remained behind on one of the cliffs.

As I said before, it is not the number of men that determine the greatness of a destiny. Figueres is far more than the mere President of Costa Rica. Between the civil war and his election to the Presidency he travelled extensively in North and South America, gave interviews and made speeches in the Universities and on the radio. He has become one of the leading representatives of the progressive and democratic classes of Latin America and at the same time an ally of the United States, which he admires and loves. But this love takes on a different aspect to that of his servile colleague Somoza of Nicaragua, who numbers his democratic neighbours among his implacable enemies and patrons of his exiled friends. He is not an eager "yes-man" but a most serious critic. It is illuminating that one of his first measures on coming to power was to start new negotiations with the United Fruit Company, which rules a little kingdom of its own of some 250,000 acres in the plain on the Atlantic coast. It paid 15 per cent of its profits to the government, which represented almost half the entire tax revenue of the land (a fact which shows what fantastic tax evaders the coffee planters of Costa Rica must be). Figueres demanded a higher share, in return for which he offered to take over the social activities of the company, the schools, hospitals, etc. His fifty per cent was only a beginning. His goal was the gradual transfer of the American undertaking to small native owners. For he maintains that the era of big capitalist undertakings on foreign land and the domination by foreign interests is over. The days have gone, too, when the Latin American countries are merely a cheap source of raw material for their northern neigh-bours. The United States must give them just prices for their products and at the same time the possibility of accumulating their own capital for long-term investments. American capital must continue to play its part in short-term investments which do not lead to political domination. Were America to recognize this moral duty, he maintains that the hatred for the Gringo would cease and the danger of a dictatorship such as communism would disappear.

Figueres said all this with a friendly welcoming smile, with none of the grim hatred I saw on the face of Guatemala's liberator. In these or in similar words, I have heard many moderate socialists speak in Latin America—socialists who to a certain extent think in terms of Roosevelt's New Deal and believe that the social reconciliation which was possible inside the United States could extend throughout whole hemispheres. The only thing one can put forward against this concept is the old argument of reality *versus* idealism. Can one expect American capitalists to be philanthropic enough to keep on with their short-term investments when their present installations have been confiscated? And it is confiscation that President Figueres is really after, despite the friendliness of his speech.

PANAMA

Racial insanity on the Canal

PANAMA CITY is a town with many faces. You could almost believe when wandering through its old quarters that you were in a European port. In actual fact the town is much younger than many of its more sober sisters. When at the end of the seventeenth century the pirate Henry Morgan plundered and destroyed an earlier insufficiently well-protected settlement—the cathedral spire still towers lonely and romantic over its ruins on the shore a few miles away from the modern city—it was removed behind the sand dunes of the peninsula to be more secure from any future attacks. In the nineteenth century the French Canal Company added a host of cool elegant palaces in their own style to the town.

A quarter of an hour's walk and you are already in a completely different tropical world. Wooden huts with gigantic verandahs border the streets. Negro children look inquisitively through the railings. Through small doorways you come into dark courtyards where washing hangs out and you cannot see the sky. The rooms teem with humanity. Here and there a Chinese or an Indian face crops up among the black woolly heads, emphasizing the strange mixture of races to be found among the half-naked squabbling children. That is the world of the proletariat, that expatriate human stream which has settled on the canal from all parts of the world.

And then you come to a *playa* with a flagpole sporting the red-and-blue starred flag of Panama. This is the frontier. Once more a new world begins—the Canal Zone, which is under American administration. Here cleanliness and piety reign. One prayer house after another stands along the broad tarred streets. Then the employees' quarters: foreigners cannot enter, and access to the duty-free import wares is forbidden. A broad staircase

leads up to the majestic Canal Administration building above
which the Stars and Stripes fly. Barracks, parade grounds and airfields make you nervous if you push on further, but they are
almost deserted. To the left of the road lies a meadow covered
with stocky bushes where a huge liner with towering smoke-
stacks waddles gravely through the grass like a cow at pasture.
We have reached the Panama Canal! A waterway which looks
so harmless disguised by a couple of bushes and yet one of the
most important waterways in the world. The road turns off to
the left and you come to a bridge. An American soldier raises his
tommy gun; you cannot go any further. The middle of the bridge
has been raised to let a steamer through, and beyond, the lock
gates of Miraflores yawn ready to swallow the giant morsel.
They snap to like the jaws of a boa constrictor behind it
and the ship begins to rise 27 feet in the air as though on a
piano stool.

It will need another couple of such lifts before it reaches a
height of 85 feet, the Continental water level over in Gaillard
Cut. Here it is constrained between steep parapets down which
the earth is constantly sliding. "Look out!" is the constant cry
that greets the pilot. When mist or twilight falls here coloured
lights blink from both banks, white to starboard and red to port
to show him the way. Sometimes when the parched vegetation
catches fire, tankers and munition ships are kept waiting for
hours, because a spark could cause untold damage. At last the
canal ends and you lose the sense of claustrophobia from which
you suffered in this Cut. To your left lies Barro Colorado Island.
All manner of strange fauna retired there when the dammed-up
waters of the lock began to flood the region. Today it is a paradise
for bird watchers. Sometimes a skipper will point out derelict
machinery rusting at the jungle's edge, a monument to the
French defeat. They were not conquered by men or treacherous
scientific weapons, but by the mosquitos which infected thousands
of tenderfoot pioneers with malaria. The Americans were the
first to accomplish a miracle and turn this tropical plague spot into
a completely healthy one.

At last on our canal journey we meet another lock. The Gatun dam is a mighty edifice which has been built for eternity. It is 2,000 feet wide at its base and its roomy summit is large enough to house a golf course. Beyond are three more locks steeper than on the Pacific side, and in the distance the houses of Cristóbal and Colón gleam on the Atlantic. The ships lie at anchor in the sea like snakes: in the locks and in Lake Gatun great activity reigns. Thirty ships on an average pass through daily, and in 1953 the Canal Company had a gross income of no less than $107½ millions with a net profit of $7.2 millions. Any child who studies the map of the world can realize the enormous strategic importance of this waterway. Instead of having to sail round Cape Horn the American Fleet, not to mention troop and transport ships, can use the shorter way between the two oceans through the canal. It is no exaggeration to say that the whole economic structure of the United States would be changed were it not for the Panama Canal. A great part of the raw material for the industry of the north-east comes from the South American Pacific coast. Chilean copper, Bolivian tin, Peruvian lead and even natural rubber from Malaya, for example, pass through Panama. The fact that today the south-east of America is industrialized, and harbours like New Orleans, Corpus Christi and others flourish, is entirely due to the Panama Canal which allows the short cut. One is inclined to ask what would happen to this very vulnerable series of locks in the case of a war. What would happen if an atom bomb. . . ? It is by no means out of the question and obviously the military authorities are fully aware of the danger. There are various possible threats; that sabotage will be carried out from a ship passing through or by a native fifth column; that it will be attacked by a submarine or an aircraft. Against the latter two eventualities the defence staff has installed radar apparatus as far as the Rio Grande and southwards to Peru with particular attention to Guatemala, only a few hours away from Panama by air. The most fruitful target for such an attack would not be the locks but the Madden Dam. This controls the tides of the Shagrés river which fills the Gatun Lake. Its water reserves form the stream which opens and shuts the sluices. If this little artificial lake vanished the Panama Canal would be out of action for months, and even the third and broader lock which for safety's sake has been built three miles away would no longer suffice. The only moderately safe solution would be a canal without locks, a canal at sea level such as the French once intended to build. The masses of earth which would have to be removed are incalculable. It would cost twice as much as the present canal and would take fifteen years to build. And a lot can happen in fifteen years. . . .

Submarine and aircraft can be dealt with, but what about sabotage? Are the inhabitants of Panama friendly to America?

Were history a heavenly power capable of guiding sympathies the Panamanians should love the States like a father, for Panama, before Theodore Roosevelt bought the bankrupt French Canal Company and sponsored with gold and naval aid a Declaration of independence on the part of the local politicians, was nothing else but a malaria-infested tropical nest, a forgotten Colombian province. It was the gold of the American taxpayers that conquered the diseases and completed the canal, the canal which was and still is the small republic's sole source of income. She agreed for the sum of $10 million, and an annuity of $250,000, to cede a zone 10 miles wide to the Americans. In a contract signed by Franklin D. Roosevelt this was raised to $430,000 on account of the devaluation of the dollar.

Easy money! Panama, people say, has the highest number of millionaires in the world in proportion to its population. Outside the city stands the most expensive hotel in the whole of Latin America. It was built on the seafront by the government and there is no road leading to it for pedestrians. You can only arrive by Cadillac. If a wretched pedestrian wants to get there, just run him down, it doesn't matter!

This hotel was built with a $4 million credit from the Export Import Bank and since its opening it has been run at a loss. "It's idiotic," said the manager (at the risk of my life I paid him a visit on foot). "The thing that strangles us completely is that we're not allowed to have a casino here. Gambling in Panama isn't forbidden. On the contrary. A national lottery and horse races bring a great deal of money to our budget, so I can't think why the government wouldn't let us open a casino. Everyone would have made money from it." The Hotel Panama with its fabulous luxury and its debts is somehow symbolic of the whole atmosphere of this port. Easy come, easy go. Everyone passes through here—tourists, commercial travellers, sailors—and all of them travel through the canal and stay in the hotels, buy in the shops and enjoy themselves in the drinking dives and cabarets. In addition to the prayer houses, the meagre slums and the old streets there is a shopping centre where the windows are filled to bursting point, and everything that the world produces glitters here temptingly in neon lights: perfume from Paris, smart sports shirts, ivory buddhas from China, gold brocade from India, with real Hindus and Chinese behind the counters. Buy and sell. That is Panama's motto.

Things went magnificently during the war, when the United States expanded their defences in the Canal zone and the troops from thirteen bases were billeted in Panama. But all this came to a sticky end when in 1947 nationalist demonstrations and the unanimous decision of parliament compelled them to clear these bases. Peace time is always a slim time for Panama, and even the Korean war has not changed it very much. Today the barmen sit like melancholy sparrows in their nests, and those ladies who for many tourists have transformed Panama city into a wild romantic brothel—an exaggeration, of course—have to content themselves with an occasional sailor.

That is the reason for the *malaise* which reigns in Panama City. As usual it has had the well-known effect: police chief Ramón, who for years as President-maker had held the effective control of Panama in his hands, assumed the Presidency and tried authoritatively to do what strong men have done everywhere. He strangled the earlier corruption, balanced the budget, presented the rich men with a taxation bill for the first time, and inaugurated a vast road-building programme, essential to any development of the country. And since he ate out of the *Americanos'* hands exactly like his colleague Somoza he can always count on their support. When he visited the White House officially in the autumn of 1953 he took a huge briefcase full of demands. "We do not want charity," he declared. "We want justice."

This "justice" implies several things, but basically only one of importance: money. Panama wants a larger annuity than $430,000—at least a seven-figure sum. She wants the "*Commissariés*," where the employees of the Canal zone buy their goods duty-free or at a small profit of 35 per cent., to be reduced or closed entirely, so that the customers will do more business with the natives. Since 1905, when these "*Commissariés*" were opened for the first time, the Canal administration has been deafened by the complaints of the Panama shopkeepers, and in the course of time they have called forth wild attacks from the press and at times even diplomatic intervention. Some of these complaints against the Canal administration are not without foundation: the contracts which bind the Great Power and the dwarf republic have been entered into rather light-heartedly by the latter.

To return to the "*Commissariés*": for a long time they sold quite unchecked to anyone who was employed by them, and when the new 1936 Treaty sharply reduced the circle of customers a flourishing contraband existed between the Canal zone and Panama. Another bone of contention is the taxes. Although neither of the contracting parties should by rights tax the Canal zone employees, the United States in 1950 cancelled this tax freedom in the case of their nationals without giving the same rights to Panama. "The other Latin American countries are treated as good neighbours," said a Panaman politician, "but we are treated as an occupied zone."

This feeling of colonial dependence is nourished above all by the different treatment which the citizens of Panama experience when getting jobs in the Canal zone. I met, for example, a young intellectual who had studied and obtained his degree at Harvard, spoke pure American and was now looking for a job. "The personnel chief of the Canal administration," he told me, "at first thought I was an American citizen and offered me a position with a very decent salary, but as soon as I revealed my true nationality things took a very different turn. The post in question was given to an American competitor and I, who had exactly the same academic qualifications behind me, was fobbed off with a very badly paid job." I heard of similar practices everywhere. They seemed to be the rule and in direct contradiction to the agreement by which the citizens of Panama should have equal rights in the administration of the canal.

In Panama City I met a young negro who had earned a great name for himself as a sociologist and a fighter for the rights of his race; a budding friendship brought us quite often into contact. Intellectually we understood one another extremely well, but I constantly found my relationship with him made difficult by the strangest possible misunderstandings. "Let's meet tonight at nine," George would say, for example. I hastened to grab some dinner and offended him because he had intended that I should eat with him. Another day he drove me by car to Colón on the Atlantic side of the canal. We arranged a time and a meeting-place for the return journey and both of us waited an hour in different places for the other. We seemed to be bewitched. When I mentioned this curious ill luck to various mutual friends they smiled sadly. "That is George's trouble," they said. "It doesn't only happen to you. He is one of the most brilliant brains in this city. He's a great sportsman who won the tennis championship and his position allows him to live at a very high level. And yet simply because of this his relationship to the outside world has somehow been broken. You know who rules in Panama? The Americans, of course. And you know how Yankees look upon the negro. He is only good enough to hump bales in the docks. A coloured intellectual? You'll meet with curled lips. And this racial insanity, which is completely alien to Latin America, is beginning to taint the country. That's why George is so insecure and so irresponsible in his relationships. He does not feel at home socially, although he is so intelligent, smart and well-dressed."

To use a cliché, one would call him "A man of gold". In Panama there are not only "gold" but "silver" men, but here it is not a question of character but of income. To make a comparison, the Americans are all "gold" and the natives are all "silver" men. Even when the inhabitants of Panama manage to find a post on the canal they are worse paid than their colleagues from the States. This discrimination found its terminology at the time of the building of the canal and has only recently become current again; the American directives were paid in gold, while the West Indian negroes, the Chinese, Spaniards, Yugoslavs and other workers in lower grades were paid out in the local silver currency. This was the origin of "gold" and "silver" men. From a purely technical form of payment it eventually blossomed into a purely caste system. Gold men and silver men were equals at work but were separated socially by an insurmountable gulf. "Gold only" was written over certain fountains and no "silver" men were allowed to drink from this water. On the other hand, no "gold" man, without endangering his prestige, would dare to visit a club or a sports ground belonging to a "silver" man, let alone invite one of them to his own house. The two groups bought in different shops and certain of the more elegant and expensive ware could only be found in the gold shops.

Employees might be doing exactly the same job, but their salaries were different. Whether chauffeur, carpenter, or book-keeper, the gold man sees his pay packet swelled to double and treble—not to mention the 25 per cent. foreign allowance which the Americans enjoy. Very occasionally a native colleague is promoted into the gold class, but he is the exception which proves the rule.

An almost amusing complication within this class system is caused by the few negroes of American origin. As United States citizens they come in the gold category and can claim the attendant privileges, but with one exception: their children cannot enter the gold school. I was told the story of a coloured employee whose children were fetched every morning by a white chauffeur and taken to the silver school for coloured children. Obviously certain Americans are opposed to such discrimination. George introduced me to the representative of the CIO Union, who is actually a coloured man. Mr Welsh began to organize the "silver" men at the end of the war. After a few years of struggle the discriminating plaques disappeared from the fountains, pleasure grounds and stores. Naturally this did not mean the end of the caste system, for these limitations have not yet been universally banished. The "silver" man now has to know exactly where he can go and cannot go, but since the outward trappings of the system have now been shed this may be the the first step towards equality.

What would be the second and third steps? This was the main subject of conversation between my coloured friend and myself. "We shall not rest," he said eagerly, "until we have full equality, and by that I mean payment according to our qualifications." It grieved me very much to have to contradict his passion. This conflict had become so bound up with his own destiny that each contradiction on my part gave rise to an angry outburst. But could I refrain from contradicting him? It was obvious: if one wanted to entice a North American to these exacting tropics it could only be done through higher pay. Native labour, however, unbidden and in too great a quantity, was always knocking at the door of the zone administration departments. Was it not merely a question of supply and demand? My friend would not see this. He would grow melancholy again, wounded to the depths by the humiliations the white man continually inflicts upon his black brother. And not only the Yankees! Even among the local inhabitants the poison is beginning to spread.

And here was the famous Arnulfo Arias, a self-styled doctor, and a politician, educated in the United States. We sat in his luxurious villa by the seashore. I was under the impression that I was speaking to a film star. He waltzed in and was now speaking in a shrill voice, fluttering his eyelashes like a young girl. You would not have thought he could say 'boo' to a goose, but this soft exterior concealed a veritable hurricane. This was the brilliant people's tribune from Panama who was able to fling the masses in wild waves against the dams of the ruling powers. But that was all. Twice he was raised to power, only to come to grief, after a short rule, through his own stupidity. On the last occasion he landed in gaol and had only recently been released. As I have already mentioned, he calls himself Arias and has brought this Aryan name to honour, inasmuch as at the beginning of the forties, when he became President for the first time, he tried to imitate Hitler's culture and race policies. But his anger was directed not against the Jews: in the name of white superiority he tried to exterminate the Chinese and the negroes.

However, purity of race is a great rarity in Panama and hardly a soul exists without a taint of negro blood—this shade is known as *"café con leche"*. This by no means destroys racial pride, but rather aggravates it by reason of a secret inferiority complex. Incidentally the colour of the skin did not matter so much to Arias as the culture. Under the war cry of *Hispanidad* he made a dead set for the Chinese, who rule small business and whose prosperity makes them a tasty sacrifice. Arias nationalized their businesses, which meant that he compelled them by a decree to sell, usually to one of his own friends, at an insignificant price; the creditors were then thrown out of the country by the police. However brutal and unfair this procedure may have been it consolidated his popularity among the natives—for robbing is always better than being robbed—and it has remained one of his permanent measures. The Chinese today are a rapidly disappearing minority and most of them work as modest employees.

His second blow affected the negroes. Panama has much to thank them for. Every other race succumbed to the heat and the diseases of the tropics before the canal was built. Only the blacks who streamed in by their thousands from the British colonies in the West Indies—from Jamaica and Barbados—could stand the climate, and after their task was completed they stayed on as welcome workers. They were particularly welcome because their mother tongue was English and thus they were able to work with the Americans. Welcome too for the most part because they had been given an excellent practical education by their English masters. There was no reason at all to hispanize themselves, since both from a practical and a prestige point of view English took precedence over Spanish—it was of course the speech of the American bosses. Arias now directed his racial laws against this "cultural blot" by taking away from all the children who had been born to the West Indian negroes the citizenship they had automatically acquired. This measure, which made these unfortunate people stateless and deprived them of their rights, did not survive long after Arias' fall. Today it only holds good to the extent that when they claim citizenship the negroes have to pass an examination in Spanish and in the history of Panama.

But was the root of the evil removed, of this evil which hardened the hearts of the "underdog" against the "bosses" and vice versa? This crazy game in which one party knew himself to be despised and nevertheless directed his contempt towards a third party? Obviously such a position was fruitful ground for revolution, and how could the presence of the arch-despisers, the Yankees, fail to bring grist to the communist mills? The Americans themselves whom I met in Panama pulled long faces. They spoke of secret agents who arrived quite legally only to disappear completely, of professors who systematically poisoned youthful intellectuals. Was there really some sinister force sowing the seeds of unrest in the heart of the American defence? But there is more hysteria than truth in it all: it is the too prevalent inclination to declare everything that is not for you as against you. My coloured friend was far from being a communist, but I can never forget his warnings: "It is dangerous to brand everything the United States criticize as communism. One runs the danger of ascribing to this word things not applicable to it, but which among many of us are honoured as being valid."

Admittedly in this respect too the new President, police colonel Ramón, did his duty. A new law passed in December 1953 forbade communists to hold posts in the government or to remain in the country. The professors who could sow their subversive seeds under the cloak of their profession were dismissed from the universities and the teaching institutes. I tried in vain to find the offices of the People's Party, which together with a small Union, the *Federación Sindacal de Trabajadores*, is under the leadership of Domingo Barria: the party never had a very great following and today has gone completely underground. When shortly afterwards a mysterious man visited the General Secretary the police were only too quick to snap him up. He turned out to be a Moscow agent who had already dealt with reliable people in various other Latin American countries and possessed a list of the communist spy net. Although Panama can pride herself on the fact that during the last World War no single act of sabotage was perpetrated by one of her nationals, the prospects for the future do not look nearly so rosy: there are considerably more communist than fascist adepts in Panama City. But even more dangerous is the hysteria through which everyone who is not for the government is indiscriminately declared to be an opponent. I was present at a dinner in a university with many politically suspect professors. I spoke with them and found a very critical attitude towards the United States, but certainly no love for Moscow. Again, although my coloured friend was no communist, I cannot forget his warning. It applies not only to Panama but to the whole Latin American continent.

COLOMBIA

Magdalena with the hardened arteries

HOW magnificent and gentle was this green. I had grown so unaccustomed to it. Since leaving Mexico I had not met with a single drop of rain. Each day the sky was the same brilliant blue until I could no longer bear to look at it. For I paid for it with the sparse wintry yellow drought beneath my feet, the perpetual dusty gracelessness of the soil. But here it was the rainy season. The aircraft bore me over wild crests and cliffs, half covered with clouds. I should have preferred to enter this new country by road, but in Colombia this was impossible. Even when the missing stretches of the Pan American Highway are completed, when the route from Texas to Panama and from Bogotá to Santiago is eventually opened, this entrance to the continent will for many years be barred on account of inaccessbile wild country and dangerous Indian tribes. It was a strange experience to fly above forbidden territory—a primeval landscape cut by no roads, with an occasional path and villages that seemed to have fallen accidentally from the full hands of the Creator. And then suddenly the aircraft landed in a first-class industrial centre, Medellin.

Colombia is the most devout land in South America, and of all its dioceses Medellin is the most pious. Monseñor Builez, the present Archbishop, has not only outlawed the aphrodisiac intoxication of the dance as an instrument of the Devil, but has forbidden the girls to wear sweaters lest their curves should disturb the hearts of the young men. Bicycling is also forbidden (naturally without success) because of the temptation of billowing skirts . . . and naturally no respectable Christian girl would ever dream of wearing trousers.

However, this almost medieval narrow-mindedness associated with a patriarchal *petit bourgeois* mentality has an exceedingly

146

modern background. Medellin is in an industrial metropolis where skyscrapers tower above the nineteenth-century houses. As in Mexico, industrialization started in Colombia with both foreign and local capital and threatens to change the face of the land in the course of a few years. It is considered one of the healthiest climates for foreign currency, since the laws allow free export of capital and profits; the best and most expensive coffee in the world gives the country an unassailable economic 'and monetary basis. The Antioqueños have the reputation of being the slickest business men of this hemisphere.

My objective was the capital, Bogotá. On the map the distance between the two cities looks like a cat's jump, and had I decided to continue my journey by plane it would merely have been a matter of hours. Anyone, however, who wishes to become acquainted with Colombia would be advised to go overland, because the true spirit of the country can only be understood by the incredible difficulties which arise in land communications. One can safely say that the aeroplane first united Colombia. A few decades ago the journey from one provincial town to another— for example from Medellin to Bogotá or from there to Cali— was equivalent to making an expedition through the tropics or in the Arctic. The provinces therefore have developed not only economically but also spiritually into a kind of autarchy. Agriculture and trade were neighbourly affairs. Even today, when roads are being built through the wilderness and the land is beginning to achieve some unity under the impulse of industry, a journey is something of an adventure.

A cosy small-gauge railway along which a train runs every two days took me through deserted valleys from the coolness of 5,000 feet steadily downwards to Puerto Berrios and the river Magdalena. This mighty stream flows the whole length of Colombia from south to north, and I had been advised to follow it at least part of the way through the primeval forest by ship. However, when I enquired at the shipping company's office as to the possibility of getting a ticket for the upstream trip, they merely shrugged their shoulders. "Perhaps this evening, perhaps to-morrow, perhaps in a week's time," came the reply, and when I

asked the reason for such uncertainty I learnt that the river had
rapidly succumbed to silting and at low water the ships with their
cargoes from Baranquilla harbour were often stranded for days
on the sandbanks. In such circumstances it was quite impossible
to stick to a regular schedule. Thus there was nothing for it except
to wait in peace for either a day or a week. In this heat! Panama
with its sea breeze was an icebox in comparison, and moreover
Puerto Berrios was not a particularly pleasant place to stay. Its
whole *raison d'être* consists in a number of huge tanks in which
the oil from the neighbouring field of Barranca Bermeso, a few
hundred miles upstream, is stored. Around them, beneath the
giant trees on the banks, cluster the negroes' wooden huts full of
indescribably filthy children. No, one couldn't stay here, and I
abandoned the idea of travelling by river. I snapped for fresh air
like a fish out of water and decided to take a bus the following
morning from the other side of the river. There I could travel
on the new road to Borbosa, where I could catch a fast train to
Bogotá.

That evening the hotel verandah was full of men—chiefly
American engineers who were building a pipeline to Medellin.
The geologist who happened to be my companion at table
scratched his bald head when I told him of my travel difficulties.
"Yes," he said, "this silted-up old Magdalena's a great problem.
The people will never solve it until they build a railway through
the heart of the land to Baranquilla. The International Bank for
Reconstruction and Development has granted $25 million. In
my opinion it would be more intelligent to look for another way
through the inhabited plateau instead of the wilderness down
here. An attempt was already made in the twenties to join
Medellin to the Atlantic, but then the business petered out. Do
you know what happened to the railway from Bogotá to Puerto
Salgar further up the river? They began to build from both ends
at the same time, and when they met it was discovered that one
team had chosen a gauge of 1 metre and the other one of 1 yard!
For a long time the passengers had the dubious pleasure of
changing trains in the middle of the journey, until finally they
decided to make it 1 yard throughout. You would hardly credit

it, but not long afterwards a few wonderful new engines arrived, designed for the metre gauge. Fortunately, on unloading they fell into the river and were lost. The insurance company paid for the damage!"

The oil people and technicians have a reason for sticking to this Magdalena Valley hell. Oil has risen to great importance in Colombia's economy, and after coffee (82 per cent) crude oil is the most important export (13 per cent). Once the childish ailments of nationalist envy and labour unrest in the late forties came to an end, a newly founded national company worked on the best of terms with British and American firms in prospecting and in increasing production. No one knows what undiscovered treasure lies in the vast jungle region near the Venezuelan oilfields. Perhaps the Magdalena railway, instead of running through a desert, will pass through the forest of cracking towers and refineries which have been planned or already erected and carry the commodity up to the settlements on the plateau.

Civil war in the name of God

I cannot remember anywhere in the world having seen so much religious zeal and display as during Holy Week in Bogotá. Long winding processions made their way through the streets in the rain—long queues of worshippers who all wanted to get into the church. Policemen stood in the doorway to control the mob. Where did the queues end? Everyone was anxious to cleanse his soul of past sins and spend Easter with a clear conscience. The earnestness of these people was somewhat cloying and their piety almost gruesome. "Our catholicism is still that of the scholastic Middle Ages," admitted Don Alvaro, a supporter of the ultra-conservative ex-President Laureano Gómez.

I scrutinized the young, haggard face of this fanatic, trying to find some spark of modern frankness in it. He had been a diplomat in Europe and one would have thought that this would have been enough to change a man. But there was nothing shamefaced in his medieval creed: on the contrary, it rang out like a triumphant fanfare. Colombia is still healthy in the corruption of the world. Nihilism, existentialism and all the other godless "—isms", even when they sport the trappings of catholicism, have been unable to reach this island of faith.

"The only modern thinker, representative of us," Alvaro went on, "is the Frenchman Charles Maurras, who unites Church and State in the same conservative thought."

"And Franco's Spain?" I added.

"Certainly," he replied, "we are, so to speak, more Spanish than the Spanish, a kind of super-Spain. We have remained truer to the spirit and the ideology of the Conquest than the mother country herself."

That is Colombia: the citadel of God, of a God that elsewhere in the world has assumed humaner and milder traits—with the exception of Spain, where our generation has witnessed a civil war the savagery of which originated from the absolute metaphysical devotion of medieval faith. From similar causes Colombia suffered a pitiless four years' civil war between 1949 and 1953—a war between the Conservative and Liberal parties.

No one can exactly explain the difference between these two parties. Once before in the nineteenth century the liberals were influenced by the lay ideas of the French revolution and of European socialism. They championed that humanity which endeavoured to protect the dignity of man against all forms of absolutism, and in particular from the Catholic Church. Under their influence Church and State were split in the Constitution of 1853. Not long afterwards the Jesuits were banished from the country, their Order was disbanded and their property, together with that of the whole Church, nationalized. All this was accomplished after the bitterest struggles with the clerical party. In the history books you find no less than seventy civil wars if you count them all, large and small. One of them alone cost 80,000 human lives and another 100,000. But then a curious thing occurred. The liberal Núñez, who became dictator at the end of the century, declared catholicism once more to be the State religion and gave the Church back its property and privileges. This ideological uncertainty, this confusion of the frontiers be-

tween liberals and conservatives, continued to be the basic mood
of the twentieth century.

"Colombia is Catholic to the marrow," the brilliant liberal
attorney Gilberto Moreno assured me when I discussed this
problem with him. "Even we liberals no longer follow the anti-
clerical trend which in the old days was bound up with our name.
There is absolutely no reason for it. Our priests are poor and so
is the Church. A recent investigation showed that they owned
only one thousandth of one per cent of the cultivated land. It
has never experienced the moral degeneration of the Spanish
and Mexican Churches. Thus there is no need for anti-clericalism
here. We liberals are perhaps more steadfast catholics than the
conservatives, for the latter are often inclined to debase the faith
and to use it as an instrument of power. Therefore the Church
has always been better placed under a liberal than under a conservative rule. We grant them larger sums of money from the
State's funds and allow them more freedom to devote themselves
to their own spiritual tasks."

In the liberal camp piety triumphed no less than in that of their
opponents, so much so that the attempt of the progressive
President Alfonso López at the beginning of the forties to institute
divorce and to renew the outmoded concordat with the Vatican
according to modern concepts came to grief against the general
resistance put up by his own followers, despite the agreement of
the Curia. The Colombians have shown themselves to be more
papist than the Pope himself.

"But wherein lies the difference between conservative and
liberal in this country," I asked him, "and why are you so bitter
against each other?" I put this question not only to Moreno but
to other liberal leaders and invariably received the same vague,
inconclusive answers. Perhaps one is justified in saying that the
liberals believe rather more strictly in the idea of freedom, while
on the other side the conservatives became tainted by a führer cult
not entirely of American origin: in these circles even today the
names of Hitler, Mussolini and Franco are all greatly honoured.
Thus it is difficult to determine the social difference between the
two parties because their leaders usually come from the leading

families in the country. And it all boils down to the fact that the conservatives are in power and the liberals are not.

"But," I said to Moreno, "you still haven't cleared up for me why the two parties are such bitter enemies."

He smiled. "The Colombians," he said, "suffer from having a very long memory. They cannot forget. For them the last century is only yesterday—the last century when the liberals had not had their claws drawn as today and when they threw the priests out by the seat of their pants."

"But Colombia was on the way to recovery," I interrupted him. "Since the beginning of this century the family wrangles have been put aside and a development on democratic lines has taken place making the land one of the most praiseworthy of this hemisphere. Why should that suddenly end? Why must the age-old hate crop up again out of something which no longer exists?"

My colleague shrugged his shoulders. "It was the 9th of April, the fatal 9th of April 1948," he murmured to himself, although this was really no answer.

April the 9th. No Colombian can hear this date without a shiver running down his spine. On this day a man called Jorge Eliécer Gaitán was murdered in the streets of Bogotá, and in revenge for this act the whole centre of the capital was razed to the ground. And who was this extraordinary man Gaitán? A liberal politician, no more nor less, but one with dynamite in his hands. He did not belong to that small section, that oligarchy from which traditionally the rulers of the party were chosen. He had risen from the people and he fought for the people. With him the nobodies of Colombian politics, the Indians, suddenly entered the political arena.

Indians in Colombia? Nowhere had I come across any of the bright, colourful folk such as I saw in Mexico and in Guatemala. They do not exist. In Colombia something happened similar to the events in Costa Rica: the peasant colonists rather than the feudal elements had felt drawn towards this country. The mixture of races swept the autochthonous Indian culture almost entirely away, so that even physiognomically the population has taken on the anonymous and colourless features of the mestizo.

This makes the Colombian plateau an almost boring country. The only thing that the natives have in common with the northern Indians is their material poverty. These masses aroused Gaitán from his passiveness. When he spoke in the House he would tear off his shirt, point pathetically to his naked chest and say, "Look, I'm an Indio too." With such demagogy he succeeded in becoming one of the most powerful figures in Colombian politics and in causing his colleagues in office an infinite number of headaches—incidentally, the liberals were in power.

Who guided the hand which fired the fatal bullet at this socialist prophet? It will probably never come to light, for the murderer did not long survive his victim.

"The communists planned it," insisted the conservatives and still maintain so today. "With this revolt they wanted to upset the Pan American Conference which was sitting at the time in the capital and taking important steps to combat the Red danger on the Continent." But many unprejudiced people shake their heads. How could a few communist intellectuals who lived in isolation in Colombia unleash such a natural catastrophe? An hysterical mob streamed into the centre from all the suburbs, completely berserk with grief and indignation; an orgy of burning, destruction and plundering broke out. It was hell let loose. The military, flown in from Pasto in the south, restored order, but the city lay in ruins as though it had been bombed. "The communists," argued my friend, "would never have unleashed such a futile tornado. Once the fire had been lit they might have cashed in on it, but they certainly never lit the fire. It was something quite different. Atavistic impulses which people thought had been tamed had suddenly flared up: the bloodthirsty rage of Indian ancestors, the age-old hatred of the coloured man for the white. Nothing was planned. It was an elemental chaos. For days afterwards you could buy the craziest things in the streets—a large refrigerator for ten pesos and a small one for twenty, because it was easier to carry. The hysteria produced the most fantastic results. I met an Indio driving his donkey to the mountains loaded with a mountain of lavatory paper, although heaven knows what he could do with it in his village. No, no one who was present will ever forget that day. Colombia was a changed country. The mob had tasted blood and now, like a wild tiger, it rattles the bars of its cage. Any day it can break out again and lay low anything within reach of its claws. No one feels safe any more. There is a spirit of nervousness abroad and that is the waxing tragedy of our days."

As long as the democratic feeling in Colombia still lived the two parties had striven naturally for power. The presidential term of office tended to foster true bourgeois virtue: the newly chosen patriarch made the rounds of his friends after the inaugural session and congratulated his predecessor with touching and simple fairness. In 1946 a split in the liberal ranks opened the way to power to the conservative Ospino Pérez—that very President who had to deal with the terrible incident of April 9th. For a time it appeared that this catastrophe would bring both parties together, because the shock caused a united national Cabinet to be formed. But it did not last long. When the new 1949 elections drew near a sinister figure, Laureano Gómez, took over the leadership of the conservative party. He was a man who had learnt his political methods from Franco and who did not hesitate to use them. In his eyes the liberals were a devil's brood and, as godless corrupters of the Christian order, were responsible for the existing chaos. Their return to power must be prevented at all costs even though they obviously had the majority of the people behind them. From then on Colombia relapsed into its ancient barbarity. The police arrested the liberal leaders throughout the land, murdered their families and drove them into the mountains. It was not difficult to strike at opponents; conviction here is not a matter of feeling but of family, as it was with the Guelphs and the Ghibellines in the Middle Ages. You were born a liberal or a conservative. There are villages which are conservative and provinces which are liberal, and in these naturally the terror was greatest. But the attacked did not take it lying down. They banded together in the mountain fastnesses and in the eastern jungle. If people had murdered their wives and children with knives, very well, they would retaliate with *machetes*. The police had murdered a friend: good, the following morning the corpses of two constables would be discovered. Then four new liberals would wipe this out and the guerillas would hang eight conservatives. Thus this war of attrition grew proportionately more abominable and more gruesome. Where was the ideology now to ennoble such a struggle? Does the tortured animal that strikes back have a credo for which it struggles? With a certain justification the conservatives called their opponents bandits, for they had become bandits. Even the liberal leaders who had remained in the cities and tried to defend their rights by letters of protest and newspaper articles jibbed at countenancing these deeds. They maintained loudly in public that there was no contact left between themselves and the guerillas, but in private conversation one felt them tremble when the conversation turned on these unhappy comrades. The most rigorous press censorship saw to it that the bloody events remained unpublished, but they were so widespread that they could not be kept secret. Under a veil of ignorance, life in the towns seemed normal. The fighting cocks of the two parties greeted each other cordially at the great ball in the feudal Country Club and danced with their opponents' wives. Outside in the Sierra they also danced—but with knives. Even in the towns, the wild beasts at times stretched their claws through the bars.

To what extent Gómez' brutality was merely an expression of the dormant collective violence was proved in September 1952 when five of the murdered partisans and battered policemen were given a funeral in Bogotá. The excitement of April the 9th lay once more in the air and once more it burst out into an irrational urge for destruction. The populace stormed and plundered the houses of the liberal leaders and destroyed their newspaper offices and printing presses. From then on Gómez' grip tightened on the throat of the country. Although the free elements of his own conservative party began to murmur against his tyranny he went on to work out a new scheme which would legalize and perpetuate his despotism. It looked as though the war of the State against the citizens was not only to be waged against the liberals but also against the conservatives. The skies over Colombia seemed darker than ever. But one of the secrets of Latin American politics falls into the category of the famous Austrian general's witticism: "The situation is constantly desperate but never serious". The game of power politics in most of these countries may to our ideas appear absurd—even criminal and catastrophic —and with our rationalism we are far too inclined to lose sight of the *deus ex machina* who is always ready in the background and holds back the extremists in the mob. Colombia seemed to have exhausted all possibilities of salvation when on the 13th of June 1953 ten tanks rolled through the streets of Bogotá, surrounded President Laureano Gómez' house (he ruled the land from his sickbed since he suffered from cardiac trouble) and arrested him. The army, which in highly civilized Colombia had remained aloof from all political affairs, suddenly entered the tragic fifth act of this political drama. The C.-in-C., General Rojas Pinilla, an enlightened elderly man, had made all his plans in peace at his headquarters and without a drop of blood being shed. Colombia, in the words of the philospher Lopéz de Mesa "had become Colombia again".

The nightmare of constant destruction had been banished from the people. A general amnesty promised the guerillas a safe return to their homes and they laid down their weapons in their thousands. Admittedly peace had still not returned to their hearts. The old resentments still smouldered beneath the surface. Although Rojas Pinilla inclined to conservatism, the irreconcilable followers of Laureano Gómez (who in the meantime had been exiled to his beloved Spain) turned against the new régime and now in turn became guerillas and touched off a new civil war by attacks on their political opponents.

The tiger was still pacing its cage, and it was obvious that before the new régime could wrest the power again from civilian elements it was faced with a mighty task of social transformation. In line with his colleague Osorio in San Salvador, Rojas Pinilla took a logical view of the situation and despite his conservative background brought about a complete revolution. The feudal families, the big industrialists and the foreign undertakings had applauded his rise to power, as had the whole population. But now, when the shadow of Gaitán seemed to loom up once more in a threatening manner, when the new master began to demand sacrifices, they started to recoil from him in terror. It became ever more obvious to the general in his presidential chair that his civil support must be sought from the peasants and the workers rather than from the politicians and the old families. Rojas Pinilla learned how to fly. He used a helicopter and appeared like a veritable *deus ex machina* at popular meetings, out of the sky, to speak to his flock. Unwittingly this military pragmatist suddenly saw himself following the same path that every leader in Latin America has to take today. The demoniacal and ill-starred fate of Colombia took possession of him, the evil spirit of Laureano Gómez seemed reincarnated. The elections were continually postponed. The censorship returned. The liberal newspaper *El Tiempo* was banned. And in the country provinces they started hunting liberals and protestants. Back to the Sixteenth Century!

Protestant martyrdom

WHEN I was in Mexico I had often noticed in the streets of small cities certain *gringos* who took every opportunity of entering into conversation with their neighbours. Their eyes lit up and they were obviously very eager. They usually turned out to be protestant missionaries and you meet them throughout the whole of Latin America. In certain countries they are looked upon sympathetically by the government and in others with horror. In all of them, however, their success is astonishing. Latin America comprises a third of the catholic world, but the apparent homogeneous catholicism is only a façade, even in fanatical Colombia.

This third is only served by 6 per cent of the total clergy, and it is a striking fact that in no single one of these countries have they been able to recruit an adequate priesthood from the ranks of their own believers. Where laws, as in Mexico and above all in Guatemala, ban the import of catholic priests from other countries, wide regions remain without regular clergy, and in other countries a similar development is only avoided thanks to Spanish aid. In this way the clergy has become the most powerful and enduring link between the former colonies and the mother-land.

The vacuum arising from the rarity of priests naturally facili-tates the work of protestant missionaries, but their success is not based on a spacial but on a spiritual vacuum which they try to fill. Catholic priests are wont to minimize their conversions by hinting that they try to buy their flock with money and other presents from their inexhaustible dollar funds, and it is possible that here and there some noncomformists resort to such dubious methods. In general, however, I found the protestant missionaries extremely exacting ministers of God, who make conversion anything but an easy game. The catholic priests, they told me, are content with formal ceremonies without bothering about the spiritual betterment of the people; in fact, they often set a very dubious example of morality. The protestants, on the contrary, would accept no convert into their ranks unless he renounced in general such attractive vices as drunkenness, smoking and pro-miscuity. Whoever decided to take such a step must also be convinced. I was constantly surprised how easy it was to dis-tinguish the *creyentés*, as they proudly call themselves, from the other Indians. The renunciation of vices has strengthened their inner and outward behaviour and they endeavour to develop their atavistic fatalism into a more positive striving for some goal. Despite—or perhaps because of—this the Church wages a bitter war against the "upstarts," and in Colombia this struggle, con-current with the excesses of the civil war, moved from the spiritual domain into that of physical violence. Under the Liberal Presidents of the years 1939-46 the missionaries, with 300 active members, had reached their peak and so, when the political war broke out, the protestants were immediately branded with the same hostile stamp as the liberals. Alvaro, the young fanatic who had explained to me the medieval aspect of Colom-bian catholicism, did not disguise from me his personal opinion of protestantism: a catholic who adopted the North American heresy was not being converted to a new faith. With this gesture he had immediately joined the dangerous host of unbelievers and nihilists, because for a true Colombian no other teaching could exist except catholicism. Not only did he imperil his mortal soul, but he basically disturbed the public morality and the whole edifice of the State. "Protestant propaganda," said Alvaro, bringing to a close his hymn of hatred, "is nothing else than high treason."

One morning I happened to be in the *Colegio Americano* with a young American named Goff. He had been away a month compiling a report on the persecution to which the protestants in the small communities were subjected. The post that morning had revealed the latest outrages: they had aroused my attention because one had taken place in Borbosa a few days after my journey through the village on the way to Puerto Berrios. On Easter Saturday at midday a preacher had collected his small protestant community in their chapel. The village catholic priest arranged a procession in front of this spiritual pest-spot. Stones began to rain through the windows, but this did not prevent the preacher from continuing his sermon. On the contrary, he raised his voice even louder, so that his attackers should hear that he was only preaching the true word of God. Thereupon the mob broke down the closed doors. At their head came the priest, who proceeded to tear down a Colombian flag from the wall—this was unjustifiably regarded as a catholic symbol—and began to fulminate against the heretics while his flock took benches, tables, hymn books, bibles and everything they could lay their hands on into the street and set them on fire. But where were the police whose duty it was to keep the peace? They merely stood by and looked on. When one of the anxious protestants turned to the captain and began to remonstrate with him, the latter merely shrugged his shoulders and replied, "My job is to support the government."

Similar stories filled all the six-page newspapers Goff had shown me and they read like some tale out of the Middle Ages. The young man's eyes flashed with rage when he told me of the small miseries to which his Colombian fellow believers were subjected. The *Colegio* where we were talking was created because protestant children were either turned away from the public schools or compelled to practise the general religion. In the meantime, thanks to the high quality of the teaching, this defensive instrument had become a very effective recruiting centre and a whole row of further protestant schools have sprung up. Goff himself taught in Ibague in a bible institute designed to train preachers and which was allied to a teaching seminary and a theological faculty. These schools were run on co-ed lines, until the authorities forced them to segregate the sexes in order to avoid such corrupt and heathenish promiscuity! Everything became a problem for the protestants. They might have been living in an alien, hostile world. Any couple that wanted a civil marriage had to possess a certificate signed by the community priest that he did not belong to the church, and the depraved pair were often kept waiting for months. Even burials became a source of endless wrangling, since the cemeteries were under the jurisdiction of the church which banished any apostates as criminals to unconsecrated ground. During five years' persecution, Goff's report ended, no less than 53 protestants were killed for their faith, 43 churches and chapels were destroyed and over 110 schools closed. In 35 per cent of these cases the attack was led by the catholic priest and in 50 per cent of the cases succeeded with the aid of the police. The new military régime had done nothing to stop this persecution. It even seemed that the new President was anxious to buy the goodwill of the Church by adopting a particularly strong attitude towards the heretics. Thus the activities of the protestants were confined to secret meetings in their churches and all propaganda was forbidden them.

After Goff's words I could not help feeling slightly uncomfortable—the same sense of discomfort that I had so often felt when talking to American missionaries. His indignation was so far removed from that humble willingness to bear the cross for the sake of his faith such as Christ recommended to his followers. Hatred for the papacy filled his soul with such bitterness that loving-kindness had been utterly polluted. "We must destroy it, for it is a menace to the world," he foamed. He was not the only North American missionary with whom I felt at loggerheads on account of his exaggerated belligerence. So many of them do not understand that their presence in a Christian country demands

Quito, Ecuador: a monastery

Bogota, Colombia: Good Friday procession outside the Cathedral

Ecuador: rafts with a cargo of
bananas on their way to the sea

Ecuador: a young Jivaro woman
preparing Chicha. She spits chewed
Mandioca into the pan where it is
to ferment

more tact than their work among the savages. In other countries I have spoken to many cultured and not particularly fanatical catholics who considered the efforts of the protestant missionaries to convert Christians to a "higher" form of christianity as an insult and as an undesired interference by foreign elements in Latin American affairs; one cannot deny that the anti-protestant resistance in Latin America has a political tinge. On the other hand, many of the American missionaries consider this resistance as aggressive sabotage.

Colombia, the most pious and at the same time the most impious land in Latin America. How can this paradox be explained? I put this question to two of the few intellectuals who not only recognize the necessity for a moral regeneration but think they have found a way to bring it about. Hernán Vergara is a leading psychiatrist and Emanuel Robledo is one of the most influential lawyers in the country. They came together one day in 1941. Discontented with traditional catholicism, which they thought too much involved in power politics and dogma, they began to study the problems of everyday life in the light of a purely personal Christian responsibility. In 1947 they published a news sheet under the name of *Testimonio*, which resulted in countless branches being opened all over the country. The Church frowned at this lay movement, which on protestant soil could be compared in many respects with the Oxford group, and for a long time it was threatened with dissolution and a ban. But how could a movement which has emblazoned on its flags the highest activity in the service of the catholic faith endanger this religion? My conversation with these two men in a modern office in the centre of the city remained one of the most remarkable memories of my journey. Vergara's serene spiritual face gleamed before me in the twilight while he outlined the fundamental principles of *Testimonio*. Behind him Robledo walked up and down listening almost impatiently to his colleague's explanation. Sometimes he could not control himself. He interrupted him and began to enthuse rapidly and gently in a monologue upon the wonders of heavenly grace. His eyes were turned ecstatically to heaven. I hardly understood a word, and when I could appreciate it intellectually it left me spiritually cold. I could not believe that this visionary was running a flourishing lawyer's practice and had such friends as the realistic and practical Vergara. He invited me most urgently to visit a group which every week in common meditation discussed the questions of economy, pedagogy and politics. But I felt that I should have been a fish out of water and that my coolness would alienate him as much as his exaggeration alienated myself.

An Athens of thieves

THE ingenuous tourist who arrives in Bogotá will see no trace of the wounds inflicted by the terror of the 9th of April. Towns heal rapidly today and there are many Colombians who in retrospect consider the event as a salutory one. "How else could we have turned a colonial city into a metropolis?" they ask. "Everywhere that roads should have been laid out for the traffic there were historic houses with pretty carved gables whose owners would have shouted blue murder if anyone had thought of pulling them down." The 9th of April did the trick and made plenty of room for the most radical solutions. Bogotá today is being developed according to the plans of the great Swiss architect Le Corbusier, and it has swollen into a big capital city. In the centre the concrete blocks of banks and business houses rise like cliffs, dwarfing the towers of the baroque churches.

Alexander von Humboldt christened Bogotá the South American Athens, and since then his judgment has been corroborated by countless travellers. On the broad Avenue Jimenez at night the bookshelves of the Libreria Buchholtz rise to four storeys like a symbol. Books are the life blood of Bogotá. I cannot explain why people read so much here, but I think it has something to do with the climate. It rains non-stop. There are two rainy seasons and it is damp even in the intervals. Nothing is so conducive to thought and concentration as rain. When the sun is shining outside, books ma! one restless. Thus the rain is probably the reason for Bogotá's intellectuality. People come back from this South American Athens with stories that they have had long conversations about Proust with a taxi driver or a porter. Unfortunately I never came across an example of this type and I do not know if it really exists. I also believe that should this be true they would probably have known much more about Horace or Spinoza than about Proust. For just as the country remains spiritually between the Middle Ages and the Age of Reason and politically nineteenth century, the intellectual interests of the city are far less contemporary than those of Mexico City or Rio. Since classical humanism is *de rigueur* you find here a species of spiritual dinosaur, giants of reading and education which you can meet nowhere else today.

An acquaintance took me one day to visit the well known man of letters Enrique Uribe White, whose Anglo-Saxon heritage comes from his grandmother, while the Uribes are one of the old Colombian familes. Enrique, who is known popularly as *el genio chiflado* (the eccentric genius), is more of a technician than a humanist in his profession. He studied at the Massachusetts Institute of Technology and for a while built streets, until he turned to publishing and intellectual activities. He lives in a very curious house outside the town with Beethoven motifs in the wrought-iron grilles and the walls covered with books from floor to ceiling. Uribe was exactly as I had imagined him. "Isn't it absolutely incredible," he said plaintively to my companion. "I've been looking all over the city for the second volume of Aristotles' *Ethics* and can't find it in a single bookshop." I must admit that I myself have never read a word of Aristotle and probably never shall. "Couldn't you get it out of the library?" I asked. "I never use libraries," he said acrimoniously, "I like to possess a book so that I can annotate and quote from it."

It is therefore not surprising that Bogotá had one of the best newspapers in Latin America. During Colombia's dark days under Gómez *El Tiempo* went through a difficult time. Nevertheless the tyrant did not dare to silence this liberal voice. When in September 1952 the printing press was destroyed, the paper appeared the following day printed on the presses of another house. Behind the scenes it was far more than a mere business undertaking: here lived the Colombian Athens, the Grecian humanistic spirit in opposition to the Spartan philistinism of the régime and the finest testimony for the existence of a humanistic reality which can be met with nowhere else in Latin America. But, alas, under the present régime *El Tiempo* has suffered the fate the Bolivian *Razón* and the Argentine *Prensa*. The new dictator has banned its publication.

The Andes University also bears the imprint of this passionate free spirit. It was founded in 1949 by a rich young patron on his own initiative with the object of giving education free from all State and ecclesiastical influence. It is housed picturesquely in a home for fallen women, high up on a slope above the town; its monastery-like gardens and courtyards with cypress-bordered paths invite the students to meditation, but the spirit of this free university is the most modern in the whole of Latin America. Here the contemplative activity of other universities has given place to intensive campus activities on American lines—actually on the lines of Colombia University. Yale, Princeton and Harvard have lightened its burden with gifts of money, books and laboratory equipment, and on its board of directors have been such great figures as Albert Einstein and Jacques Maritain. When Eisenhower visited Bogotá on his Latin American journey he was made an honorary Doctor of the Andes University. Actually it is unlike any other Institution, a bridge between the United States and Colombia. Its outspoken aim is to give its students a preparatory education so that they can complete their studies in the North American colleges. After five semesters which include an intensive study of the English language, they are sent to a special Institution in Pittsburg, Illinois or Texas to take their exams. The *Universidad de Los Andes* has today a staff of 45 professors and 250 students from all social grades, for no candidate whose intellectual capacities are apparent is refused for lack of financial means. Local and American patrons have provided bursaries for poor students. The big industrial enterprises also give their aid by financing the training of future technicians.

During my stay in the capital I had the pleasure of enjoying the hospitality of friends who live in a spacious house in the residential quarter, but there was no reason to envy them. Each night on retiring to bed the lights were left on in several rooms. My hosts kept loaded revolvers beside their beds and had grown accustomed to sleeping very lightly. At the least noise they jumped up to see what could have caused it. When they went out during the daytime without leaving a servant in the house the radio was left on full blast. Only in this way could they hope to find their possessions still there on their return. In Bogotá, apparently, the thieves as well as the humanists are men of genius. They too possess a grounding which one might almost call Aristotelian. They bundle the entire household goods, from the master's best ties to the ladies' garters, on to a Persian carpet and make away with the loot. It is never seen again. During Passion Week, while the householders prayed in the churches to God to protect themselves and their property, robberies took place in the city amounting to millions of pesos. If you go to the police they merely shrug their shoulders. They can do nothing about it. A friend of mine whose entire silver was stolen one day lodged a complaint against his cook's lover and with a great deal of difficulty managed to get the fellow arrested. In the meantime the silver had disappeared, for the silversmiths are always eager buyers. "Do you expect us to punish the man?" asked the police captain. "Naturally." "Then will you be good enough to pay five pesos for his keep per day during his term of imprisonment." "What do you mean?" "Five pesos a day, or else the rogue will go free." As the lady refused to pay, this is exactly what happened.

The only possible thing to do is to shoot. If you shoot a thief in your house, nothing can happen to you. Another alternative is to insert a notice in the paper such as I myself saw one day. "Señor Ladron, I ask you most courteously not to sell to a third person for practically nothing the camera and the typewriter you stole last Friday from my house. I am ready to buy back both objects at a considerably better price and you can rely upon my complete discretion." In Colombia, as in other Latin American countries, you are far more likely to succeed with politeness than with energy. Thus the true lords of Bogotá are the thieves. There is a magnificent mountain path along the Montserrat hill at whose foot the city stretches out like a grey sea, but no one dares to use it, for it belongs to the thieves. I heard of a lady who, while her husband turned the car round, was relieved of her jewellery and her gold watch. The stories that circulate are legion, rather like those told by the Italian Jesuit Father Lombardi, who preached the new social responsibility of Christians throughout Latin America. In Bogotá he gave a very impressive sermon. "Is it not understandable," he said pathetically, "that poverty provokes the needy to steal? As long as the rich flaunt themselves and the poor hunger, how should it be any different?" The enthusiasm was enormous. The mob closed in round the stout Father and shook his hand warmly. When he got back home he discovered that his notecase had disappeared. The three detectives from Scotland Yard who had been invited by the government to train the local police fared little better. They had no sooner set foot on Colombian soil than their entire luggage with their professional instruments had disappeared.

In Colombia there is also a curious indirect path to theft—to steal legitimately. When the legal owner of a property or a legacy omits to claim it straightaway it can be treated as ownerless property and put up to public auction. Such actions are instigated by a private informer who pays for the proceedings and is given half the proceeds. The law demands that the owner be ordered to report to the law courts and a notice is inserted in the paper—the most obscure paper possible is chosen, which nobody reads—whereupon after thirty days the judge and witnesses inspect the ownerless property, and after a further space of time to allow the transfer to be effected in the Ground Book, the property he has acquired is then sold as quickly as possible so that the third owner can claim that he has bought it in good faith and is therefore insured against any claim. This robbery of so called ownerless properties—which is a highly lucrative business and many lawyers make it their speciality—gave rise to a strange incident. Shortly after April 9th the Colombian government showed the Russian diplomats to the frontier. The eighteen diplomats had lived in a roomy country house built in the colonial style; after their hurried departure it was sealed up, and guarded by an armed policeman while waiting for its fate to be decided.

After a certain time one of the corsairs who specialized in vacant properties hit upon the idea of stealing the Soviet Embassy in this way. Unfortunately he was unlucky. The reporter of a big newspaper discovered the notice in the obscure paper and published the story. The Russian government, warned by friends, reported as the owners within the official period. It was decided to visit the sealed building once more and the visitors were in for a great surprise. While the policeman had kept guard with a loaded rifle at the door the thieves had broken in from the back and had celebrated real orgies in the building. Empty bottles of vodka lay piled up on the floor and the only other object that remained in the whole Embassy was a portrait of Lenin. Furniture, linen, kitchen utensils, even the film projector for propaganda films, had disappeared. Of the three luxury cars which had stood in the garden, one had entirely disappeared and the other two had been stripped down to the chassis. Three horses grazed like ghosts in the garden.

My reader will undoubtedly shake his head: did the watchman at the front door notice nothing at all? Obviously he did, but he remained silent, for as a matter of fact both the police and the thieves come from the same *milieu*. When I visited Gilberto Moreno one day in his prison a young policeman accompanied me up to his room. On the way he asked me if I could recommend him a good lawyer in the city. "Why?" I asked him with surprise. "Well," he said, "my colleagues have stolen my pistol and I can't make them give it up."

Even at diplomatic receptions where the highest society is present, small costly objects disappear in some mysterious manner unless they are carefully locked in showcases. For example, a German doctor told me of the visit of some eminent colleague from the provinces. "When he left I noticed that a valuable silver ashtray was missing from my desk. What could I do? I couldn't go to him and say 'Give me back my property.' In short, I let things slide. After some time I had occasion to go to his own town and I took the opportunity of looking him up. My ashtray was standing proudly on his desk. As I left I said very politely 'I suppose you don't mind if I take my own property away with me?' It was a very uncomfortable situation, but only for me, the one who had been robbed. Not for him. 'Why ever not?' he said with a smile. 'Did you miss it then?' This is typical of the people. They have no idea of what they are doing when they steal. Since this episode I have no inhibitions. I look them clearly in the face and when I see one of them pinching something I say, 'Leave that where it is, please'. Do you think they ever look ashamed or blush? Not on you life."

"I can hardly credit it," I said. "Even in good society—even the intellectuals? How do you account for it?"

The doctor shrugged his shoulders. "It is a difficult psychological problem," he replied. "I've been studying the people now for years. They're a curious lot. They seem to lack a sense of form and order which we Europeans take for granted. For example, I pass some photographs over to a friend. He takes them upside down as I have given them, looks at them and says 'Very fine.' They are still upside down. Or tell the gardener to build you a path. He will certainly cut it slantwise through your property, and probably through your flower beds. If you're in the street you constantly bang into people because they are dreaming and never look where they're going. If my wife asks the maid to bring her evening shoes, which she has already seen a dozen times, she is quite certain to bring in her rubber boots. It is more than thoughtlessness. It is an extraordinary way of reacting which we shall never understand. There is no concept of 'Mine and Thine' and you will find that the millionaires steal too. We can't possibly reproach the simple people. Do you understand their civil war? I don't. It comes in the same category."

Only one place is safe from the thieves because it is not a paying proposition. The Gold Museum is safely housed in the bank of Colombia, and to get to it you have to pass a row of watchmen. But then, when you enter the neon-lit underground hall, you would think that you were in a drawing room rather than a museum. The floors are covered with thick carpets and

the custodians sit unobtrusively behind two tables and work.
It is one of the most inspired and noble museums I have ever
visited. In the showcases twinkle enormous objects of gold, as
large as soup plates. These barbaric, ostentatious tiaras or necklaces aroused the greed of the Conquistadores and made them
rush off in quest of an imaginary Eldorado lake in which legend
maintained that the ruler, his entire body adorned with gold,
bathed each year and threw in inestimable wealth or jewels as a
sacrifice to the gods. But my attention was caught much more by
the remarkable geometrical treatment of human and animal
figures which can be found in a score of variants. I had already
seen the famous gold treasure of Monte Alban in Oaxaca and
other treasures which are the pride of the San José museum in
Costa Rica. But nowhere had the human figure appeared so
barbaric and been subjected to such sinister transformations. Here
too there were examples in which a certain æsthetic canon could
be felt, but they were far behind the perfection of the Mexican
goldsmith's work. In the archæological museum I had already
been almost terrified by the idols of San Augustin from Southern
Colombia—those remnants of an age-old unexplained culture.
They too were more irrational than anything I had seen in
Mexico. I felt that this primitive Colombian art had its foundations
in a deeper region of the human soul, almost in the pre-human.
I felt that I was seeing a display reminiscent of the crazy, obsessed
and occult artists whose work in Paris was known under the
concept *art brut*. Did not this inhuman background threaten to
emerge from the Colombian soul and to shake the humanist
Athenian tradition to its foundations? One thing was quite
clear. Anyone who looked upon the recent civil war as a political
squabble was making a great mistake. It was far more than a
struggle between two parties. It was rather an intellectual combat
between the dark powers of this collective soul and present-day
culture. The front line lay not between the weapons of the
opposing sides but in each individual heart.

ECUADOR

Amiable Ecuador

THE *bon mot* of a certain historian is often quoted in South America: according to him, in Venezuela you breathed the air of a barracks, in Colombia of a university, and in Ecuador of a monastery. That does not hold good today. Little Ecuador has a much more liberal and freer atmosphere than Colombia and the monastic mood is completely lacking. This does not mean that the Ecuadorians are any less pious than their Colombian brothers. When for example the Air Force wanted to build modern machines a few years ago, special Masses were said and processions were organized in order to dissuade the Christian flock from their warlike projects. The difference lies in the fact that since the end of the nineteenth century, when their fat, wilful, gruesome President García Moreno was murdered, Ecuador has been ruled by an unbroken line of liberal Presidents. Its history has by no means been peaceful. Here power for each ruler was like a beautiful capricious courtesan, short and intensive in devotion, abrupt and bitter when the time of departure came. In Colombia history is a tragedy, but here it has an element of comedy which basically is merely a parody of the former. During the twenty-five years from 1925 to 1949, this land has had no fewer than twenty-seven Presidents and six different Constitutions. It has had a series of strikes and *coups d'états* in which the main figures still remain more or less the same: the people, 75 per cent Indians, have watched this game of marionettes played by the thin white upper crust without being fundamentally affected. In this lies the complete difference between Ecuador and Colombia. Here no Gaitán arose, no caged tiger made preparations to lay the capital in ruins. Ecuador is actually the only Latin American country where you can still observe something of the former patriarchal age which has completely dis-

appeared elsewhere. Here the feudal lords still rule uncontested on
their *haciendas* and according to their whims they are the father
or the slave driver of the Indians, for whoever owns the land
also owns the men who are born on it, and whoever buys it also
buys the *huasipungos*, which is the name given to these serfs.
Admittedly in theory laws have put a stop to this practice, but
throughout Latin America the laws never represent the true
state of affairs, only the powers which make them. Ecuador
possesses one of the most progressive codes of law in the world,
but I shall never forget the terrified expression of the hat maker
as he accompanied me on a visit to his weavers in Cuenca when
I questioned him. "I beg of you never to mention the word
codigo in front of my women workers," he said. "You could
get a big flea in your ear."

While for the moment the gadfly of class and race struggle has
not yet stung the people, the atmosphere in Ecuador is very
peaceful. As a modern socially-conscious man you cannot of course
suppress a feeling of revolt when you learn that less than 500
owners possess three-quarters of this mountainous country. You
will be even more up in arms when you hear the famous story of
a big landowner who gave a huge party, and in order to display
his fabulous wealth let the water for the tea be boiled on a fire of
banknotes by servants who barely earned 5 cents a day. But from
the æsthetic point of view—and I am fully aware that politics
have nothing to do with the æsthetic, but must be judged from
the purely moral standpoint—this unbroken feudal order does
not fail to make an impression on the visitor. And I should not
care to say that the Indios of Ecuador are any more unhappy than
their rebellious brothers of the other countries. Could so honest
and friendly a people really be unhappy? Even the landscape here
seems clement. The road which winds through rocky hills is
small and has a crumbling plaster surface as if it were an old
Roman way. Agaves grow at the roadside and here and there on
a giant stalk blossoms rise like the branches of candlesticks to the
sky. You feel that you should not be sitting in a bus but in a four-
in-hand mail coach from the last century.

I had hardly got out of my bus on the frontier when a

picturesque Indian woman with long black plaits waddled over to me. "*Siñur*," she chirped. "*Siñur*." Since I was immediately captivated by the singing intonation and the enchanting distortion of the Spanish vowels, I was easily persuaded to participate in the illegal adventure she proposed. She had been into Colombia and crossed the frontier at night with a load of industrial treasures all of which were dutiable in Ecuador. "No one will search you because you are a foreigner," she chirped, and without a trace of embarrassment began to stuff my baggage full of linen cloths, aluminium cooking utensils, matches, ground coffee and other booty. I looked with growing concern at this unwitting addition to my property, but consoled myself as soon as I saw that various other travellers were equally willing to oblige. The chauffeur had put a thick bale of stuff beneath him as a cushion, and the contraband covered by the passengers' cloaks peeped from under all the benches. One thing I could not understand. We had come to a halt in the Ecuadorian frontier station and the Customs lay behind us. Why all this game of hide and seek? I soon learnt that two more Customs houses had to be passed further inland. It seemed to me very peculiar, but then Ecuador is a very peculiar land.

After a few miles we came to the first control. The man put his nose in the air and saw absolutely nothing. The disaster happened sixty miles further on, as we were approaching the first large town, Ibarra. Probably the inspector there was in a bad temper or for some reason or other he had decided to make an example. We were told to get out of the bus. "It's unheard of," said everyone. "What an impertinence! Leave the poor woman in peace." The Customs soldiers were obviously annoyed at having to carry out this disagreeable duty. "We're very sorry," they said as they hauled the smuggled goods from under the benches. As the Indian woman had prophesied, I was treated with astonishing leniency. My photostat apparatus lay on top of my case. The inspector looked at it with a professional eye. "An engineer, I see." "A philologist," I replied. Obviously he was much impressed by this unfamiliar profession, for he let me through with all my goods. My friend the Indian woman, who was whining at the back of the waggon, had to undergo the shame of being searched. She stood up and shivered as though all her limbs ached, then, as quick as lightning, stuck the packets she had conjured from beneath her skirts under her fellow passengers' coats. She was very slim indeed as she finally got to the door. None of the passengers had refused to help. On the contrary. They all had a feeling of solidarity with the smuggler, although none of them knew her, nor did they hesitate for one moment to defend the interests of a citizen against the brutal interference of the State. The foreigner did not naturally belong to the company; a common misfortune had brought him into the circle. *"Muchas gracias, Gringito,"* said the Indian woman when I returned her goods once the storm had passed. I had to smile. The word of contempt which from Mexico to Colombia expresses the hatred of the foreigner had in its diminutive form become a term of endearment. *Gringito*. How pleasant it sounded. Here not only the Yankees but all foreigners are called this.

This feeling of having somehow returned home grew even stronger when I left the bus in Otavalo. It would be a great mistake to miss the markets in this small town. The Indians of Otavalo are quite unique. Their skin is lighter than that of their brothers and they are incredibly conscientious. This has saved them from the slavish fate of their comrades. Perhaps the reason for this well-being lies in the serene friendly atmosphere which illuminates the whole region. Here the youngsters run after you on the streets and chatter while they show you the way—not because they expect a tip, for they finally leave you without holding out their hands. It is the mere pleasure of being able to converse with a foreigner. These people are eaten up with curiosity. Wander about the region, look at the flocks of white cranes rising from the holy lake of St Pedro at the foot of the volcano which the natives call *Padre Imbabura* and worship as a god. No one will meet you without saying something. Even the smallest children waddle out of the doors of white thatched houses and lisp *"Donde vas?"*

Inside the father sits at an ancient loom and the mother keeps her spinning wheel turning to prevent the strands from slipping,

while the little girl on the floor tangles a snippet of wool or
nibbles a sugar cane she has picked in the garden. You should see
how amiably the father jumps up, with what perfect courtesy he
asks the guest in and explains the secret of his craft. A well-
trained city salesman could never present his wares with more
elegance. You will find here the finest homespuns with English
patterns. How did they come here? This was the greatest piece of
luck that occurred in Otavalo. Previously the Indians had only
woven for their own needs, until one day about thirty years ago
a rich landowner brought one of them a piece of English material
with the words, "I like this pattern. Do you think you could
make something like it?" From then onwards the weavers of
Otavalo have produced a homespun, and their wandering
journeymen, who are easily recognized by the long thick plait
hanging down their backs, wander as far as Colombia and Peru.
And how cheap these Otavalo materials are! You can get a
complete suit length for 110 sucres—$7.00.

Sucres: it is typical of the sweetness of Ecuador that here you
pay—at least in name—with sugar. "What is the price of that
scarf?" "40 sucres." In any case paying is a real pleasure in Latin
America. In Guatemala you pay in birds—the quetzal, the jungle
bird with the long green iridescent tail which is also the crest of
the country. In the other Central American lands you pay with
historical characters: in Salvador and Costa Rica with Colum-
buses, in Honduras with Lempiras—called after a wild Indian
leader from pre-Spanish times. Nicaragua, on the contrary,
allows its conqueror Cordoba to pass from hand to hand, while
Panama tries in vain to supersede the dollar with the discoverer
Balboa. Ecuador, however, has chosen the most poetic coin.
Their sucres are not called after real sugar cane but after a French-
born general who defeated a Spanish army on the slopes of the
volcano Pichincha and freed the capital from the Audiencia.
Bloody sugar, therefore.

With the new industry prosperity returned to the gentle
valley at the foot of Imbabura. The Indios bought the homestead
they had previously leased from their masters and the former serfs
suddenly became capitalists. That was the miracle of Otavalo,

a miracle which proves that the Indian race has not lost its independence, but that the active strength which once created the immortal monuments of pre-Colombian culture still slumbers within it.

The Indians from Otavalo, however, weave the noblest cloths for themselves, and they are not for sale. They weave the thick meshes by hand. The blue poncho he wears each Sunday to market is three times as heavy as the loom woven cloth. In this dark overmantle he looks like a great lord. His wife, however, wears a hat with a broad curling brim below which a bright-coloured kerchief hangs down over her shoulders.

These Indios have retained one great vice, the love of alcohol. In the wake of the golden chains and the flute playing follows the *chicha*, the sour fermented corn drink native to this country. I know only too well what it tastes like, for you cannot pass a small group of drinking men without being offered some. The alcohol content is very small, but it is drunk in enormous quantities as the Mexicans drink their *pulqué*.

The air of Quito is famous throughout the Continent. It blows down fresh from the mountains. Even when you are almost astride the Equator you are still 8,000 feet above the heat, and you live in perpetual spring. This is a city where contemplative men should settle—an adobe city where communion with the earth has not yet been lost through contact with asphalt. More than any other capital it belongs to its people. Go for a walk on the great Plaza San Francisco. You will find Indios sitting there in their red ponchos. They squat peacefully on the pavement and watch the cars pass without being in the least impressed, or you will see them praying in the gilded church. Old, smooth heavy gold adorns the broad carved frames of saints and visionaries. Even the gold here smells of the soil, of that same soil that clings to the feet of the praying congregation. Foreign art mingles perfectly with the native, Arabia lives in the ornament of the roof, and in the faces on the altars you will constantly be reminded of Buddha. Missionaries brought these forms here from China.

Quito is a town of hills: they rise on all sides. These high hills from which you can look down on a sea of churches, each more beautiful than the other, never fail to attract you. They are not drowned in concrete as in Bogotá or Mexico City. They still raise their heads knowingly above everything transitory.

What a splendid slumbering kingdom! A breath of melancholy haunts its colonial walls. If you visit the house of some aristocrat you will be amazed. He may own his *hacienda* and earn a great deal of money, but he lives with a modesty that does not betray his prosperity. Through an open door you may catch a glimpse of a wonderful drawing room with gilded chairs along the wall, sofas and an array of cushions and occasional cuspidors, but the curtains are drawn. Only once a year does the sun shine in, when guests are invited to a family party. Otherwise they live . . . where? I never found out. Certainly not in the bedroom, for the beds are unmade. On the tablecloth in the dining room all the menus are recorded back to the Incas. All that remains is the kitchen. It is no wonder that the householder constantly wears his overcoat as if he were on a visit. The street and the club are his world. The house is not to live in. It is purely an accessory like his wife.

And yet, on the other hand, little Ecuador has done more for its cultural life than many greater nations. The Ecuadorian *Casa de Cultura* stands in a fine park. In its halls can be seen wonderful colonial paintings, for Ecuador is the home of the best young South American painters. This art musuem shows their pictures. The young author over whose work the private publisher shakes his head on economic grounds will find a printer here. In all the greater cities you find a similar *Casa de Cultura*, with lecture halls and well-stocked libraries. They are the centres around which nearly all the intellectual life of the region revolves. These institutions were created in 1944 and are supported by a tax on exports.

Otávalo, Ecuador: return from the market.
In the background the volcano Imbabura

Journey into the plain

YOU cannot fail to be impressed when you shiver in the Quito market under the mountain wind and see the most magnificent tropical fruits on display. I have never seen such wonderful bananas as those which are brought by streams of lorries from the lowlands. A strange thought: here you are comfortably installed on green wooded hills without a thought that you are on a ridge and that on both sides the mountains fall steeply into the plain. And yet you need only to go for a trip in one of these lorries for one of the most exciting adventures to await you. It is by no means an undiluted pleasure, for although paying passengers are acceptable nothing is done to encourage them, and they have to sit perched up on wooden seats behind the driver. After a quarter of a hour my limbs began to ache as if they had been caught in a pair of pincers: if I tried to ease them I could not help treading on my neighbour's corns. After a time the lorry stopped and the driver began to collect small coins. "What's the idea?" I asked. "They're for the saint who protects us," was the reply. I can assure you we needed some protection! The mountain road that leads down into the tropics from the Quito plateau wanders at first along the Cordillera pass and then through wild ravines so narrow that it was intended for one-way traffic. But in Ecuador everyone pleases himself, and therefore on a dangerous curve we suddenly met a spluttering car. Give way? Not likely! We were already perched perilously near the abyss, and now we had to move slowly further out. People may call me a coward, but I would like to wager that anyone in this position would be sweating profusely. The seriousness of the matter was proved by the rusty wrecked cars we had already seen at various places far below us, like dead dogs, with their four wheels in the air. "Go easy," I said gently to the driver. "Do you want to end up in the ravine?" The man grumbled amiably, "Don't worry, Señorito. This year no one has gone over the edge and only five last year." The driver of the approaching car waved us on. The precipice edge disappeared under our carrier. I closed my eyes. "*Dios*," cried the woman behind me, who was escorting her niece to her husband in the plain. "Let me out of here." She began to rattle the door. The driver only gave a grim smile. "We've all got to die once, *Señora*," he cried, "why not. . . ." He was going to say "now," but the other car had passed us all right. This had to be celebrated with a cigarette. The driver stuck a cheroot in his mouth, took a box of matches from his pocket and tried to light it. An Ecuadorian chauffeur is not a good improviser. He leant daringly with his elbows on the wheel and went on driving. While he made several unsuccessful attempts to light his match the curves and the abyss sped past and the cold sweat ran down our spines.

And then we were suddenly in another world. The warm damp air assailed our nostrils. Our clothes stuck to our bodies and our heads ached from the swift change in atmosphere. Outside, the broad leaves of the banana palms and the jungle trees lashed the roof of the lorry. Quevedo is a hideous spot like all the other village settlements in the tropics. The houses are built of wood and have begun to turn a mouldy grey under the constant stream of rain. The warped beams have come apart and yawn as though they were hungry: the heads of the nails are all rusty. You feel that it would be child's play to pull down the whole matchbox village with your bare hands. A calm river flows through the banana plantations, and the small boats from the capital steam up and down on its waters. The following morning the *Vinces* was sailing for Guayaquil. That evening I strolled through the streets and ended up in a bar run by a German. There are quite a few of them in Quevedo, and Hallmann had once been a Nazi. Obviously he had not been a good one, for in 1938 he had suddenly tired of civilization and had left Germany for this country. He and his wife now ran a tavern. She is actually a Chinese, but she gets along perfectly with her "Aryan" husband. I even witnessed how she saved his life. A drunken man staggered in, slumped on a stool and ordered whisky. Hallmann took the bottle from the shelf, but put it back as soon as he noticed his customer's condition. When the drunken man saw this he put his hand in his pocket and aimed a rather unsteady revolver at the landlord. In a flash the Chinese woman rushed at this dangerous individual, put a half-hitch on him and managed to throw him into the street. Hallmann shook his head. "We can't even lodge a complaint against him," he sighed, "because he is a Senator. You never know in this country. A man who looks like a hobo turns out next morning to be a powerful politician. It's fatal here ever to lose your head."

The *Vinces* made her way slowly and peacefully downstream. The river wound through the plain in wide curves. Every few miles the boat turned and struggled against the current to come alongside some primitive landing stage where a man in white with a broad straw hat waved. Gangplanks were laid to the boat from the bank and robust negroes began to unload the hundred-weight sacks of rice from the holds. They flung them on to their shoulders as if they were cotton-wool, or else they piled mountains of bananas in the bows, making it sink ever deeper in the green unruffled water. The passengers began to get very bored. The scenery was monotonous: banana plantations with their leaves fluttering in the hot wind.

Let no one harbour any romantic illusions about the tropics. The plenty which grows here is always tinged with the fine healthy boredom that lies in all organic growth. Man has something in common with the plants which bloom with so little effort around him. The whole Ecuadorian lowlands breathe the wonderful peace of a Garden of Eden. Here ripen the harvests which form the bulk of the exports. In the old days it was mainly cocoa that left from here for the world markets until, in 1924, a parasite began to ruin the bushes. Even today production has not reached the old level, although in recent years it has begun to rise again, thanks to the planting of bushes which are immune. Today the banana has taken its place. Ecuador is the largest producer in the world, although coffee is still one of her largest trade assets.

But to return to the deck of the *Vinces* once more. The humping negroes on the narrow gangplank were still balancing their rice sacks on their heads, when something happened that I should by rights have foreseen. We had run aground. The whole crew, together with the captain, immediately jumped into the water, which soon reached up to their thighs, and began to stick poles under the keel. The screw raced madly, but we were stuck fast. Twilight fell. The passengers slung their hammocks on deck while the crew went on working. When I woke next morning the scene had changed. Another steamer had dragged us off, but we were no further advanced because we were stranded again. This time it was for a different reason. The desperate efforts to get away from the bank had thrashed sand into the propeller shaft which had rubbed away the mounting. Now it was necessary to unload all the fine heavy rice to discover the hole. . . . We could look forward to another night aboard. Huge rafts made of balsa trunks floated past on the calm water. These balsa trunks are as light as reeds when you pick them up, and they are exported from Ecuador to the United States for aircraft building. The rafts were loaded with bananas and allowed to drift down the river. The lumberjacks had built small cabins of shady banana leaves fore and aft, where they took it in turn to doze while their comrades kept the traffic in the stream with a pole. I looked at them almost enviously when they waved to us as they passed.

One of my fellow passengers caught my eye on account of the patience he showed at our imprisonment. His face looked wise and energetic beneath his greying hair. "Isn't this a wonderfully rich land?" I said as an opening gambit to our conversation. "It seems almost inexhaustible."

"Don't be deceived by your first view of the river," he replied. "Land somewhere and make your way to the interior. After a few hundred yards you will come to barren thicket. About 34,000 square miles of the most magnificently fertile land is uncultivated. Of course this coastal region is an enormous Eden full of unbelievable wealth. No one knows it better than I do, for I'm a farmer; but I tell you less than a third of it is under cultivation."

"But how is that?"

The man shrugged his shoulders. "Well, you see, the settlement structure of our Andes countries is slightly crazy and that holds good not only for Ecuador. Up in the mountains a million men eke out a paltry existence from the soil and down below in the plain, where nature is more than generous, live only half a million. There is of course a reason for this. When the Spaniards came here malaria was a scourge and only the recent medical discoveries have made life possible in this region. But we are faced with a gigantic task—to winkle the people out of the over-populated Sierra and transport them down here, where the land is only waiting to feed them. It is not only an economic need, but actually the most vital question for our policy. Strikes and revolutions, you know, are our endemic diseases, and to this you must add the tension between the coast and the Sierra which can lead to an explosion at any moment.

"Take a look at those young sailors. Look at the men on the bank. Have they anything in common with the Indios of the Sierra? Here the *montubio*, as he is called, has woken up and is open to all influences. He knows how to take care of himself in quite a different fashion from the humble Indians up in the hills. He combines the cunning of the Indios with the arrogance of the Spaniards and the gaiety of the negro. He is a mixture of all three. These people from the coast are the shock troops of liberalism. Progress has always started from here and been carried with violence into the Sierra. It is our misfortune, of course, that our capital is situated in the mountains. In Quito the feudal lords sit in their places: there the clergy have a hearing. Even the most intelligent projects lie and rot in office drawers. A Senator from Guayaquil, for example, proposed a law to tax property and compel all the dog-in-the-manager *latifundie* to cultivate their idle land or else relinquish it to others for exploitation, but it has not gone through and the Indians don't bother. They belong to an age-old passive society. They succumbed to the Incas without a struggle and later in the same way to the Spaniards.

"And so, you see, the coast and the hinterland will always be at loggerheads. The people from down here will continue to protest: What are those old corpses doing up in Quito? They're right. Guayaquil should really be the capital. The whole wealth of the land pours in there before being shipped abroad. Foreign currency is piled up there. In Guayaquil you will find the activity and the currents from the outside world which lead to progress."

I must admit that Guayaquil looked like a big capital when our boat came within sight of its lights at dusk on the second day. The moon during the last part of the journey had graced us with an even more enchanting pageant. Now to the left, now to the right, broad tributaries joined the main stream until we were sailing on an arm of water, which has made Guayaquil *the* harbour of the South American west coast—an ideal harbour except for the silting which makes it dangerous for big ships. Today it is fast sloughing its sleepy unhealthy tropical skin. The wooden pillars of her houses not only collapsed under the nagging tooth of the termites, but under the fresh breeze of an expanding trade, and in their place are rising city buildings of steel and concrete. The following day, as I strolled through the broad avenues of the business and harbour quarters, I could not help remembering the words of my ship companion. He was right. What a very different atmosphere reigned here from that in contemplative Quito. It was almost impossible to believe that the two cities belonged to the same country.

And was not the President, whom I had met in Quito, a typical example of the political rhythm of this country? Velasco Ibarra is one of the most picturesque personalities of all the living politicians in Latin America, a typical product of this tragi-comic small country Ecuador. The folk call him alternatively as a term of abuse or of endearment *el loco* (the madman), and in actual fact he is one of the most erratic and eccentric characters who has ever sat in a presidential chair. He has already been President twice, and twice, in 1935 and 1947, a military *coup d'état* overthrew him. On each occasion he went peacefully into exile, and since he is a magnificent jurist he could always get a job as a professor. The first time he taught in Venezuela and the second time in the Argentine. As a progressive, he was elected once more in 1952, winning the election against a Conservative opponent strongly supported by the clergy and two liberals. "Velasco may be crazy," a colleague of mine said in Guayaquil, "but to some extent he personifies the fate of Ecuador."

Velasco, as I have already said, is a professor, has a bald head and wears pince-nez. Like all professors he is absent-minded, and in addition to this, incredibly self-willed—so absent-minded in fact that he never remembers what he said yesterday and will undoubtedly say something quite different again tomorrow. Incidentally that is one of the reasons for his unqualified success. He leaves the decisions to his audiences to such an extent that he always says exactly what they want to hear. He talks like a socialist to the workers, like a papist to the catholics and like a liberal to the school teachers. Moreover, this is not a mere demagogic stunt. He is a chameleon. He has introduced a new fashion into the politics of his country—the art of talking to the people. Previously politics were confined to the gentlemen's clubs: Velasco took them into the streets. And what an orator he is! His promises are even more remarkable. One day he was making an electioneering speech in a small town. "I will build you a new school," he said. Loud applause. "You shall also have a fire station." More applause. "And I'll see that you get a bridge." At this there was quite a stir among his audience. "But we haven't got a river," someone said. But Velasco was in an extravagant mood. "All right, my dears. You shall have a river too!"

But he not only promises, he fulfils. Public building has always been slightly original in this country. When it is a question of building a road or a railway Parliament grants a few million sucres. Some politician then buys the machinery and begins to build; after two or three miles there is no money left. The affair comes to a standstill until the next credit is granted. This is so very much the fashion that no one raises an eyebrow. When a Swiss contractor in all honesty wanted to build a vital railway from Quito to Esmeralda he landed in prison after a lot of intrigue because the line endangered some very powerful interests. When the Swiss Ambassador intervened with the President, the latter wrung his hands with embarrassment. "I know full well that your countryman is innocent," he said, "but here's the rub. If he were guilty we could arrange matters for him, but not now that he's innocent. How could we let him go?" That is Ecuadorian logic.

Velasco is a stickler for honesty. Theft makes him furious. For a Latin American statesman this is a great disadvantage, for in this hemisphere you are supposed to understand the weaknesses of human nature. He makes hosts of enemies not only because of his virtue but because of his absent-mindedness, for he orders one thing one day and another the next, and he is always right. Categorically right. When the situation does not fit in with his views the matter is dropped. If Parliament will not play ball he dissolves it. Thus the soldiers who throw him out are always liberators. But Velasco—and that is the irony of his fate—is no tyrant; in his heart of hearts he is a confirmed democrat. On the evening before the election he praised Switzerland as being the statesman's ideal, and with this ideal at the back of his mind he plays the dictator. He is a man who wants to improve the world. He wants to shake the country out of its feudal lethargy, wants to bring it to the ideal of a people's sovereignty. He has not enough patience to smooth out opposition. He simply smashes it. "I'm no St Francis," he cried when I met him. "I have to use force to bring about a democracy." That is Velasco, Don Quixote Velasco. Today he is at loggerheads with the politicians who supported his candidature. He has driven them out of the country and suppressed their newspaper. The opponents of yesterday are the friends of today and heaven knows what will happen tomorrow. "But why do you insist upon being President?" I asked. "I don't. But my duty. . . ." A man always becomes what he wants, and above all in this remarkable country Ecuador.

Wanted : A human head

"I HAD not been two months in the Amazon jungle before I saw one of the most remarkable and rarest performances that the primitive forest offers. One day when I visited the hut of a Jivaro I found him preparing a human head. Everyone knows that these savage tribes have retained the custom of cutting off their enemies' heads, shrinking them to a fifth of their original size and spending a year of carrying them triumphantly on the end of a spear. The Jivaro had cut the neck open and was now carefully probing the skin of the skull with a blunt blade, much as we should skin an expensive fur. A pot of herbs was simmering on the fire. The face, that had been reduced to a bloody shambles, would be cooked for several hours in order to transform the perishable flesh into the imperishable. When my friend finally removed it, it had been reduced to a fraction of its former size by the magic action of the herbs. Next, all the orifices were sewn up so that it formed a kind of pouch and was put back once more into the boiling kettle. Finally my Jivaro took his trophy out and before it grew hard carved the face with a sharp instrument to make it resemble its former possessor. Now take a look at the chap."

The head which the young Spanish scientist Hector Acebes held in his hand must have belonged to a handsome young man. The brilliant black hair sprouted thick on his head, the eyes were closed as though he were asleep, his mouth was thrice sealed so that the dead man could not betray who had murdered him. The nose protruded almost like a muzzle from the forehead, giving it a very wild appearance. Acebes had acquired this year-old *zanza*, as this trophy is called among the natives, from a civilized Jivaro friend of his. I told him that I should very much like to be present at a similar cooking. Acebes laughed. Only two months in the jungle, and it was highly improbable that one would be present at the shrinking of a head, because, fortunately, this only occurred at the most twice a year—otherwise the jungle would have long since been depopulated.

When I visited the German photographer Bodo Wuth, a few days later, my eyes fell on a coloured picture from an American magazine pinned on the wall. It portrayed a savage youth dipping a man's head in a cooking pot.

"You too, eh?"

"Of course," said Wuth. "But you can easily photograph one too."

"What do you mean?"

"You'll simply have to take the zanza with you from here.

You can buy scores of them in Quito. You'll never find them down there in the Oriente."

In this way my plan matured to visit the eastern jungle which in all the Andes countries forms the unapproachable regions, called the regions of the future, the Oriente. No Ecuadorian can speak of this Eastern Province without giving vent to grief and anger.

Ecuador's Oriente once stretched far into the Amazon basin, until in the forties the warlike Peruvians stole the region from their weaker neighbours in a frontier dispute. This struggle for the jungle was the indirect result of the negligence of the Spanish rulers. They defined their frontiers with true Spanish grandeur. You will find *haciendas*, for example, whose boundaries go "as far as the eye can see" from the mountains, and in the Amazon the frontiers were simply laid down by the river "where it ceases to be navigable". What did that mean? Navigable by steamers or navigable by canoe? Four hundred years later, to rectify this lack of precision on the part of Spain, thousands of young men lost their lives in the struggle, and since international opinion favoured the Peruvians, Ecuador was obliged to sacrifice her Eastern Province by the Rio de Janeiro Protocol in 1942. Even today the frontier has not been defined *de jure* and in practice it lies where the hostile frontier posts face each other.

Since for this reason the Oriente teems with soldiers it is prudent to provide yourself with a pass signed by the War Minister. In actual fact, when I got there I was told that it was quite unnecessary, but in Latin America the local military authorities usually differ in opinion from their Ministry: I could not pass a single post without showing my pass, and should undoubtedly have been flung into the nearest gaol had I not had one.

Nor did I have to wait long before I found my shrivelled head. As I have already mentioned, Quito abounds in them. It is an under-the-counter trade, because the Ecuadorians consider it casts a slur on their national honour. In practice you only have to go to the nearest souvenir shop, or someone will come up to you in the hotel lounge and offer you one of these heads. How can such a rich harvest exist in view of the meagre production? The explanation is simple. Very few of these heads have seen the jungle. Most of them are the heads of monkeys and other animals which have been changed by skilful hands to look like men. In addition to this there are heads made out of leather "Made in Quito". For some time Japan delivered them made out of *papier mâché*, and in short the fabrication of fake zanzas is a flourishing industry. Now it is not very difficult to recognize a false shrunken head, and I am quite convinced that mine, which I borrowed from friends, once really belonged to a man. Ears and nostrils could easily be traced and a tender fluff blossomed in its nose. But who could maintain that it did not come from the anatomical institute of the University? There must be medical students who spend their time making these heads, for it is a profitable job. A good example fetches between 800 and 1,000 sucres, and corpses cannot answer back.

I met the first living Jivaro in Zamora after a two days march from the southern town of Loja over an icy romantic mountain pass. It lies in a deep ravine. You will find no hotel there. You have a choice of the monastery or the barracks. I chose the former, and was received by a young, friendly Franciscan bishop. The monastery was being rebuilt. The clay walls of a new church were already half finished, and outside my door a lay brother was carpentering window frames and an altar. This young bishop had brought life into the wilderness and was trying to attract the converted savages from the surrounding country. He was the first Ecuadorian to take over the post from his Spanish precedecessors, and his approachability was very different from the latter's caution. A decree from his friend the President had empowered him to entice young men and girls from their primitive settlements, if necessary by force. I soon had a closer view of the young people. I saw them at grace before meals, saw them at evening kneeling round his chair and allowing him to stroke their hair. "A hideous brood," the young bishop said to me. "It would be easier to swim against the tide of that river over there than awaken anything like a soul in these animals." What an ineradicable hankering for sin lived in the parents of these children!

Polygamy, sloth, nakedness and sorcery were their special vices. They worshipped no god but only a devilish spirit in the figure of a wild goat. How could one make such savages realize that they were created by a heavenly father? It was desperately difficult. To this end the bishop had used severe measures and taken the children from their families so that they could be in his spiritual care. Now he was planting the seed of faith in their souls. The people out in the forest, however, were completely lost. It was futile baptizing them, even when they showed their willingness. The Franciscans had taken a very promising Jivaro to Rome and introduced him to the Holy Father, but this had not prevented the ungrateful creature on his return from shedding his seemly European costume, grabbing himself a few wives and reverting to the lowest forms of heathenism. No; one could only baptize these sinners on their deathbeds, when there was no possibility of them soiling the sacrament as a result of their hideous lives.

I listened to his tirades in silence. "And what do the Jivaros think about it when you take their children away?" I asked him.

"They loathe me," said the bishop unconcernedly. "They loathe me so much that my life would be in danger, except for the fact that the barracks are not far away."

I was sorry for the bishop. Fancy spreading the message of love with such violence. But not only the Jivaros hated him. The major who was in command of the station would have cheerfully given his head over to be shrunk, had his duty not compelled him to act as a protector. This aggressive priest interfered with everything. He wanted to build roads joining Zamora to the outside world. He was even in favour of the proposed airfield. Not only did he take the children away from the Jivaros, but he compelled them to work for nothing for the good of his monastery. The officers told me with a grin what an ominous name the poor Jivaros had given to the educator of their children. For them the bishop was always *el gran macho*, which in plain English means "the great goat".

The bishop was not very pleased when I told him that I thought of paying a visit to Don Alfredo, a man whose name was known as far as Loja. "Ah, so you're going to the Oriente to visit Don

Alfredo," he said acrimoniously. The man in question was a
German who had built a house in Jivaro fashion at the confluence
of two rivers and lived the life of a jungle hermit. "An unpleasant
fellow," said the bishop, "who only encourages the heathens."

The major invited me to sail down the river with a military
transport, and I accepted his invitation gratefully.

"*Guten Tag, die Herrschaft,*" I said as I met Don Alfredo and a
friend who shared his loneliness and helped him to build boats.
They had carried a tree trunk outside the hut and were filling it
with water. Later the sides would be burnt out to give it an
eliptical form so that they could fasten the thwarts to it.

Don Alfredo was rather embarrassed at receiving a visit from
a European. "I can't offer you very much comfort," he said
apologetically. But that was the last thing I wanted. I wanted to
see Jivaros, real wild Jivaros, and suddenly one who had just
returned from the hunt with his blow tube stood before me. Half
a dozen small ruffled birds hung at his belt and he was already
aiming at a new victim which had perched on the roof. He put a
thin arrow swathed in wool, hardly thicker than a match, into
the blow tube and fired. A weak flutter of wings and the bird fell
lifeless at his feet. The wooden splinter had hit its mark, and I still
cannot understand how this feather-like arrow had managed to
pierce the plumage. Don Alfredo, however, told me that it
would go through the thick pelt of apes and wild boar. In these
cases, of course, the point had to be dipped in *curare* poison, which
the Jivaros from the southern tribes procure on the Brazil-
Bolivia frontier. It can kill in a few seconds, but only creatures
which never eat salt. Thus men and goats are immune from it.
Don Alfredo was very enthusiastic about the advantage of the
blow tube for hunting. You come up quietly to a tree on which
some birds are sitting. A rifle shot rings out, one or perhaps a
brace fall and the others fly away, but with the silent blow tube
one after the other fall silently from the branch like ripe apples
without any of the others being aware of it.

When Don Alfredo noticed my limp I had a further opportunity of admiring the wisdom of these wild savages. I had borrowed a pair of riding boots for the journey from a friend and they

did not fit me particularly well, as I found out after my two days walk. I had an enormous painful blister on my heel. Furthermore in Zamora I had been bitten by the tiny mosquitos which make life there a misery. Their bite does not hurt but after a few hours it swells; it is worse and more irritating than a wasp sting. Your limbs all feel inflamed and you can do nothing but keep on scratching. This of course makes matters worse. Don Alfredo noticed my trouble and brought a couple of twigs from a bush which in any other place I should have admired for its beauty. The long white umbels of the guando, as this bush is called, hang down in demure festoons. Their juice alleviates pains of all descriptions, and after taking a foot bath and rubbing my bites and blisters with its leaves the pain disappeared completely. An extract from this plant is used by the Jivaros as an opiate for their surgical operations. You have to fast for two days beforehand and two days afterwards to be immune from the poison. It is a powerful narcotic and slows down the bloodstream, but beware of not taking the necessary precautions. One of Alfredo's white friends, intoxicated with guando juice mixed with another native potion, *natema*, paid for his irresponsibility with the loss of his senses and finally died a painful death in delirium. A medical commission from the States, Don Alfredo told me, had recently visited Jivaro country in an attempt to win the local drugs for modern pharmaceutics. The most exciting discovery, however, was made by another American. Could the herbs which were used for shrinking heads be made to serve a more useful purpose? he wondered. Cancer, one of the unconquered human flails, was a growth of the tissues. Would it be possible to treat the body with these tissue-reducing herbs? He settled in Guayaquil and began to experiment. In actual fact many of his patients began to feel very much better, and although the last word has not been spoken on this new discovery, it may be that one day it will be found to be a decisive weapon against the insidious disease.

In his youth Don Alfredo had travelled in the United States. At the age of 30 he returned to Germany, and finding no work left again for the jungle, where he made a comfortable living from gold washing. All the rivers in the Oriente bring down gold, and if you know your business you can collect about a pound of dust a month. But then war broke out with Peru and Ecuador lost her best gold areas. In addition to this there were too many washers and the yield had begun to fall. When this happened Don Alfredo followed the example of so many others whom the jungle had swallowed: they wanted to return to civilization but found they could not bear it. The most marvellous land of plenty lay here to entice them. You only had to claim your share from the government and you were immediately the owner of 50 hectares with the sole responsibility of clearing and planting it. Don Alfredo with his friend had done this. A fine orange grove stretched out behind his house and coffee grew in the shade of the banana palms. Achiote bushes flaunted their red thorny pods. He had raised chickens and pigs. There was plenty of fodder for them here. It must be wonderful to live in this land of the lotus eaters!

Only an inexperienced romantic could have such a thought, a romantic who had read of the magic of the jungle by the fireside and had never experienced it in person. Don Alfredo had experienced it. He knew that in the primeval forest everything grew—everything, even the destructive powers. One day nearly all his chickens died of the pest. The pigs here are half wild and break through the hedges and destroy the crops. A wild dog must hold them in check by biting them in the hocks; worms will get into the wound and the beasts will be eaten by parasites unless they are painted each night. They are also prone to catch the pest. One is prone to everything here. The jungle assails the crops like an overflowing river. It is no accident that here man constantly has to carry a knife as the medieval knight carried a sword. He must struggle untiringly; he must constantly destroy so that the wilderness does not drown him. One moment's weakness and immediately . . .

Don Alfredo had been ill for a few weeks and he did not know how he could clear the thicket from his property. "Everything I make goes back into the struggle with the jungle," he said sadly. "We have worked and slaved here for years and you can see the result. I still live in a hut like the savages. I live from the fruits of my own soil—today cooked bananas, tomorrow mandioca roots which serve as potatoes; and we brew our drink from distilled sugar cane. Try it, it's very healthy, and contains all the vitamins. We eat meat very seldom, except when we kill a chicken. Both the river and the forest have grown poor in game, because the Jivaros shoot everything they see. You can travel for days without meeting a wild boar. As for women—what white woman could possibly come and live in these conditions, and the Jivaro woman brings her whole family along with her, apart from the fact that. . . So you live a solitary and wretched life in the jungle. For many years mine has been nothing but work. The jungle, that magnificent accursed jungle over there, keeps consuming her own gifts. Perhaps when the road comes as far as this things will be different. When a few more settlers pour in, I shan't be alone in my struggle."

Yes, that is the jungle—a polluting luxuriance of life. Lift up your plate and a huge beetle will run away. Lift up your rucksack and you will find hundreds of insects under it. There are *cucurachas* of all sizes, small ones, middling ones and big ones—as big as the palm of your hand. They eat your shirts, they eat everything that thrives on dirt. When you forget to wash they even nibble your cheeks while you're asleep.

Outside in the garden the leaf-cutting ants are at work. They have settled on the edge of a banana leaf as if a foreman had posted them there. Their sawing jaws are quite audible. Then a column of workers comes and takes the stolen piece of leaf in its pincers. They are incredibly industrious. If you plant vegetables you will find the whole bed gone in one day. Nothing helps except to follow the thieves, find their nest, dig it up and burn the whole colony.

Yes, that is the jungle, the romantic primitive jungle. How wonderful it is up in the barren mountains to plant a tree or to sow your maize in the ground. Those are the creations of the peasant. He cares for them, presents them with his labour, gives them water and sees them sprout. They are like well-beloved children born of one's own flesh. That is a worthy task for men, but here in the jungle what use is man? He is a child in a conflict against dragons, helpless even as a destroyer before so much

exuberance. That is why his huts grow mouldy so quickly.
This world is not for him, it is not for creatures whose aim is
creation. Man here is debased because he is not strong enough
and the spirit serves no purpose.

After two days I said goodbye to Don Alfredo. He procured
me two young Jivaros from the neighbourhood. They would
travel with me downstream and take the opportunity of visiting
their tribesmen on the way. I did not particularly care for Itza.
He had tasted too much civilization; his hair was shaved and he
wore a shirt and trousers. He sat in the bows of the canoe and as
the current bore us along threw out his hook baited with worms.
It was made fast with a red string and the fishes must have been
particularly idiotic, for they kept biting. Behind me sat my
favourite, Schiki. I did not much care for calling him this name,
because it meant "Urine". Itza, on the contrary, meant "The
Moon" which is far more poetic. Schiki, however, still wore his
hair long and nothing but a loin cloth. When he laughed his
teeth gleamed black between his lips. They were stained with
piu to prevent them from falling out. He hardly used the broad
paddle. The green river had become broad and mild and carried
us swiftly forward. At one moment we heard a roar ahead: I
had to get out and wade through the forest. The two youths made
the canoe fast with a liana and dragged it over the rocks, protecting it from the wrath of the rapids. We embarked again further
downstream and glided as in a dream beneath gigantic branches
which hid the sky, listening to the stream that gurgled and sang
beneath our boat.

At times Schiki let the paddle go free and let out a long piercing
cry not unlike the note of a factory siren. Then from the clearings
which break the monotony of the jungle a similar cry would
echo. "*Hut huye hutschoi,*" Schiki would scream back, and out
of the ensuing jabber I managed occasionally to distinguish a few
Christian names and Spanish numbers. They told me that Schiki
was explaining to his invisible friends ashore the object and goal
of our journey, and passing on the news which he had learnt
from other tribesmen on the way down. This jungle telegraph
is used by all travelling Jivaros. Everyone tells his neighbour

anything new that has happened, and in this way news spreads
with the speed of the wind over hundreds of miles. Had some
misfortune happened to us we should not have been abandoned.
All their comrades in the neighbourhood would have known
where we should have appeared and what was our destination.
We should not have had to wait very long for help.

The Jivaros have no villages. Each family lives in a huge oval
house of bamboo poles in his own clearing in the jungle. Towards
evening my two friends paddled fast to reach the next settlement
where we could find a lodging. On each occasion I enjoyed the
venerable ritual with which the host greeted his visitors. The doors
are narrow and open at both ends of the hut. You have to make
yourself very small to slip inside.

No one casts a glance at the newcomers. They behave as if
you were made of thin air. Schiki makes a sign to me to sit down.
We wait in silence at the entrance. Suddenly a woman slips from
the group. Very cautiously she carries a calabash filled to the
brim with a white liquid not unlike milk. It is *chicha*. Each of us
takes three deep draughts. Only after this friendly cooling drink
is the tongue free for greetings and welcomes, for question and
answer. I go over to the head of the family and spread out the
presents I have brought with me from civilization. Needles and
thread are the favourites, for here sewing is masculine work.
The chief will be very happy if you give him powder, for here
the shotgun has gradually replaced the blowpipe. The youngest
of the women, a sweet plump creature from whose broad lower
lip a small wooden stick protrudes coquettishly by way of ornament, leaps immediately on a small mirror to admire her youthful
features and the magic of the tattooed lines. In return for my
gifts I received a duck, one of those I had seen waddling about in
front of the house. Schiki wrings its neck cold-bloodedly and it is
put into the pot without its throat being cut.

The duck indubitably belongs to me, and were I to observe
my occidental rights I should eat it down to the last bone. But
I had learnt enough of the customs of the Jivaros to know that
this would have been looked upon as unseemly barbarity. For
here there is no "mine and thine"; everything is communal.

The women watch from their corners as the oldest among them plucks the bird for the feast. In these bamboo houses, where there are no blankets or cushions, small children crawl about the floor, dogs are tied up on leashes, chickens scrabble and guinea pigs get under your feet. It is one great living community without any privacy whatsoever. In any case, I was selfish enough to fish the most delicate pieces of my duck out of the pot and as I chewed it there was general smacking of lips from all round the hut—a smacking and a cracking, for even the bones were eaten. Schiki fell upon the one I threw away and began gnawing it like a dog. And not only the bones but the entrails, everything is eaten. In Jivaro country a duck certainly does not die in vain. I suppose it is a miracle that they do not also gobble the feathers as they do the fish scales.

It has grown dark. The children cuddle up to their mothers like small well-fed pigs. My two friends, without saying a word, have stretched themselves out on a guest bed and have generously left me a small canoe to sleep in. A clucking hen has perched near my head. I light her up each time I put my torch on. She makes her way with her brood to pick up the crumbs which fell on to the floor after the meal. A very uncomfortable night, the reader will probably think. Personally I have seldom felt so contented and happy as sleeping among these savages.

Next morning the great sensation occurred. Itza, with complete Jivaro impartiality, had rummaged in my pack and discovered the shrunken head. I could see him whispering into Schiki's ear, repeating it to the women, until all eyes were turned expectantly upon me. I took the zanza out of its wrapping and handed it round for inspection. A surprise. They were all really horrified and no one dared to touch it. The women put their hands over their mouths with that expression of "I can't touch it" which old ladies assume when looking at implements of torture in a museum. I asked Schiki to let himself be photographed with it, but I had to fasten the object of terror on his spear myself; then he put on such a grim agonized expression that it might have been the shrivelled head of his own living brother. Finally the head of the family brought out his feather headdress which he wore only on feast days. It was made from the golden, wine red and blue plumage of the pepper-eater, and today has become as rare as the zanza, because very few Jivaros can resist the temptation of exchanging them for the sweets of civilization.

The time has come to say goodbye. The Jivaros are off hunting and we have to return to the canoe. The women prepare a calabash of *chicha*. While they suckle their children they put cooked mandioca in their mouths, chew it peacefully and spit the mixture into a pot, where it will ferment. This is what I had drunk on my arrival the day before!

After a few hours a river ran into the main stream and a soldier waved to us from the bank. We had to land and the sergeant examined my papers. He was hospitality itself—an almost unpleasant compulsory form of hospitality. No, I could not possibly continue my journey. The next Jivaro settlement was far too uncomfortable—in fact, out of the question. The head of the house was away and my presence alone with the women might prove dangerous. It would be much more comfortable to sleep at the post. He was obviously right, for the soldiers lived in a roomy house and had plenty of provisions. A charming tame toucan with its huge curved beak was an added attraction for me to stay, but my two comrades would not hear of it. They seemed anxious to avoid the military. When we arrived at the ill-famed Jivaria I saw at once why the soldiers had wanted to keep me away. The women were extremely pretty and for my taste could have been slightly more virtuous. On the door a strip of paper was nailed on which the absent husband had written "I beg the soldiers to leave my wives in peace. Otherwise I shall demand payment for the chicken they stole from me last week." Well, well! Itza told me that the soldiers sought out the Jivaro women in secret, and in this settlement only a few weeks before a young girl had been raped and killed. So that was it. That was the progress the white man carried into this world of "savages"—Christian morality enforced by "The Great Goat" and the peace of military disturbers of the peace.

That evening the *chicha* flowed once more in streams. I counted the bowls my friends had gulped down. They must have drunk at least two gallons each. Heaven knows where they found room for it in their slender bodies. Very soon, in spite of the small alcohol content it began to have its fatal effect. Itza and Schiki quarrelled so bitterly that they declared they would not continue their journey together on the following day. It needed all my powers of persuasion to reconcile them, although they probably understood hardly anything I said. Had I not succeeded I should probably still be sitting in the jungle today.

It was not the excitement which kept me from sleeping that night. I was brooding over the fatal responsibility of the white man, whose presence, like a slow poison, had penetrated this ingenuous and wonderfully conceived world, dooming the Jivaros to extinction. They were prevented from cutting off each other's heads and turning them into trophies, but, instead, their bodies, weakened by the tropics, were ravaged by influenza, smallpox, measles and tuberculosis, all European diseases. Urges were aroused in these simple men which formerly they never knew, and they, for whom indolence represented the highest human virtue, were now compelled to work for small wages by the usurpers.

All this was tantamount to the destruction of their world and the physical end of their race. Even a common cold could prove fatal in their state of unpreparedness.

PERU

Pizarro lives on

PERU welcomes the traveller with a Customs zeal surpassing anything I have experienced behind the Iron Curtain. At the frontier an official takes down all your particulars in duplicate and this is repeated at the frontier post of Tumbés. Well, that's that, you think with relief, but you are very wrong. At each town through which the bus passes the Gringo is hauled out like a criminal and once more his particulars are noted in a police official's book. The same thing applies at night. The military atmosphere that reigns in this country is very apparent. In Colombia I was called *Professor*, in Ecuador, *Maestro*, but here in Peru the porters called me *Jefe*.

The hilly Ecuadorian country stops at the Peruvian frontier as though cut off with a knife and an entirely new landscape begins —the desert. Sand, nothing but sand and sea. Occasionally the road climbs through undulating dunes only to descend in breakneck curves. You pass one cross after the other. Traffic victims here are buried by the wayside as a warning.

In Talara the desert changes to an industrial landscape, oil pipes wander through the countryside. Not a human being in sight: only pumps serviced by power stations bend their heads like birds drinking in the sand. It reminds one of Salvador Dali. It is a mistake, however, to consider the desert zone on the Peruvian coast as a boring stretch of country. Many travellers decide that it is better to get it behind them as quickly as possible in an aeroplane. Desolation: on one side the dark wall of the Cordillera and on the other the boundless sea. From June until November the countryside is draped in a napkin of fog; its fringes extend over the dunes and behind them the sun's rays crawl tardily over the ground. Here and there towards evening the light grows clearer and the golden sand dunes cast violet shadows in the desert. Sometimes the road winds through loam cliffs and descends once more in hairpin bends into a broad green valley. You can hardly believe your eyes. The valley is dotted with friendly farmhouses and sugar cane or cotton fields. For here there is plenty of water, life and wealth . . . and a mile further on you come to the desert again with no sign of a tree or a house.

At times out to sea a tiny hillock rises from the waves like cream on a raspberry ice. It is not cream but manure—the most famous manure in world history, manure that made possible a civilization. Without this guano the Incas would not have been able to feed their people and the crumbs of soil on their mountain slopes would have produced no harvests. Without guano there would have been no Peru or at best an insignificant and historically unimportant nation. Before mineshafts were sunk in her mountains and oil wells in her desert her entire economy was built on this manure, which seemed to be an almost inexhaustible source of export wealth. Today however the reserves have almost disappeared and the guano company, which is controlled by the government, can only spare 150,000 tons a year for agriculture. The export has also fallen. The producers of this wealth are the most tireless workers in the world. They toil day and night, ask for no pay and they never strike. Moreover, their work is the easiest and the most pleasant in the world; they merely have to digest and to multiply, nothing else. Twenty to forty million birds! And they are treated with respect, I might almost say with reverence, as though they were a mighty union. No aircraft may approach with the drone of its engine, no ship may blow its siren and no hunter can fire at them. For in these cases the flock would rise in the air in terror and their coveted excrement would fall in the sea. When you approach the island in a boat you have the unpleasant feeling of trespassing on forbidden ground where man must run the gauntlet of thousands of angry birds' eyes. For heads are raised from all the cliffs and terraces where the parents are guarding their eggs or their young. It is a single protest from waddling cormorants, gannets, pelicans and divers, whose only tolerated guests are a few clumsy sea lions.

All this creates a huge causal chain: the desert on the coast, the Humboldt river, the Arctic cool near the Equator. Thus the coast of Ecuador where it curves on the Pacific is a burning hell, and the desert extends here because the damp air above the cold water is condensed to fog—a fog which never throughout the whole year turns to fertilizing rain. The Humboldt river provides the birds with their food. Countless millions of anchovies live on the microscopic plankton which it carries down, and they in turn disappear into the hungry bellies of the sea birds. Sometimes a mysterious cyclic condition brings about a catastrophe among the anchovies. About every ten years, for some undiscovered reason, the temperature of the Humboldt rises and kills off all the plankton. Then the anchovies starve and as a result the guano birds also hunger and die. The last of these catastrophes happened in 1951 and 100,000 precious birds died on their white islands. The anchovies have still not reached their former number. Possibly not only nature but man was responsible for this. The guano birds have found a competitor, the fish nitrate industry, which sends its products to the poultry and pig farmers in the United States in exchange for good dollars. The guano administration is far from pleased at this competition and the Peruvian government is faced with an almost philosophical problem: should the anchovies be digested or pulverized in order to give the greatest return.

The motor buses are magnificently organized. They run strictly to time. At 3 o'clock in the morning we were in Trujillo, another colonial town. The façades seemed stiffer and even more florid and the wrought iron balconies, reminiscent of Arabian harems, more richly ornamented than I had seen elsewhere. I already felt that I must be nearing the imperial city of Lima.

The following day I journeyed northwards to Chan Chau, the largest ruined city of the continent, a memorial to the Chimu culture which flourished here long before the Incas, at the dawn of Christianity. The earthwork walls cover an area of 15 square miles; the capital sheltered one and a half million inhabitants whose kingdom once stretched from Guayaquil south as far as Lima. Temples, palaces, strongholds and aqueducts can still be recognized today after 2,000 years. How was that possible? How could this transitory kingdom survive the destruction of time? We know the reason. It never rains here.

Had Peru been a land of rain and sunshine Chan Chau would long since have vanished from the face of the earth. On one single occasion, in March 1925, the weather god suddenly changed his mood. It poured for a few days and the giant city melted under the stream like butter in the sun. Later came the bulldozers of farmers only too eager to enlarge their spacious *haciendas*. They assailed the thousand-year-old walls and soon levelled them to the ground. Even the small-holders found the land worth an attempt. They planted their beds among the ruins of palaces and temples from which wonderful reliefs looked down upon their vegetables—reliefs with birds and dragons wreaking their vengeance on a small human being, reliefs from a far-off mythical world, reliefs made of earth which could be scraped off with a finger nail. Only thanks to a miracle—presumably because they were covered with sand—did they survive the rain. In 1945 the Peruvian government suddenly came to the tardy conclusion that such treasures might possibly be worth while saving. From then onwards the farms and small-holders were kept under supervision. They could no longer be evicted, according to the ruling laws, but the remaining reliefs were given roofs and protected by glass windows.

The people of Lima sigh for the sun. If only the sun would shine! Sometimes a patch of blue appears in the shroud of mist and a diffused light filters through the clouds. It is not particularly cold and yet you shiver in your overcoat, although you are only a few degrees south of the Equator. Nylon shirts which elsewhere dry in four hours need two days here because it is so damp. It is related that the Indians suggested this place to the Spaniards as being particularly suitable for building their capital, merely because they thought to themselves "They're all bound to die here." This seems to me highly credible, but the city has survived.

The summer is not particularly hot, and although one shivers in the winter the thermometer never falls below zero. Everyone suffers from debility here after a few years as a result of the magnificent climate. Since the body is subjected to no tempering it falls into disuse. Not even the bacteria can stand this fabulous climate. Now and then a flea is imported with the jute sacks from India; it spreads the pest, but there is no need for alarm. The disease peters out on its own account. A worm appears in the garden and begins to eat the plants. It will die a natural death, say the gardeners, and in due course it disappears. Everything comes to an end on its own account here—except the chickens. Roofs are a superfluous luxury for which a new licence is necessary. The citizens of Lima have discovered a use for them: they keep chickens up there. Cocks crow at all hours of the day—at midday, at evening and at midnight, because the street lighting makes them think it is dawn. This is what I liked most in Lima. You are in a capital city and you would think you were in the depths of the country. One of my first visits in Lima was to the cathedral. The twin towers of St Rose rise proudly above the *Plaza de Armas* and the government palace. In a side chapel rests the mummy of the conqueror and founder of this city, Francisco Pizarro. It is a beautiful golden yellow and magnificently preserved, but the skull grins from the disintegrated face. Nearby can be seen the coat of arms which this plebeian chose—instead of being suckled like Romulus by a she-wolf, Pizarro was supposed to have been suckled by a sow. The murder of the son of heaven, Atahualpa, is portrayed above it. The treachery is not concealed with shame, but flaunts itself boldly. Outside on the Plaza I saw the equestrian statue of the Conquistador: with dagger raised, he rides a fiery stallion. Some stone masons were dragging it from its plinth. Was another twilight of the gods being prepared here. Would Pizarro be disenthroned in the same way as his more noble colleague Cortés in Mexico?

Not a bit of it. Pizarro looked slightly dislocated but not degraded. On purely æsthetic grounds it had been decided to move the 6½-ton warrior hero from the parvis and erect him in the nearby square that bears his name. In Peru no one thinks that the Indian heritage could be greater than the Spanish. No, Lima feels herself to be a Spanish city and still honours her founder who was suckled by a sow.

The museum is quite remarkable, full of testimonies to all the cultures which have sprung from the rich soil. You are greeted in the courtyard by a reconstruction of a Chavin temple, decorated with a hundred faces and eyes. Eyes everywhere, but not the omniscient eye of the Christian God which follows the onlooker wherever he goes. This omnivision squints in all directions like the facets of a precious stone. Be careful when you stand in front of these idols that you do not feel as you did in Bogotá: how alien and hostile, how remote from all humanity, is this world. And yet, on the other hand, so incredibly modern. Apart from their temples their art is most utilitarian in character. You will find showcases full of pottery—pots, nothing but pots! Heads of the most subtle design laugh from the necks of these jars. The whole pre-Inca daily life dances in comical little figures round their rims. They drink at banquets, play, hunt, fish and sew their garments. Even their love making, to the embarrassment of many puritanical observers, has been immortalized on these *huacos*. And then the materials! In Paracas, somewhere in the desert, the tombs of the nobility were discovered. The occupants had sat there in their loneliness, buried in the sand for 2,000 years, bundled and tied up with string as if they were just going to be sent off by post. When they were unpacked it was an enormous surprise. The clothes which had covered their withered bodies were as fresh in colour as if they had been woven today. Yes, today, if people could still produce anything so marvellous. The eye never grows tired of deciphering the fabulous monsters who grin on their resurrection as though in amazement at the present day. A whole hall is devoted to the surgical arts of these incredible ancients. You can see trepanned skulls with the orifices protected by a little artificial lid, probably the surgeon's reparation of war wounds.

The riddle in the desert

THE largest halls and the greatest number of showcases in the Lima museum are filled with objects originally from a culture in the south of the country—from Nasca, which flourished at about the same period as the Chimu kingdom. Any traveller who does not propose to follow in the wake of the ordinary tourist must underline this name three times in his notebook, for in the nearby desert lies the most exciting riddle known to the archæologists of South America.

Now, obviously there is a reason why travellers have given the cold shoulder to these most grandiose traces of early mankind. They are very difficult to observe. Fundamentally they were not created for earthly beings, but for some birdlike eye which can decipher their pattern from a great distance. This is why they remained unnoticed for centuries until the aeroplane revealed this marvel. One day, Dr Kosok, an American archæologist on a flight from Arequipa to Lima, looking absentmindedly out of the cabin window, suddenly gave a start. What could he see down there in the desert? Strange geometrical drawings, straight lines of different thicknesses projected for miles over plains and slopes, a tangle of parallels and angles. It was like a picture painted by some abstract painter. Whole figures now stood out clearly against the dark ground—right angles and trapezoids, resembling airfields.

Dr Kosok immediately hired a car in Lima, journeyed to Nasca and began to survey the desert. The patterns he had seen so clearly in bird's-eye view had suddenly been transformed into banal shallow ditches. The desert here is thickly covered with dark red oxydised iron flints. Some secret hand had removed the flints to one side and uncovered the pale desert subsoil. What could these ditches mean? Were they traces of an earlier agricultural development? Were they irrigation canals? But how could the water flow uphill and cross river valleys? All the laws of gravity contradicted such an explanation. And these triangles which began on the high plateau. What could they possibly have to do with water? A pure coincidence gave Dr Kosok a new idea. He stood deep in thought on a line running westwards just as the sun was setting. To his surprise it ran straight to the point where the heavenly light-giver sank below the horizon. He consulted his almanack. It was the day of the summer solstice. How fantastic! Were these kilometre-long lines and geometrical figures a gigantic astronomical observatory designed to record the path of the stars and the planets in relation to the seasons, the moment of the rainfall in the mountains and therefore the best time for ploughing and sowing?

This was no longer an archæological problem, and Dr Kosok had no more time to spend wandering about in the wilderness. Only as a result of very careful study, a complete survey and measurement of the various lines, and after year-long observations of the stars, could one hope to solve this problem. He discovered a German mathematical mistress now resident in Peru who was prepared to take over this difficult and thankless research task. I met this woman, Maria Reiche, in Lima. She was just about to retire for a few months to her hermit life in the desert and she invited me to go with her. A cotton planter had placed a watchman's hut at her disposal; the fields made a flowery-white patch among the yellow and red of the waterless desert. Early in the morning, armed with a ladder, a sextant and a theodolite, we climbed the gentle slope from where the desert observatory extends from the fertile green valley. In actual fact one would need a helicopter in order to study all the lines at leisure. The ladder was to some extent a substitute and allowed us a little panorama. This improvised aid had enabled Maria Reiche to make a discovery which had previously been overlooked from an aeroplane. Mysterious animal figures were mingled among the geometric lines, birds with long beaks like cranes; a fish, a spider, a scorpion, a cat with a fish's tail, etc. They were thinner and flatter than the geometrical symbols and in the course of the centuries the wind had obliterated them, so that now they could only be reconstructed with the greatest care. At early dawn and at sunset when the oblique light allowed her to distinguish the most delicate folds in the ground, this tireless woman climbed her ladder trying to pinpoint the lines and directed her helpers who followed her instructions, carrying a plummet line weighted with a heavy stone. Excitement increased as a new miracle was revealed. Without the aid of trigonometry or theodolites the ancients had managed to draw gigantic animal figures of the most perfect type on the ground. Why and for whom? No plane will allow you to see them from above, and when you stand on a ladder, as I now did, the eye could only take in a leg or a head; the whole figure became lost in the distance. What technique did they use to enlarge a drawing so perfectly to this gigantic size, and what was the meaning of these animal figures? Perhaps the spirals which broke them here and there gave the clue. In ancient Egypt spirals had a numerical meaning. They signified rolled-up measuring lines and represented the number 100. Did some arithmetical meaning lie hidden here as well as in the heaps of stone which had been erected here and there in ordered rows. Hypotheses, nothing but hypotheses which cannot be answered.

Even the astronomical meaning hangs fire. Nothing could be more simple than this, a layman would think. This woman wanders about for days on end in the desert. She sleeps in the desert. Therefore it must be possible within a few years to establish where certain constellations rise and set—for example, the Pleiades which we know played an important rôle in the life of the ancient Peruvians. It is only necessary to look for the lines which run to the horizon and we shall get a result. Maria Reiche replied to my simple argument with a smile and a sigh. There are many flies in the ointment, because in the course of the centuries—and who knows if the age of the lines would not oblige us to reckon in thousands of years—the zenith and nadir of a rising and setting star constantly changes.

If today one hit upon a constellation which conformed to a certain line it would not necessarily imply that it did so at the time of the ancient Peruvians. Another problem. Nothing but riddles.

And yet perhaps this new difficulty, which is one step further towards a solution, will bring about the answer to a very important question. How old is this gigantic observatory? Were a constellation one day to be identified with a certain line one would be able to reckon the date by the degree of variation. The mathematical teacher continues to make her calculations in the desert with great tenacity. She has become obsessed with the subject as in earlier days other research workers became obsessed with the Pharaohs. She will never rest until she has wrested the secret from this wilderness.

A thriving barracks atmosphere

IN March 1954 the cosmopolitan Avenue Arequipa, which leads from the heart of Lima to the residential quarter of Miraflores, presented a curious picture to the unprepared visitor. Trenches ran across the drives, camouflaged with a few drainpipes. But instead of workers, bands of armed police lounged about the neighbourhood. Police sat on the roofs of the surrounding buildings keeping a certain house under observation. Anyone who wanted to visit the Colombian Embassy—for this was the building in question—was closely searched by the police post. When a car left the Embassy it was followed by a police car, in short, the most secret atom research laboratory could not have been more carefully guarded. The object of these attentions was a white-haired man with a fine eagle profile, Haya de la Torre, the great Peruvian revolutionary, a descendant of that noble wayfarer Pizarro who has been immortalized on the walls of his monumental chapel. He had not yet been arrested. He could move about freely in the besieged building and in his isolation could read and write whatever he pleased, but had he set a foot outside his citadel the police would have snapped up this bitter opponent of the ruling President General Odría. Nowhere had the custom of sanctuary as practised in Latin America created such an absurd situation as in the case of Haya de la Torre. Sanctuary has survived more or less as a necessity owing to the frequency of revolutions and *coups d'états* which determine the political life of this continent. When a *coup d'état* succeeds, the men who have been thrown from power seek refuge in the Embassy of another country. If it fails the revolutionaries take refuge beyond the frontier. Provided he has no evil crime on his conscience—relating to this particular incident, of course—the foreign Ambassador has the right and in fact the moral obligation to take in the supplicant and give him the safe conduct abroad which he will demand. For no one knows whether or not he himself will be obliged one day to knock on the door of an Embassy. Sanctuary is therefore a *sine qua non* in Latin American politics. Let us consider the case that in a *coup d'état* the losers were to be sent for trial: the amusing and lucrative lottery which politics represents here would then become a highly dangerous business and no one would dare to stage another revolt. In that case of course politics would be finished. Thus it does not matter if the attempt fails: one goes for a holiday abroad and waits for the next opportunity. Sanctuary is therefore to a certain extent the politician's life assurance. In certain countries the law is so highminded that overthrown opponents are allowed to retain their plunder until they return. The reason that Haya de la Torre was besieged for five years in the Colombian Embassy is because in his case opinion was so divided that since the 3rd of January 1949, when he fled there, the good relations between Colombia and Peru developed into a bitter conflict. Haya de la Torre, General Odría maintained, was the leader of a political party which had proved its criminality by countless attacks and murders, not to mention a bloody riot in Callao harbour. He was a common terrorist without a right to political sanctuary. He started a rebellion, retorted Colombia, and what pray are the political methods of our continent except rebellion? Haya is a political refugee! The conflict was brought before the International Tribunal at The Hague, which gave a truly Solomonic judgment. It decided that Colombia had no right to harbour the revolutionary leader, but on the other hand was not bound to deliver him to his enemies. Upon this both parties became more confirmed in their viewpoints, although in the meanwhile the Colombian government had become far less friendlily disposed towards revolutions. The sanctity of asylum surmounted ideological differences. Not until March 1954, when the repre-

sentatives of the hemisphere met at the Caracas Conference, did
the Peruvians allow de la Torre to leave unmolested for Rio de
Janeiro. General Odría could with reason hope that the revolutionaries could no longer batten on the fortified body of his
country.

When a dictator bottles the bacillus of revolution and in this
way tries to render it harmless he knows only too well what he
has done. Not only on the faces of fellow travellers but also on
those of the convinced Liberals a shadow of deep compassion
can now be seen whenever the name of Peru is mentioned. The
country is, to use their own terminology, one of the most
"reactionary" in South America. Not only in the amiable patriarchal sense that Ecuador is conservative, but in that evil sense of
a conspiracy of the dark powers: feudal lords, church, army and
foreign capitalist companies. For not only as in the neighbouring
State does the arrogant Spanish upper class rule over enormous
properties of the Sierra without feeling menaced by any agrarian
reform, but all the strong Liberal tradition which at least wrested
from the church its property and political power is lacking.
Peru is rich from the wealth to be found in its soil, but the
foreigners reap the harvest. Copper, silver, gold, lead, zinc,
vanadium, bismuth, tungsten: the American Cerro de Pasco
Corporation together with the American Smelting and Refinery
Company and the Vanadium Company takes the lion's share of
them all. The International Petroleum Company, which owns
the most important oilfields, is a subsidiary company of the
Standard Oil of New Jersey. The British Peruvian Corporation
owns the most important railways. The German family of
Gildemeister together with the American Grace Company are
the sugar kings, and the Banco Italiano does half the banking
business of the country. What remains then to the Peruvians in
their own land? Cotton: yes, to a large extent that is their domain,
except for a third British interest, but even this commodity is
not independent of the whims of foreign markets. Was this not
material enough for a fine public orator like Haya de la Torre?

In 1925, as a student, he hoisted the flag of protest for the first
time against President Leguía. Since then, either at large or in

exile or behind prison bars, he has almost unceasingly disturbed the peace of Peru. He travelled to Mexico, where with other exiled students he founded the social revolutionary movement of APRA (Alianza Popular Revolucionaria Americana). He met Stalin and Trotsky in Moscow and studied British socialism at the London School of Economics. Of all the revolutionaries of the Latin American Continent he is undoubtedly the most brilliant, a friend of Romain Rolland, Einstein and Walt Disney, and a master of all the arts. He is to a certain extent intoxicated with the same idealism as Simón Bolívar, and like all intoxicated people he has two sides to his character—the loving affection which burns to unite all the proletariats of the world, but also the blindness and incapacity to face reality when it comes to concrete facts. The programme of APRA embodied the noblest ideals: distribution of the land to the peasants, liberation and education of the Indios, the muzzling of native and foreign capitalists, nationalization of the mines and transport, and the creation of a great Latin American State community. Far less thought was given to the possibility of realizing these aims. The most important precepts were changed from one moment to the next without anyone raising a finger. For some time Haya de la Torre was an opponent of the United States and later their friend. Anyone who tries to portray exactly what APRA stands for immediately becomes involved in a chaos of contradictions and unrealities, but this has not damaged the movement. Quite the contrary. The conservative powers which previously ruled Peru have tried with force and oppressive measures to keep it away from the polling booths as an illegal party, but Peru urgently needs socialist reform. All the youthful elements are on the side of *Aprismo*. In the forties de la Torre was acceptable in society drawing rooms and yet he was never President. But the movement helped the Liberal Bustamente into the saddle; he surrendered to its majority in Parliament and in local government. The party headquarters became to a certain extent a presidential palace not unlike the the Court of the Pharaohs. Gold flows in streams, but where does it come from? From the public coffers, of course. The APRA ruled communities are bankrupt. The tragic laws of Latin

American revolution are in force here. The liberator becomes the new exploiter because idealism is only a hair's breath away from corruption—from the most shameless corruption. President Bustamente tried to tame the tiger which rattled at its bars, but he merely managed to madden it. Chaos descended on the country. In Cerro de Pasco the Alcalde was murdered by an infuriated mob. The terrified American engineers keep their bags ready packed. The revolt of the naval officers in Callao brought about a crisis, but Peru suffered on 9th of April. The army saved the situation and took over the government. Bustamente retired in favour of his police chief, General Manuel Odría. A general! everyone sighed. A straw man put up by the great landlords and the reactionary powers. Poor Peru!

But there are also pleasant surprises in politics. The General who after a year and a half was elected President without opposition and who rules with a Parliament of his own choice, is no soldier of the old ludicrous type. He knows that one cannot suppress a revolution; one must appropriate its aims and bring it about by other means. Exactly like his colleague Osorio in Salvador, Odría is trying to bring about a conservative revolution. He himself is the son of a poor widow who earned a living as a sempstress in order to pay for his military schooling. The country he has taken over was economically in a deplorable state; the currency debased by inflation, the economy lamed by all manner of controls, the export business on the decline for years, the national debt burdened with $32 million and a powerful budget deficit. His first task was to rescue it from this impossible position.

He had plenty of advisers and plenty of assistants whose support could easily have been won over by the gift of some small post. But Odría had the courage to go his own way. During his military studies he lived for a long time in the United States and learned at first hand to appreciate the advantages of a free economy. To this end he brought in a private firm from Washington, Klein and Sachs, as economic advisers. The director, Dr. Julius Klein, was head of the Latin American branch of the Trade Department during the Hoover Presidency. His team, which comprised no more than ten men, after an all-embracing study of the position gave the following basic recommendation: take off all the controls! The decree of November the 11th, 1949, introduced complete liberalism in place of a controlled economy, a policy similar to that adopted by Erhardt in Germany. A Peruvian economic miracle resulted, which cannot fail to have an impression on the other Latin American countries.

From now on the whole endangered economy began to breathe once more. The mining enterprises, which previously had to exchange all their foreign currency into the almost worthless native *sols*—hard currency which was urgently needed for imports and the necessary machinery—could now buy and sell freely. Immediately money for investment streamed into the country: $50 million from the Cerro de Pasco for waterworks: $100 million from the American Smelting for the exploitation of newly discovered copper fields. French capital financed steelworks and Dutch capital a chemical industry. In the Sechura desert between the Northern Andes and the sea, and beyond it in the Amazon basin, fourteen oil companies started a wild scramble for concessions, among them four native companies. Odría offered favourable treatment to the concessionaires. They are allowed to exploit their strikes for forty years. After this the entire plant reverts to the State, which also takes half of their net profits. The law is based on that of Venezuela, which also gives a spur to the economy by a similar distribution of national and private interests. In the case of the mining companies, too, Odría has shown generosity—from interested motives. The result is prosperity such as the land has never before experienced.

Prosperity for whom? For the rich, the shareholders, the industrialists, the big merchants. And how stands it with the poor, with the mine and factory workers, with the Indios on the land of the Sierra?

When the General seized power and announced that his principal aim was the betterment of living conditions for the peasants and workers, many observers shook their heads sceptically. Everyone talked like that and no one did anything about it. But since during the growing inflation under the APRA régime the position of even the revolutionary classes had only deteriorated, the "Peruvian economic miracle" also had its influence on them. The removal of controls brought no rise in prices, as many pessimists expected, because now the "under the counter" wares streamed in from the free instead of from the black markets. In any case, during the first years of the fifties the cost of living index figure only rose a fraction compared with other Latin American countries such as Mexico, the Argentine or Chile; wages kept pace with or went ahead of prices. The profits from mines and oil companies that swelled the State coffers did not vanish into the pockets of the politicians—Odría did not shrink from prosecuting his best friend, who had abused his position for personal gain—but was diverted to schools, hospitals and workers' settlements. During the past few years more than a quarter of the budget—of a balanced budget—has been devoted to education and health.

Odrías's government is of course Conservative in so far as it does not interfere with the existing order. There has been no mention of a distribution of land, because the big planters with their experience produce better and more cheaply than small holders. Under Odría a non-ideological managerial viewpoint reigns: it is more profitable to introduce the methods of big business to small holders than the other way round. Thus in co-operation with the *Servicio Cooperativo Interamericano de Producción de Alimentos,* run by technical experts from Point Four, agricultural centres have been founded which already take care of more than a million small holders; they plough the whole year round with their tractors, learn modern methods in experimental laboratories and schools, with the result that their harvests are four times greater than before. An expert from the Bank of America in California has helped Peru to create a State bank for agricultural credits: it advances short-term harvest loans at cheap rates to *peons* who want to become independent. This is of the utmost importance to the great plans for colonizing the Oriente, which lies deeper and more lost in the wilderness in Peru than in Mexico. The Trans-Andean road, which stretches as far as the Ucayali river, has opened up a colony in grand style in a region where a few score years ago only a few timid Indios lived. "Why should we have an agrarian reform," a Peruvian asked me, "when we have such an enormous expanse available for settlement?" Actually this cheap solution takes the wind out of the demagogic sails provided the opening up of unused land continues. The experts of Point Four were also responsible for the great settlement plan of Tingo María in the Oriente. Today 20,000 men already live in the midst of this wilderness.

Odría encourages anyone who wants to push on further. In Lima I met a group of very strange pioneers, language experts from the Summer Linguistic Institute of Oklahoma University, who are busy studying and recording the dialects of various remote tribes from the Amazon basin. They number about a hundred, for the most part young girls who land one day in a small plane near an Indian village without knowing a word of their language and settle among them. Presents and other courtesies are the quickest methods of obtaining co-operation. They have to start like a child with an unknown and completely alien dialect by pointing out various objects and learning the names from the natives. A word of caution. If you point with your finger you will always be told the same word, the word for "finger." In Amazon country you point with a protruding lip. In this way you make a collection of the nouns and then start on the verbs until ultimately you have grasped the grammar. The ultimate goal, however, is the translation of the Bible. Part of this research work is paid for by protestant groups in the United States, even when the philologists refuse to participate in any kind of missionary activity. They are trying, they say, to bring to the savages who still worship the most fabulous idols the elements of the Christian faith, the Ten Commandments and the Sermon on the Mount. But even this has aroused the deepest mistrust in the Catholic Church and evoked a repeated campaign by Cardinal Archbishop Guevara against the foreign intruders.

Is this just or unjust? A charming anecdote I heard betrays the secular gulf which separates these jungle Indios from the most civilized of all whites. Even in the bush the American scholars are unwilling to renounce the pleasures of a comfortable life.

They are in contact with their bases by radio, and aircraft bring
loads of tinned food, which is their staple diet, into the jungle.
One of the young folk who for years had tried unsuccessfully
to wean his coloured friends from praying to the boa constrictor
engaged the chieftain in conversation. "Why won't you accept
Jesus Christ?" he asked. The man dismissed the idea with contempt. "*Jesú Cristo* is no good," was the reply. "You're wrong,"
said the linguist; "I think that he possesses enormous power." But
the Indian was completely unimpressed. "*Jesú Cristo* only sends
tinned food," he said. "He obviously hasn't heard of mandioca."
Another American, the multi-millionaire and philanthropist
Letourneau, who nursed different plans, had to submit to a storm
of protest from the Lima clergy. He had obtained from the
government a concession of a million acres of primeval forest on
the Pachto river, which at an estimated cost of $2 million for the
first two years he proposed to change into a flourishing garden
and to build a road at his own expense joining it to the Trans-
Andean road. Once more the President did not give way to the
clerical campaign, and in January 1954 the millionaire, after the
arrival of the first shipload of machinery and equipment, was able
to start his project.

On the other side of the Cordillera, too, mighty agricultural
plans are in progress. Fifty-six mountain streams which previously had been allowed to trickle away in vain are to be brought
together by artificial tunnels, led into the lakes and used by an
enormous power station. In other parts of the desert artesian wells
have been sunk from which water will be pumped. Odría's aim
is to make the land completely self-supporting, and he is well on
his way to achieving it. Previously Peru had to import 20 per
cent of its comestibles.

The foreigner feels happier in Peru than in almost any other
country in South America. "You see," an American business man
said to me, "here a feudal society has understood the secret of
progress. Even Marx recognized that the natural path to socialism
must first undergo a capitalist phase; Odría merely wanted to
change naturally and fundamentally the whole structure of
feudalism. He developed the potential of the country, introduced

industries, factories and better wages. That kills feudalism in the natural manner. When the worker in the mines or in the factory earns three times as much he will never work for a landowner at a starvation wage. The same or a similar problem arises in all the countries of this continent. Most of them, however, want to take two steps at the same time—*i.e.,* overthrow simultaneously feudalism and capitalism. This impatience is their greatest error and basically this is why their social revolutions must fail. Only foreign capital is strong enough and only foreign technicians have enough experience to awaken these lands out of their sleeping-beauty trance. Admittedly it is a difficult theory to maintain in view of the prevalent anti-colonial feeling, but it is no less important all the same. That is why democracy here is in such a desperate position. The people have no love for the foreign companies. The more uneducated the proletarian the quicker he can be roused by the idea that the foreign exploiters should be driven from the country. That is the tragedy. These people are not mature enough to understand the real necessity for their existence. They want to kill the goose that lays the golden eggs. Only one course remains—to prevent them from doing so by force. That is the problem of the Americans here in their sister continent. None of us here are at all in favour of military dictatorship, but it is the only power capable of enforcing a realistic policy. The man here who courts popular applause will immediately be in danger of being swallowed up in chaos and fantasy. The generals, however, are still courageous enough to be unpopular and they have the armed power behind them to enforce the necessary measures until they stand on their own merit. Unfortunately most dictators are not angels, but we must be all the more thankful when one comes so near to perfection as this Odría."

As in the case of every dictatorship, it is also difficult in Peru to estimate to what extent the people are content with their ruler. Only two large newspapers appear in Lima, *El Comercio* and *La Prensa.* Both of them are Conservative and even without a censorship would not kick against the pricks. In the editor's office of *El Comercio,* which belongs to the powerful old family

PERU   217

of Miro-Quesada, the visitor's eye will be caught by a blood-stained suit in which Antonio, the former owner, was murdered in 1935 by a young APRA fanatic. This is to a certain extent a symbol of warning: Be on the alert! A strange journalistic product is a weekly magazine on the same lines as the American paper *Time*. It merely bears the number of the year, for example, 1955. Its home political section supports Odría, but as regards foreign politics it is a true vehicle of Communist propaganda and prints quite faithfully the atrocity stories of the germ war in Korea. These strange contradictions can probably be traced back to different money sources. When I tried to bring the editor down to facts he simply did not turn up to our appointment, in the normal Latin American way.

How secure in the saddle Odría feels can be judged by the fact that in August he made a very strange speech for a dictator, admitting the right of workers to strike. Could he have risked this because he knew that the unions are in the hands of people —actually Communist leaders—who are favourably disposed towards him? In any case, on this presidential invitation there were a few strikes caused by unjust dismissals, unfair treatment and low wages. They were successful. Of a more serious nature were a few student demonstrations in the universities of San Marco in Lima, of Arequipa and Cuzco. A student of national economy from the latter university told me that a rivalry existed in the student organizations between Communist and APRA groups but that the latter showed the greatest restraint. Does this signify that APRA continues to exist underground? It is difficult to say because conspirators, even if they exist, refrain from advertising. In any case the abominable behaviour of the party when in power sobered up many middle-class intellectuals who at one time were favourably disposed towards it. I was dining one night with a man who had belonged to it and held quite a high position. When I tried to get him to talk about this period he dismissed the subject with a gesture of horror as though it were an unpleasant memory. The APRA was not broken by Odría alone. To a very large extent it destroyed itself.

And what of the people? A taxi driver summed the matter up

quite well. "I hate the arrogance of the officers," he complained. "They never pay you what you ask and simply give you what they think is right. That's natural. Whoever is in power gets a bit above himself. We boycott them as much as we can and look the other way when they hail us. The police too. They're bastards. They don't give you a chance. They kill you with fines."

Peru may have the atmosphere of a barracks parade ground, but paradoxically it is a flourishing barracks.

The Sierra of Slaves

NOTHING can happen to me, I thought, as I took my seat in a Central Railway carriage to continue my journey through the valleys of the Sierra. All right. The railway takes you in five hours from sea level to the altitude of Mont Blanc. Was this any reason for being nervous. I had climbed hundreds of times with irons and a heavy pack to similar heights, and it was ridiculous to think that I could suffer from mountain sickness.

I had not breakfasted, and bought some provisions from the busy sellers on the station platform. For example, in the famous *Bartolomé Jardin* I bought 2 lb. of *chirimoyas,* of which I am particularly fond—a fruit the size of a fist whose soft flesh reminds you alternately of pineapple, strawberries and whipped cream. I chewed happily at my fruit while the engine snorted up the mountain, through tunnels, over wild torrents and embankments. No, nothing could happen to me.

The fresh air entered my nostrils and we continued to climb. I looked at my watch. We had already been travelling for three hours. The air became thinner. "I'm all right," I kept saying to myself. A doctor in a white coat walked along the corridor carrying an oxygen tube. I, the great mountaineer, looked at him almost disagreeably.

Higher and higher. . . . My pulse was beating fast, but all the same. . . . Snowy glittering mountains ahead. Now we were driving through the wastes of snow. The light glared in my eyes and dark glasses no longer helped. My stomach began to rumble, but I was still all right. I felt I was turning pale and ought to lie down. Ridiculous. There was too much to do; I must watch the view as we passed, the snow on which I should have so liked to ski.

At last we were on top of Galera, the highest railway station in the world—15,673 feet I read on the signboard. I was all right, but suddenly everything turned black. I leant back in my seat and cold sweat broke out on my forehead. I was terribly sick. Fortunately no one took it amiss.

Gone were my illusions that I was a good mountaineer. I was hopelessly sick and I was not even carrying a heavy rucksack and an ice axe. You cannot stand being inactive at 15,000 feet. Then we started to descend, but it brought no relief. In Oroya I pulled myself together and staggered round the smelting plant of the Cerro de Pasco Corporation. It is a dreary spot, one of the most godforsaken places in the world; although it is so near the sky it reminds you of an entrance to hell. The poisonous smoke from the countless chimneys has destroyed all the vegetation on the surrounding mountains. The scree rises cold and grey before your eyes and makes you feel giddy. "In a few years it will be green again," remarked one of my companions, and he pointed out a giant chimney below towards which a steel-ribbed gigantic worm seemed to crawl. The age of multiple chimneys is over. Now everything has to go through this gigantic filter plant. On my next visit to Oroya I should be able to pick flowers, but at the present moment my limbs ached as if I had got 'flu. Unfortunately, there was no decent hotel for ordinary mortals in this dump—the site of the largest smelting works in South America— only wretched bug-ridden hovels. Ah, I forget! Bed bugs cannot stand this height, but fleas can. Finally a fellow countryman who worked with the company took compassion on me, inviting me to share his room in the busy factory hotel. He too was sick of Oroya. It was all right piling up dollars, but he was young enough not to want to live for ever in this pestilential wilderness.

The following day I felt better, but my pulse was still 120. This would continue until enough red corpuscles had built up to offset the lack of oxygen in the air.

I decided to risk going a little higher—to the Huaron Mines, which belong to a French company. I plunged into the snow armed with a letter of recommendation from a friend. Although I was unexpected, I was received with open arms. They were a delightful bunch of young fellows, all French engineers and one Austrian. The landscape was not much better than in Oroya. It was green, although just as bare, and without bushes or flowers. The human atmosphere, however, was warm and cheerful. What a pity I was suffering from height and kept coughing. It was quite ridiculous to cough, for I had not caught a cold and my bronchial tubes are quite healthy. It was this accursed air. I could do nothing. I went on coughing all night until I nearly choked.

The following Sunday I visited the famous market in Huancayo, south of Oroya, on the road to Ayacucho. Once more I saw one of my Mexican experiences corroborated: the industrialization of the land had penetrated into the world of the natives and had almost destroyed the magic of their indigenous creative powers. One or two shops still sold native work of art. Here for example begins the kingdom of that unmistakable gay knitted cap with the hanging ear-flaps, worn by the mountain children all the way to Lake Titicaca, or you will see a sky-blue deer prancing through a fairy forest full of pheasants on some fragile black scarf. Nearby leers the coarse leather mask of a human monster with staring glassy eyes, bushy scowling eyebrows and moist lips. Best of all I liked the terra-cotta cows which had found their way here from Ayacucho. The holes in their backs can serve among other things as a flower vase; their swollen udders make them all look as though they should be milked. In addition to these, also in clay, I saw magnificent churches with huge clock-dials in their towers, so fragile that I hardly dared to touch them. And then those calabashes with entire *fiestas* and caravans with llamas and drivers carved on their dry brown rind. I could discover no practical use for these and I think that they merely serve as popular picture books. Then there were hand-knitted woollen jackets, socks and mittens which leave the fingers unprotected. All these had been banished to one end of the market, while everywhere else the products of the city were on view. I suspected that these peasant survivals were bought more by tourists than by local customers. That is the tragedy. Economic prosperity has to be paid for with the loss of the soul. That is perhaps why Ecuador has preserved such a high and yet ingenuous culture, because the much-vaunted "progress" has made the least headway there.

On the map in the travel office a thick line joins the little city of Ayacucho, famous for Sucre's decisive victory, to the old Inca city, Cuzco. It should take one day by bus, I thought. But there are no more buses in Ayacucho. A lorry stood on the plaza with "Andahuaylas Leaves Today" smeared in white paint on the windscreen. "What time?" I asked. "At midday." "Why not earlier?" The man shrugged his shoulders. "All right, at eleven if you like." What a nice obliging chap! At 11 o'clock punctually I took my place among a crowd of Indians. It was lovely and warm in the sun. The lorry stayed where it was until 1 o'clock, when at last we drove out of the dusty street into the country. Then we had another halt for lunch. Here the last passenger turned up—a travelling salesman with a mouth like a coffee mill. He was furious that the seat he had ordered next to the driver had been taken, for no respectable man would ever sit at the back, where I was sitting among the Indios. He grumbled and growled, threatening the police, etc., until finally the owner of the lorry gave up his own seat. Peru has the almost legendary Leguía, who ruled in the twenties, to thank for this road. He kept a firm hand on his own people and his palms outstretched towards the foreigner. His age was the age of loans, of borrowing money for the future in order to expand the production capacity of the land—until suddenly the slump tumbled the price of farm products and Peru, like so many other countries, stopped paying interest. This irresponsible period is now a thing of the past. The North American banks study the repayment possibilities before they will grant a country new credit. Just as the plantation owner became an accountant instead of being a king, the hybrid optimism for the future of the various countries was superseded by sober planning. Today the foreign companies are milked by dues and taxes. That is the new and more solid way of raising loans. Odría also builds roads, but with his own money. He is more secure than his great predecessor. Perhaps he looks more closely into his engineers' accounts! Leguía had to pay his foreign road builders by the mile. It is fantastic how slowly the road meanders up to the mountain, how broadswept the bends in order to avoid a few yards of hilly ground. That is why the short stretch on the map is in reality a three to four days' journey.

But it is of no importance. Time does not exist in the Sierra. Our chauffeur drove with hair-raising *verve*. Somewhere above the town in the previous week a truck loaded with passengers and pigs had overturned in the early morning. The chauffeur had been drinking all night. The result: twenty dead, not including the pigs. We stopped at the scene of the accident and strolled about for half an hour discussing it before we drove on. After another half an hour another truck approached us from the opposite direction. We could see it a long way off, but the driver only put on his brakes at the last second, and crash! there was a head-on collision. It did not matter. The dents could easily be beaten out with a hammer. Another excuse for half an hour's gossip. We drove on. Trucks, men, pigs. . . . It was all a matter of indifference. They were all freight. Somewhere on the road a man with a pile of sacks at his side waves. The truck owner bargains with him, drives on, only to stop in order to raise his freight prices by the manœuvre. Time plays no rôle at all. One of the Indian's hats is blown off. He screams like a stuck pig and bangs on the roof of the cabin until the chauffeur stops. We have to wait another quarter of an hour until the fellow has retrieved his hat. The sun beats down and we drive through a lonely high plateau covered with dry yellow grass.

After so much waste of time it was already pitch dark before we began to climb again after the first *quebrada*. In one little village we were stopped by the police. Because of the previous week's accident a new order had come into force forbidding night driving, so we had to spend the rest of that particular night in a very primitive inn. Since most of us were changing vehicles in Andahuaylas next day the lorry owner agreed that we should leave at six in the morning. Everyone was on the spot at the appointed hour except the owner. From the very first moment I had looked upon him with suspicion. He had a gammy leg as the result of a youthful accident and hobbled about on a crutch; but instead of arousing compassion this disablement made him look rather sinister. His face was so evil that his club-foot merely enhanced his diabolical appearance. The chauffeur knocked loudly on the door of the room where the cripple was sleeping—obviously he must be awake now, or crowing over the impotence of his fellow travellers. We all shook our fists and swore loudly at him, but it was of no avail. An hour, an hour and a half, the mood in the lorry rose to boiling-point. At 8 o'clock the fellow limped over as pleasant as you please; as though everything were in order. "Good morning," he said. "You bloody rogue, you irresponsible pig," was the obvious reply. Not a bit of it. No one made a murmur—not even the big Alsatian dog. "Good morning," everyone replied. "Did you sleep well?" I could not believe my eyes or my ears. Where had all their rage disappeared? Already twice before in Ecuador I had seen similar ruthlessness met with silent indifference. On the first occasion I started to reproach the man and only earned the disapproval of my fellow sufferers. This time I said nothing. In actual fact this prank would probably cost us a whole day's wait in the wretched village of Andahuaylas. What did it matter? As I have already said, time does not exist in the Sierra. It seemed typical to me, though, that the fellow felt no responsibility towards his lorry full of passengers and was secretly enjoying the abuse of his power. It was typical, too, that he got out of it without being punished. Here people shrug their shoulders and let the impertinent lout triumph, whether he be the ruler of a lorry or the ruler of a country.

Cuzco unadorned

THE entrance to Cuzco is as regal as such a city deserves. The snow-covered chain of 20,000-ft. mountains rises majestically behind the yellow plateau upon which sheep graze as far as the eye can see. The car takes a gentle hill, winds through a ravine and there at your feet, embedded in pinewoods,

lies the town of the Incas. On a green mountain slope behind it
stands a giant white inscription *Viva el Peru*.

Anyone who questions this unæsthetic patriotism will learn
that the hammer and sickle which once crowned it have been
covered up. As long as there were free elections the city of the Incas
always showed strong Communist tendencies. It is in its tradition.

At the time of my visit Cuzco did not show its gay side. The
fate of all South American cities has not spared this mountain
fastness. On the 21st of May 1950 a great part of the town was
laid in ruins by a serious earthquake—exactly 300 years after a
similar one must have terrified the new Spanish overlords.
Fortunately the catastrophe happened at midday, when most of
the people were out of doors in the sun, and moreover a big
sporting event had attracted half of them to the stadium. The
casualties—forty dead—were therefore comparatively light. The
old churches, however, were shaken to the foundations, and the
coats of arms fell from the proudest palace gates. Was it the
revenge of the old Sun God for the sacrilege to his golden
sanctuary that Santo Domingo which was built on its walls
suffered the greatest damage, such great damage in fact that the
architects to whom the rebuilding of the ravaged town had been
entrusted were considering whether this minor work of Christian
art should not be razed and the old Inca sanctuary restored. It is
worth mentioning this episode because Spanish public opinion
was up in arms, fearing a twilight of the gods in Peru similar to
that which they had suffered in Mexico. For the old rulers here
still consider themselves to be at home. It was they who would
have to pay for the rebuilding of the cathedral. Cuzco today
has been given over to the stone mason. At every street corner
their chisels are carving stones for restoration purposes. There is
no time for dreaming and enjoyment. Even when the towers
stand again much will have been irretrievably lost. The earthquake has done here what mob rage accomplished in Bogotá: it
broke down the dams which stood in the way of modernization.
Even if the churches remain, the mystery of the old narrow
alleys, of the *genius loci*, has disappeared for ever. The same applies
to the monuments as applies to many masterpieces of the Colonial

Lake Titicaca, Bolivia

age: the splendour of the frame often overshadowed the worth of the picture.

In spite of this a great deal remains to attract us to Cuzco; the solid walls of the Incas and their predecessors stand unshaken. Now, when you walk through the streets, a few reddish stones appear out of the adobe walls. That is a piece of the old City of the Kings. In the centre greenish square stones make a compact wall along some small street. Their edges fit like wheel-cogs together. One of these stones is particularly intriguing to the visitor. It is a dodecagon breaking its contour no less than twelve times. How could the stone masons of that age produce such masterpieces of accuracy? It remains a secret, like so much else in old Peru. Some people suggest that some corrosive liquid was used to give the stone such smoothness.

What a proud self-confidence their architects must have possessed. All these walls were built for eternity. Except in cases where, from lack of respect or fanatacism, the conquerors tore them down to use the blocks for their fragile churches, they stand completely undestroyed. The fortress still towers on the hill to the north, with stones so cyclopean that the conquerors were powerless against them. Among all these monuments of strength and size, one is very poignant. A children's slide falls from the top of the hill through the rock, and this makes one remember that the Incas were also human.

Cuzco is not only a town of ruins but also a tourist centre. On Sunday mornings one luxury car after the other speeds over the hill to Pisac in the Valley of the Incas to visit the local market. The Indians here are quite different from those in the rest of Peru. They have remained true to their old costume and wear red ponchos with intricate geometrical patterns, while the women with their platter-like silver-embroidered hats conjure up the magic of medieval courtly ladies. I could not believe my eyes—a fair-haired child with blue eyes twinkling from an Indian woman's *rebozo*. "Are you the mother of this child?" I asked the young Indian girl with astonishment. Her face lit up in a bright smile. "Como no?" she replied in Spanish. "Un gringo me ha hecho el favor" (Why not? A white man did me the favour).

P

Peru: the stone monument of Huaron
below: Peru: the sun stone in Machu Picchu

The greatest attractions of this market are the Alcaldes who each Sunday wait on the priest after Mass. I found the service in the homely little church where the sunlight penetrated through the roof unconsciously comic. I shall never forget it. A whole host of American tourists invaded the holy precincts with a barrage of cameras and film apparatus. They were so alarming that the Alcaldes, instead of proudly leaving by the main door in their ceremonial costumes with the tall red hats, crept away from the foreign invasion like nervous children or thieves with eyes averted. The llamas which a peasant had brought along for the amusement of the tourists were much more patient. It is time for me to say a few words about this charming beast of the Andes. I had already seen a few of them grazing in Ecuador. In Huaron they carry minerals from a remote mine on their patient backs, and the further south I travelled the more frequently I saw their long necks stretched skywards. What a wonderful experience it is to see a herd of llamas wandering through the *puna*. Speed is not one of their virtues. With an almost ballerina-like grace they bend their knees and put one hoof forward after the other. Fifteen miles a day is the maximum that can be expected of them. The llama is as obstinate as a spoiled woman: it is one of the few beasts that will not allow men to torture it without giving back tit for tat. Self-conscious dignity lies in its gaze as it does in the eyes of its relation the camel. Put an ounce more on its back than the 100 lb. which it is prepared to carry and it lies down on the ground and refuses to budge. No blows will bring it to its feet. It would rather let itself be beaten to death than carry that last ounce. The same thing happens if a man tries to put it to work on its own. Nothing doing. It is only prepared to work in the noble company of its fellows. Its method of self-defence shows its aristocratic nature. It does not kick like a common donkey. It spits, spits with such an effortless, magnificent, dispassionate elegance that as the spat-upon person you cannot take exception. In any case what can you do about it? Beat it. Ridiculous: one doesn't beat women. Just follow the example of the Indio, who is an expert in llama psychology. He pays like with like. When he wants to punish a llama he spits in its face.

Like all noble characters, this beast has been subjected to the
most abominable libels. It is, as I have already said, in many
respects like a ballerina, and one cannot deny its grace and sex
appeal. It has been said that the Indian sometimes confuses it
with his wife, and this has given rise to the legend that the flail
of humanity, syphilis, originated with the llamas. However,
science has long since disproved this fallacy.

Puritanical American females can therefore let themselves be
photographed in its company without losing their own moral
dignity. They must only be careful to avoid the spittle: it will
not help their complexions and llamas, too, very often suffer
from fits of anti-Imperialism.

If one can compare a llama with a ballerina, its shy relation, the
vicũna, is Pavlova personified. Normally you can only see them
from a ridge at a great distance, for they are shyer than chamois.
In spite of the ban, hunters persist in shooting them—and they
are therefore quite justified in being shy. Their hair is the silkiest
that has ever grown on an animal's body, and is twice as fine in
texture as that of the merino sheep. At the time of the Incas this
costly wool belonged exclusively to the ruler. Spanish greed,
however, tore it ruthlessly from the bodies of these fairy-like
creatures so that today their numbers have sadly decreased. In
Potosi I saw a soldier leading a tame vicũna through the streets.
She followed the man's heels with such a light step that she seemed
to float through the air.

On the other hand, the llama has a plebeian relation, the alpaca,
a real slut, utterly devoid of grace. Only on account of its thick
pelt do the Indios allow it to graze on the *puna*, and on railway
stations the women crowd round the train to sell tourists warm
slippers made of its hide. They are covered inside and out with the
same delicate bloom, encouraging you to stroke them as though
life still throbbed in them. You simply have to put your hand in
your pocket. In any case they are astoundingly cheap.

Machu Picchu! This is the word you constantly hear as soon
as you set foot on Cuzco's soil. Have you seen Machu Picchu?
Have you seen this most miraculous of all the ruined cities of the
world? The tourists in the hotel nod and admit that they have

never seen anything to resemble it in their lives. It is quite easy to
visit it. A railway built by the government winds down through
the ravine of the Urubamba river and brings you in a few hours
to the bridge from where the eagle's eyrie can be seen far above
one's head. You begin to feel the tropical heat and you sweat as
soon as you start walking. But this too has been taken care of: a
road has been blasted in the cliff face and a car carries the inquisitive visitors peacefully to the heights, where they find refreshment
awaiting them in an hotel.

Today there is nothing remarkable about reaching Machu
Picchu. It was a different matter in the old days, when the Sun
Virgins fled from the orgies of the Spanish authorities in Cuzco
along giddy mountain paths to the solitude of this mountain
fortress. The Conquistadores never discovered this sanctuary.
They never considered it worth while exploring the depths of
the gorge. There was no gold there. Nothing but cliffs. Nothing
but vertical towering rocks covered with undergrowth. Here the
splendour of the old sacred ritual continued for a time until that
too was extinguished. Only the legend remained alive among the
Indians of the neighbourhood, the legend of the lost city. At the
beginning of this century the American archæologist Hiram
Bingham followed its trail: he found the palaces and temples
swallowed up by the jungle and brought them once more to
light. The descriptions I had previously read did not at first sight
seem to be exaggerated. It is above all the setting which over-
powers the visitor. This is how an eagle must live in his eyrie.
Far below the river foams through its ravines, and before your
eyes the towering realm of Huayna Picchu raises its restless
snowy peaks to the sky.

On a similar peak stands the town, with its terraces clinging
to the rocks: the walls grow so naturally that they seem part of
them. I immediately made for the highest point where lies the
most mysterious object of the Forgotten City, the Intihuatana
Stone. It resembles a statue by some abstract sculptor, and it
could be displayed in a museum of modern art under the title
Reclining Figure. Yet its purpose here remains a secret. Was this
the bloody sacrificial stone? Why then the unequal inclines of

the steep surfaces? Were the shadows of the sun and moon read
on it? Or, as one theory maintains, did the priesthood on the
shortest day of the year harness the sun to it by magic so that it
could not disappear for ever? It remains a riddle.

That is Machu Picchu. It is an integral human universe perched
on a dizzy mountain ridge. Palaces, watch towers, provision
chambers, sleeping quarters. . . . Waterfalls trickle from basin to
basin down the precipice. The walls of the common buildings
are artlessly terraced. The temples of the gods and the houses of
the nobility, however, are built of those same mortarless squares
which in Cuzco even managed to withstand the earthquake. It is
impossible to look at these walls without a secret feeling of
discomfort. Discipline went too far here. Here the wall ruled,
nothing but the wall, and with a certain gruesome self-satis-
faction, the refractory stone was hewn into perfect obedience,
becoming a mere part bereft of its own expression, of its own will.
No more accurate expression can be found for the state system
of the Incas. The citizens became the submissive tools of a
collective. They possessed all the material security they needed
for their physical existence, but without enjoying the most
elementary rights of free men. Not even the right to be idle. This
was high treason in this busy ant heap. Thus, Machu Picchu has
left in my memory no impression of human creation like Copan
of the Mayas. Of course the bleakness of these heights may have
produced a spirit quite different from the tropical luxuriance of
the Central American lowlands—a crisper, more puritanical and
poorer spirit. Even the temples of Royal Cuzco seem like modest
mountain shrines rather than cathedrals when compared with the
ceremonial buildings of the Mayas. But another spirit resides in the
works of the Incas. They were, to speak in Indian terms, a warrior
caste far removed from the universal wisdom, astronomy,
mathematics and other arts possessed by the priestly hierarchy of
the Brahmanic state of the Mayas.

Or will some unknown wonder emerge one day from their
civilization? The last capital of the Incas who had been driven
out of Cuzco, which Bingham identified with Machu Picchu,
lies, as we know today, much lower down in the jungle, and yet

no man has so far discovered it. In the summer of 1953 an expedition of the American Geographical Society followed one of the tiled roads which joined the Inca towns through the jungle. In the spring of 1954 a British expedition went in search of the secret city Paititi: a generation before the famous Colonel Fawcett had disappeared on a similar quest. The most fabulous legends are woven about the unattainable; legends of Indians with mysterious gold objects from the old Inca gold treasure crop up; stories of tribes who still speak the pure ancient Quechua language of the Inca kingdom and who will kill any white man who sets foot near the Holy City. But one day these last riddles of the Incas will succumb to the tireless curiosity of man, that adventurous curiosity which will not be silenced even if the secret only ends with a sacrifice of his life.

BOLIVIA

Titicaca, the sacred lake

THE story has been told countless times, but whenever one speaks of Bolivia it always comes as a revelation. In the year 1868 the Bolivian dictator Melgarejo invited the British Ambassador to a reception in honour of his new mistress. The noble Englishman politely refused. At this the angry General had him stripped, bound backwards to a donkey and handed him over to the mockery of the mob. When the mortified Ambassador informed Queen Victoria of the outrage and said that no satisfaction was possible, the infuriated monarch struck Bolivia off her map with a stroke of her quill pen. For a few decades the country ceased to exist for the British Government. Whereupon it is reported Melgarejo, with a smile, removed England from his own map. Those were magnificent times and cavalier methods of mutual destruction.

The Aymará folk who live in the high plateau are very passionate and the visitor can easily distinguish them at first sight from the mild inhabitants of the Royal Inca valley. They blink at you out of those small eyes with hostility. Look at the faces of the bystanders: they seem to have withdrawn into themselves like snails. They do not look; they dream. The costume, too, strives for one effect only, to isolate, to imprison. The women pile skirt upon skirt, five and sevenfold in all colours, red, blue and gold, and when they dance they unfold like roses. At other times this surplus of clothing billows in a crinoline over their hips, a fortress wall that forbids any approach. The Aymará woman never removes these skirts. She sleeps, makes love, gives birth in them, and when you see one of them crouching on the streets in some village you know exactly what she is doing.

You stand on the threshold of the land before the Sun Gate of Tiahuanaco, one of the few remains which have come down to us from the ancient culture of these troglodytes. It would be a highly profitable task to trace the relationship between the architectural forms of different cultures and the physical structure of their peoples. The strange inexplicable stone blocks in Tiahuanaco which rise out of the coarse grass of the steppe would be a fine example. They stare at you just as morosely and coldly as the people. Even the chisel of the sculptor seems to have rebelled. It merely grazed the surface in the thinnest reliefs which can only be observed on close inspection. Even though Philistine spades have used the ruins as a quarry and destroyed so much irreplaceable material, Tiahuanaco remains a site of interest which vies with the far richer Maya and Inca survivals. I think that this is because it is not an enclosed and well-preserved ruined quarter, but is dotted about like seeds, thus helping to increase its surrealism. Here and there a few grim archaic heads stand by the roadside or are woven into the village like leashed dogs outside a church. Here and there you will find an open door and nothing lies behind it. Or you wander around the flagstones of the palace, known as the Tribunal: an earthquake has scattered the stones and destroyed the passion for straight lines and right-angles which in this world stylize even the magic countenances. You would imagine that this is age-old, perhaps as old as that unexplained world of San Augustín in Colombia. But you would be wrong. Modern science has dated these monuments far closer to the present day. If it be true that the Sun Tower was erected between the seventh and the tenth centuries, then many of our Romanesque cathedrals are just as old. But in the last analysis, does physical age ever play a part? It is so timeless that the whole of modern Bolivia is projected into the prehistoric era. Perhaps she moves you more than any other Latin American country, including Mexico which is so much more beautiful, because here every stone, every face, still bears the imprint of demons. The prehistoric features of the creator god Viracocha stare from the gable of the Sun Tower, while a triple row of fabulous beasts look up to him from below. No one knows what the picture means. This is a daring statement on my part, because I shall doubtless call down upon my head the wrath of the so-called "Tellurists"—in other words, the blood and soil boys who reign in the archæological chairs of Bolivia, and who never cease trying to give mysterious meanings to the ancient monuments. They dispute the recent dating of foreign professors as criminal, as a kind of Gringo attack on the prestige of their country's monuments.

I still do not know today how I ever managed to find a bed in Copacabana. Hosts of pilgrims jolted along in tall trucks to visit the shrine of the miracle-working Virgin. The great *fiesta* was approaching and all the inns were full to bursting-point.

Then a miracle happened. "Hé, Gringo," someone called after me. I recognized the man. He had travelled with me in the bus and from his clothes I had taken him for a commercial traveller. However, he turned out to be an ordinary lorry driver who had earned a pile of money in the mines which he was now spending on a holiday trip. I still do not know whether it was want of companionship or pure good nature that persuaded this complete stranger to share his room with me. The word room of course is a euphemism. It was a dark hole in an old house on the ground floor looking on to a courtyard. It purported to be an inn. No beds, only boards, but the proprietor made an effort and brought in mattresses. No bath of course. The water seeped from a spring into the courtyard, and as regards the usual office which in Spanish is called *excusado*, I was shown a door which merely led out on to the opposite side of the court-yard. I entered and turned round questioningly to the proprietor. I was in a bare room with an earthen floor, but curiously enough there were no traces of it having been used. The man nodded encouragingly. Good. When I was ready, a beast wandered in through a hole in the wall which I had not noticed. It was followed by a second. . . . They began to grunt all round me, waiting for a titbit. That evening I enjoyed my pork cutlet with great gusto!

Not long afterwards my attention was drawn to another animal which a young Indian girl was cooking on the oven in the courtyard. It must be a rat, I decided, for it was about that size. A thick stick had been stuck in its mouth and the girl held it to roast over the charcoal. But I was wrong. It was no rat but a *cui*, as the guinea pig is called in this part of the world. I was eager to taste it and must admit that it had a tender tasty flesh.

Copacabana like so many other centres of pilgrimage in Latin America, has stolen its prestige from an older sanctuary. Even today certain mysterious stones in the neighbourhood puzzle the archæologists. They cannot say what purpose they served. Half an hour away up the hill you will come to a strange erection, an angular stone bridge which two flames of stone join to the out-jutting cliff. The Indians have christened it "The Inca gallows," although it probably never lived up to its sinister name. Behind it lie the coastlines like a jagged pair of antlers and the vast lake. This is Titicaca, and it is the highest navigable expanse of water in the world. One is almost loth to call it a lake: as on the open sea the sky and the water encircle it on the horizon. Here and there an island in the distance breaks the blue solitude. But soon it no longer forms part of the lake. The mirage seems to elevate it into the sky and it sways there as though on a pilgrimage to heaven. It is easy to let your imagination run riot, for this lake is of divine origin. Titi, the sacred mountain puma, gave it its name and ahead where the promontory joins the horizon lies the island on which the sun gave birth to the first Inca ruler. An afterglow of perfection from this island probably fell upon Copacabana. From here the pilgrims go in sailing vessels to visit the Sun Temple. When the Spanish brought their Christian Virgin the hands of a converted Inca carved the serious almost melancholy features she still bears today. Here you will find nothing of the clemency of the Brown Virgin of Guadalupe: a tragic land like Bolivia needs a tragic saint.

The Virgin has inherited the same appalling taste that distin-guishes all American saints; gunpowder smells just as sweet in her nostrils as incense. Her feast is not for people with weak nerves. Every five minutes mortars fire on the Calvary hill above the town as though it were under artillery bombardment. Smoke bursts drift above the hosts of pilgrims as they pant up the stony Via Crucis. They stop at each station of the Cross, pick up stones and fling them at its feet. Soon there is a mountain of discarded sins, for this is the significance of this custom. Other pilgrims stray among the slopes and seem to be picking flowers, but they too in actual fact are busy with their salvation. They weave the coarse grass into pretty plaits and thus bind up all their wicked deeds. Free and absolved, they reach the crest, where the "magicians" wait for them.

Guatemala is far away and Mexico farther still. The belief of the Mayas was very different from the sun cult of the Incas, but the gestures they make when blessing the candles of Chichicastenango are almost identical. The holy men are unadorned. They wear the same knitted caps with the dangling ear flaps as all the local peasants wear, but the worshippers kneel before them as though they were distinguished by some secret glory, raising their censers in prayer, letting the image kindle their passion while their lips babble unceasingly the old reverent formularies. At the end of the service the holy man comes to the edge of the platform, where the abyss falls steeply to the lake. In his hand is a beer bottle, an ordinary bottle from the national brewery. He fills a glass, raises it to the sky, and pours it with a murmur on the soil. It is an offering to the watery God Titicaca down below. The pilgrims follow his example and everyone pours his libation on the ground. Occasionally you will see a bottle with a hock label from Rudesheim. The allegory of the transitory is so poignant here that it needs no camouflage.

You should then follow the pilgrims to the second outer peak of the Calvary hill. What is this display? Is it a toyshop? Women sit behind brightly painted little houses of all types and tastes. One resembles a country dwelling, the other a modern town house. Men and women put their heads together, jesting and gossiping about the advantages of the one and the other, as though they were going to live in them. Then you scramble up the steps of a flourishing rock garden in search of a "plot." The whole peak has been parcelled by the gardeners into small allotments which you can buy symbolically for a few cents. Now that the house had been chosen the pilgrims with unburdened hearts start the descent. Now not only are they cleansed of their sins, but their consciences are now clear, since symbolically they have acquired a house on the sacred hill.

The island of the sun

I HAD no idea, the evening I made my way to the landing
stage at the foot of the Calvary, how instructive a journey to
the sun island could be. I had been invited to one of the two
haciendas into which the island is divided, and was looking forward to a fine evening sail of three to four hours. But Lake
Titicaca, the divine Puma, is truly feline in nature. It may accept
you with an affectionate caress and a surface like a mirror and
then as soon as you are on its waters lash out with foamy claws
that can smash the canoe on the cliffs. Not in vain had the boatman
cast a troubled glance at the sky and the scudding clouds. The
Indians know the moods of their lake as a married woman knows
her husband's. They have given names to the wind which are
homely in the extreme. You can safely trust "Grandfather
Esteban," but *Perro Perro* the "dog-dog" whips up the waters so
threateningly that it is better to remain in port. Many an impatient
tourist who thought to tempt its rage has returned from his
adventure in terror with callouses on his hands.

I too almost regretted that I had attempted the journey. The
boatman glanced alternately at the circle of women huddled
in the stern of the boat and the wild racing clouds overhead and
postponed his sailing from hour to hour. We had spent the
previous night on the hard wooden deck of the boat waiting for
a favourable wind. Now the women had gone home. It was
already dark when the crew cast off and hoisted the patched sail.
The weather began to tease us: hardly had the sail bellied than
the wind changed like a frenzied hare and brought the boom
about our ears. Rain began to pour in streams from the low-lying
clouds. I crept below deck in the bows and with increasing
anxiety felt myself being flung about between mountainous
waves. When I cast a glance over the gunwhale, sky, land and sea
seemed to be a single boiling cauldron, and only the iron features
of the boatman enthroned like an idol in the stern defied the
chaos. I was doubly grateful for such a consolation when I
suddenly felt seasick for the first time in my life. I was more than

embarrassed at my weakness when I vomited, but not a single
Indio blinked an eyelash, not even my immediate neighbour
when I returned to my seat. I think that had I died on the spot
none of them would have stirred. When the storm abated the
men reached for their primitive oars, poles nailed to boards. The
creaking of the rowlocks and their joints disturbed my sleep. It
was 8 o'clock in the morning when we finally entered Challa
Bay. "The bailiff is in Copacabana. There's no one at the *hacienda*,"
said the boatman curtly as I got out. I felt hungry and miserable
and should have enjoyed a little hospitality. "Why the hell didn't
you tell me so before?" I shouted.

"You never asked me," was the reply.

I was immediately surrounded by a few Indios whose occupation I could not discover. Apparently they had to work in the
hacienda four days a week in exchange for a patch of ground the
fruits of which belonged to them. Since the bailiff was away they
sat about for the most part doing nothing or romping like young
puppies. Later, when authority returned, an atmosphere of
idleness still reigned. Even when they worked they were so
lackadaisical that their efforts could hardly be described as
exhausting.

"Can you give me anything to eat?" I asked them. "*No hay*,"
was the answer. "Haven't you even got any bread?" "There's no
bread on the island." "Then what the devil do you eat here?"
They looked at me in silence. A rather vapid-looking youth
opened the kitchen door and brought me a jug of maize . . . I
enjoyed chewing the soft baked ears. Another dish contained
soya beans, which the Indians looked upon with distaste but
which I enjoyed. This boiled stuff was no meal for a Gringo. The
following day, when the bailiff's wife arrived and looked after
my well being, I had to put up a great fight to be allowed to eat
these tasty fruits of the soil instead of hideously overcooked
noodles she had brought with her from Copacabana. Soya is
considered fit only for *peones*. I was under the impression that the
old woman silently despised me for such plebeian tastes.

One of the brightest memories of my life is the time I spent
walking about the sacred island. Bright in the true meaning of the

word. No sooner had I left the adobe huts on my daily walk than the road climbed through the sand dunes which the sun had turned to silver. Sky and lake lay in a circle like a blue dome at my feet, and every creature I met, even the donkey stumbling along under its load, the sheep nibbling at the sparse grass on the slopes, was like a heavenly apparition with its own aura. Even when you know nothing of the Inca sagas, the sanctity that pervaded everything here is most apparent. In the distance, where a chain of snowy giants formed a marble rood, loomed a gigantic sacrificial stone on a small neighbouring island dedicated to the moon. Its significance has undergone a miraculous change in the course of time. It now serves as a penal settlement, and people told me with secret satisfaction that the politicians and land-owners who in the old days had built it for this purpose were some of the first inmates to enjoy their new creation. Foreigners were therefore forbidden to approach it, not only by the whims of the lake but by police regulations, although it still possesses many important Inca ruins.

It would have been a waste of time visiting the Island of the Sun merely to see the ruins. Had the silver ubiquity of magic rays not illuminated them, the artlessness of their construction would hardly have reminded you of Cuzco's passion for geometry. You have no idea, when you clamber over the wall which separates the northern tongue of the island from the ruins, that in the old days the sacred precincts of the Sun God began here; only when you reach a second level *plaza* dominating the hill does its ceremonial significance become revealed. Here stands the rough-hewn stone on which the sacrifice was made and the blood allowed to run down the gutters.

One day I visited my compatriot Alberto Perrin, who owned the half of the island nearest to the mainland. His father had migrated here from Neuenburg in Switzerland and had married the daughter of a General and President. The farm with its remarkable profane Inca relics was a legacy of this marriage. I met Don Alberto as he was grubbing in a ploughed field for old tombs. His passion for archæology drove him to explore the island for pre-Inca traces. His efforts had procured him a rich fund of

pottery without however giving him any insight into the unexplored prehistoric ages. He had excavated a perfectly preserved
chamber only a couple of feet below the surface and he showed
me the half-mouldering bones. Was this not a remarkable
coincidence? For years the peasants had ploughed and sown this
field. Had the Indians only tilled the earth so superficially that
they had never dug down as far as the roof? Had they, in pious
respect for the remains of the dead, spared the place on purpose?
Don Alberto was inclined to accept the second theory.

We went back to the garden of his hacienda and cooled our
hands in the Inca bath. From three cavities in the solid wall the
water poured into a basin shaded by eucalyptus trees. A stairway
overgrown with weeds fell steeply down to the beach, where a
watch tower—according to the archæologists—overlooked the
narrows and the nearby mainland.

Don Alberto was a very thoughtful young man who was
passionately interested in the problems of his adopted country,
and he had plenty to occupy his mind. What sort of a country was
this that fed its population with difficulty and with partriarchal
methods, importing four-fifths of its food from abroad, from
Argentine and Peru? Here on the lake there was little sign of
the fate which the Indians suffer in other places on the Altiplano. Here Lake Titicaca mellows the winter frost and the summer drought, but only a few miles inland are stony steppes which
often refuse to produce any seed for the sowers. There is only
one alternative. Starvation or migration to a region which is not
subject to such misfortunes. Fundamentally this fatality has
nothing to do with the social status of the people in question:
whether it is a question of feudal haciendas or those collective
communities the *Ayllus*, a survival of Inca days; whether free or
enslaved they are still the same step-children of destiny in a land
where a bull takes six years to mature for the slaughter, where the
drought thins the wool of the starving sheep into worthless
strands. You only have to look at these beasts. They seem to have
come to life from some medieval engraving. They are the
descendants of cows and sheep which the conquistadores imported
400 years ago. All progress in modern breeding has by-passed

them without leaving a trace. The major agricultural problem of
the Sierra not only in Bolivia, but also in Peru and Ecuador, is not
so much the feudal order but quite simply the question: how can
one wrest from the soil sufficient food to feed a steadily growing
population? Richer and better grass must sprout on the *puna*.
New and better stock must replace the degenerated herds. There
are mighty valleys in the flanks of the high plateau with practically
no roads and railways. The surplus population which today still
clings obstinately to the desert could settle there in a magnificently fruitful climate. Bolivia is wealthy, fabulously wealthy.
One only has to bend down to pick up the treasures, one only
has to build, to organize. . . .

"And also, not to have so many revolutions," I interrupted my
friend's explanations.

He nodded his head thoughtfully. "The new social order must
and will come," he said. "It may surprise you to hear this from
the mouth of a landowner, because all my colleagues speak quite
differently. But I am something of a black sheep. They take me
for a communist. For years at the meetings of our club I have
repeated the same thing—that the good old feudal times have
gone for ever, that the trend is against the old landed gentry
whether they wish it or not. We must take the law of the coming
reform into our own hands so that it does not fall into the hands
of the enemy. My colleagues' reactions were always the same—a
smile, a shake of the head, some ridiculous evasive answer. They
maintain that the Indios are not human, that they are merely a
rather superior race of animals. They are cursed with an atavistic
laziness and unless you beat them they would never do anything
again."

"The same old story," I sighed, "but unfortunately it's not
true."

"It's both true and untrue at the same time," replied Don
Alberto. "It all depends on how you look upon them. Admittedly
our Aymarás don't like work. They waste a hundred days of the
year feasting, dancing and drinking. For two months they travel,
and this perhaps is the real key to their psychology. With their
savings they buy a little salt from the Sierra mines, load it on their

At the frontier between Chile and the Argentine:
the "Thunderer" in the background

*Copacabana,
Bolivia: a devil's
mask on the national
feast day.*

*Potosí, Bolivia:
a house being
constructed with
bricks of mud.*

llamas and drive the beasts over icy mountain passes down to the Yungas jungle, where there is a lack of salt. They exchange their load for fruit and have to make the terrible return journey. Two months of exhausting and fatiguing work—and they are broke two months later. The profit to be made from this exhausting journey is insignificant and yet the people fall into the same error year after year. If they were sensible they could cultivate their own land at home without too much trouble, but they just can't help it. They love going on a spree."

"So fundamentally your landowners are right," I said. "No," replied Alberto excitedly, "they're not right. You mustn't forget the reason the Indios are like this. It is merely because hundreds of years of serfdom have demoralized them. The psychological side of agrarian reform is no less important than the technical. It is necessary to awaken the spirit in these men, the spirit of those forgotten men who once created the marvels of Cuzco and Tiahuanaco. If we do not behave humanely towards them they will rise and seize from us what we are not willing to give. This violent solution, however, is doomed to failure. I do not think it could be achieved by a parcelling out of the *haciendas*. We must share them with the *peones* in a comradely fashion until we have awakened a sense of joint responsibility in the Indios or in their children. We could transform their desperate, almost hostile, dependence into a flourishing co-operation."

"But how could you persuade the landowners or ask them to sit down at table with animals?" I replied.

Don Alberto was silent. Was not the tragedy of the revolutions a failure to recognize that they could not possibly succeed. Don Alberto's colleagues were foolish not to heed his warnings. In the meantime the law which they believed to be firmly installed in their hands has taken away their power and turned like a boomerang against them. During Passion Week 1942 the streets of the capital were filled with battle cries and the *Movimiento Nacionalista Revolucionario* overthrew the military dictator who protected the old ruling class of the *haciendas* and the mines. Dr Paz Estenssoro, the revolutionary party leader, was brought back in triumph from his exile in the Argentine. His very first words betrayed the fact that the country was about to experience a social upheaval. Nationalization of the mines and land reform were the slogans which the agitators carried to the remotest villages of the Altiplano.

Things began to stir among the Indios. Not only did they regard their landlords as· unwanted usurpers on land which, according to the new laws, belonged to them, but here and there after some riotous feast day they cut the throats of their master or his bailiff. On 2nd August 1953 the President appended his signature to the decree that slavery was abolished. The land which previously had been leased to the Indians as payment for their toil now became their own property. Should the former master require their services any longer he would have to pay for them. After twenty-five years the *latifundie* would be given compensation for their expropriated land. Not a single one of them believed it.

However, the execution of the decree had not taken place on the Island of the Sun; but the Indians with subtle cunning had exploited the terror felt by their former masters to drive the bailiff from Don Alberto's property. One day one of them approached the young man and under the seal of silence betrayed his comrades' sinister plans. It was only a vague suggestion, but it was better to take notice of it. . . . A few days later a second Indio appeared. With his own eyes he had seen a tommy gun unloaded from the sailing boat. The bailiff felt a shiver run down his spine. He sent an SOS to Don Alberto that he should be sent some weapons, retired to Copacabana and only paid a nervous visit to the island once a week. Finally he gave notice. Since then no administrator has lived on the *hacienda*. The cunning Indians had achieved their goal. No one controls their activities any more and even less their omissions, except that from time to time Alberto sails across to the island to supervise the major details of the work.

Revolutions, Bolivia's national sport

THE malice of frontier lines has contrived that the land route from Copacabana to the capital runs across Peruvian territory and is therefore subject to tiresome controls. Thus travel is diverted over the lake narrows of Ticquina, which affords the tourist a highly curious spectacle. A few miles before you arrive there the cars begin to put on speed trying to pass each other, eager to arrive first at the critical spot on the winding mountainous road. Down below whole columns have formed and you have to wait for hours. Nothing can hurry the oriental dilatoriness of the sailing boats which act as ferry as they did in the days of old. Their flat sterns are pushed against the stony bottom, and while boatmen and passengers with all their strength try to make fast the wallowing keel with ropes, the heavily loaded trucks make their way on to this unsafe platform. A tattered sail flutters aloft and peacefully the wind and the rudder bear the vessel to the other bank. It is a miracle that there are not more accidents on this breakneck venture. The reader will probably ask, why don't they put powerful motor ferries on the job? This was actually done a few years ago, but unfortunately after a few weeks they were all wrecked, and a deserted boat-house still stands there today, a melancholy witness. The drivers continue to hoot like maniacs, but the frenzied age of the machine is far removed from here. Indolent fishermen cross the path of the car ferry in their balsa boats. They are woven out of reed grass, and with their padded look and towering beaks they resemble floating sofas. Wooden canoes could provide lasting shelter for the boatmen. The balsas rot within a month, and even if the building of a new one only demands a few hours from a skilful hand, the quest for endurance and stability—for they capsize easily—has begun to diminish their use and soon they will have disappeared completely from Titicaca.

You think that it will never end. Parched, dusty fields, with here and there a herd of sheep tended by a grey-haired woman or a ragged youngster, and behind it all the mountains no longer as imposing as on the lake, but icily near.

And then comes a great surprise. The high plateau seems to have been cut with a knife. Below lies La Paz, one of the most dramatic capitals in the world. The road descends from here constantly through deep valleys. No tree grows in the grey desert of the Altiplano, but after three hours by car you can pick oranges. La Paz seems perpetually to resist the lure of the enticing lowlands. Its houses cling desperately to the slopes so as not to slide down into the valley. It is a city of inclines. The vertical rules. You are continually climbing upwards or downwards.

Through the narrow streets you catch a glimpse of the most beautiful mountain in the world, Illimani, a white sugar loaf beneath a sky of that lyrical blue which only the purest heights know. Nowhere else can you find glaciers at the gates of a capital city.

But this has its disadvantages; cars are worn out after a few years because their engines cannot stand the rarefied air. Potatoes will never soften in boiling water, and bread, even from the best baker, tastes revolting. When you climb up to one of the skyscrapers on the central avenues your heart beats as though it would burst.

But are there no lifts in La Paz? Of course there are, for Bolivia is equipped with all modern conveniences, but while I was there none of these amenities was functioning. This was no fault of the heights but of *homo sapiens* who should have looked after them. La Paz had to do without electricity for a purely internal reason.

The Canadian company which provided the town with electricity had tried for several years to obtain a renewal of their contract, but the business had been left in abeyance. A Bolivian official never moves unless he receives a bribe. When the Gringos abandoned such baksheesh because they realized that they were indispensable the contract was not signed. No new works were built and no new cables laid, and now the worst had happened. The lifts did not function and you could not ring a single bell. The administration swore and raged and fined the Gringos. The newspapers were furious and insisted upon the nationalization of the inefficient company. The normal man went on quite un-complainingly.

To bring things to a head, the pipes which brought the water to the city burst because the responsible authorities had allowed them to rust, and for a whole week the city went dry. I had ceased to be surprised. In Bolivia even inanimate objects rebel when the State takes a hand.

You will easily understand this if you happen to visit a Ministry. I am not particularly keen on Ministries of any description. Almost everywhere in the world they are impregnated with a mouldering spirit of boredom. In Bolivia it is quite different: they are as pleasant as you can possibly imagine. Each Ministry has a distinct personality. If you visit the Ministry of Education you won't find a soul there. You climb the stairs of a pretty colonial house to be faced with a spate of empty rooms. No porter comes to ask what you want. Only empty rooms yawn before your eyes. You make your way past all the doors: not a soul. Probably the inmates are gossiping somewhere over a cup of tea. Finally you sit down insolently in a chair in an empty room and begin to dream that you are a Bolivian civil servant. It is a matter of opinion as to whether such dreams are happy ones. Admittedly you have nothing to do, but the salary is only 3,000 Bolivianos a month, which corresponds to about £5. Now, £5 is not a very high salary even for doing nothing, but that does not alter the fact that after each revolution all the members of the victorious party are given civil servant jobs, and the party is very numerous. Even if the good folk are prepared to work, there are far too many. Dozens of them are crowded into the same room. They play chess, box or polish their nails. The Bolivians themselves realize that this cannot continue. They applied to UNO that they should be sent a technical Commission to create an efficient administration. No less than twenty experts from every possible country, eleven nationalities in all, appeared one day and installed themselves in the different Ministries—experts on agriculture, mines, finance, national health, road building, social problems, etc. They began to work out recommendations and suggestions without knowing if they would ever be carried out. One of them reported to me that he had achieved an unqualified success. He had persuaded his office colleague to read detective stories instead of boxing. In this way at least his spelling and his style were improved. But one can become accustomed to anything. *Viver pericolosamente*, was Mussolini's slogan. He should have lived in La Paz. On any peaceful Sunday afternoon it is quite probable that shots will suddenly ring out. In such cases it is useless to try and discover the cause; the best thing to do is to get under cover quickly in the nearest doorway. Yes, there they fire on each other in the streets in broad daylight, a miracle which did not surprise a single of my fellows who had gone to ground with me. They have grown too used to it. The music of bullets suits this town. Bolivia is the classic land of revolutions. The most recent was the 179th since its liberation from the Spanish yoke. That means about one and a half revolutions a year.

The very latest, however, on April 9th 1952, differed from all its predecessors and yet it was still not the ultimate. This time it was no longer juggling on the part of ambitious *politicos* fighting for power. The people had risen to bar the gates once and for all to the "old guard" and had taken the weapons into their own hands. Now, these children occasionally poop off their weapons in the street for pure joy and occasionally for other reasons. Who could take these people seriously? Who could really say whether the smiles on these round, apparently good-humoured faces were born of friendliness or brutality? One day a procession wound its way peacefully through the streets unlike any other political manifestation I have ever seen. Yet there were no grounds for any such rejoicing. A few days beforehand it had come to shooting again and a few young people had been arrested on a charge of preparing a counter-revolution.

Of course it was the *Rosca* again. For months there had been no peace from this bogey man. Day and night the radio thundered against the perfidy of the *Rosca*, and anyone who did not understand the meaning of this word had only to look on the posters plastered on the walls. A young hero wrestled with a many-tentacled octopus captioned with the same letters *Rosca*. This word apparently described all the undefined hotchpotch of reactionaries and imperialistic powers which had enslaved the land both in actual fact and also in the imagination of the people—starting with the old feudal families, the soldiers and the mining companies, and finishing with the United States Embassy.

So these *Rosca* were showing their teeth again. A great rising of the whole people must counter them. The syndicates, the corner stones of the new order, must collect in their hundreds on the great plaza in front of the government building and manifest their unchanging fealty to the President. In the middle of the week the shops closed and a dominical peace enveloped the city. The march began—workers with brass bands and fluttering flags. More than that: they slouched along as if on a Sunday afternoon stroll, gay and high-spirited, delighted to be away from work. Some agitator lout suddenly shouted: "*Viva la Revolución.*" "*Viva,*" replied the crowd. "Long live the constitutional President," he shouted once more. "*Viva. Muera la Rosca.* Death. Down with Yankee imperialism. *Abájo. . . .*"

How terrible, the reader thinks. But I must ask him to look at the faces from which these expletives issued. They were the same foolish round Indian faces which a few weeks before in bright masks danced to the melody of Pan flutes. Yes, then it was the melody which stirred them; now it was the slogans. But it all reverted to one and the same thing. This too was a *fiesta.* "*Aájbo,*" they kept on crying, and a broad good-natured snigger could be seen on their faces. "*Muera,*" and the shrill laughter ran through the ranks. Were those really revolutionaries?

Or again, look at the women. They too screamed *Viva* or *Muera.* Their babies with wrinkled faces echoed their cries. It was immaterial, *Viva* or *Muera* where life is so difficult and to die is too easy. The leader of the Amazons screamed so passionately that she was soon hoarse. Not a seat was to be had on the benches of the plaza. She turned politely to an old gentleman who was enthroned on one of the stone seats. He did not move. Obviously he was a *Rosca.* The hoarse creature raised her arms in the air. "Would you refuse a seat to the Indian people?" she screamed. "Down with the traitors. *Abájo,*" echoed the voices behind her and the whole company sat down on the ground.

Nor was there any lack of ideological heroes. A drunken beggar in tattered clothes staggered between the benches. "I don't belong to your bunch," he said. "I'm a Liberal." He swung his prayer book with one hand and with the other requested alms. All the citizens who would have liked to scream and did not dare to, gave generously. He was the herald and the jester of the counter-revolution.

This crowd with the waving flags made its way past the President's palace. Its façade was spattered with bullet holes as if it were suffering from the measles. That is the only true decoration for a country that has experienced 179 revolutions since its own Independence Day. On the balcony stood the men of the most recent, the people's revolution. The President is an amiable professor who smiled down on the crowd and made the V sign, aping Churchill.

Down below, however, in the centre of a swirling crowd directly outside the government building stood a lamp post, a magnificent massive lamp post. It is the most famous bronze lamp post in South America and it gleams like gold. In July 1947 President Villaroel was hanged from it—a friend of the people who had tried to favour it with countless decrees, murdered by his own kind. When the new revolution was victorious the lamp post was decorated with flowers and the *Rosca* were accused of having murdered the noble man with its machinations. But no sophistry in the world can alter the fact that the people hanged him, the people he loved so much. And why? For some whim. That is the nature of this crowd; changeable and capricious to excess. Today they cry *Viva* and tomorrow *Muera*. No wonder Bolivian history is one of the most tragic in the world. It was unlucky to have had very powerful neighbours who seized its coastal area and forced it back to the highlands. And when in the Chaco war of the thirties it attacked its weaker neighbour Paraguay, the terrible climate of the tropics mowed down these mountain dwellers in their thousands. This time defeat was accompanied by an economic bankruptcy from which Bolivia has not yet managed to recover.

And then the mines, that accursed blessing! When the Conquistadores overthrew the Inca kingdom and ravished the gold treasures of the temples they had no idea that immeasurable wealth lay hidden in the southern mountains. Pizarro's colleague Almagro, who received the land as payment for his services, frowned and lost his life in a crazy attempt to wrest the far more speculative wealth of Cuzco from his companion. Only later, when energetic explorers set out in search of adventure, did the mountains begin to reveal their wealth. Silver was brought to light from hundreds of seams. When this began to run out in the age of tinned foods, a new silver was discovered, tin, and tin has until today remained Bolivia's fateful mineral. When I call it "the new silver," this is no exaggeration. It was found in fabulously wealthy veins and in many places could simply be picked off the surface with bare hands. Into the deep ravines climbed the willing Indian beasts of burden. In the dust and the infernal heat they worked thirty-six hours at a stretch, numbed their flagging senses with coca and died after a few years like flies from silicosis. While they perished in filth and poverty their masters rose all the faster to become multi-millionaires, just as earlier the Conquistadores had grown rich from their silver. There is, for example, the story of the junior clerk, Simon Patiño. A defaulting debtor offered him a mine claim in settlement of a debt, so he and his wife started to exploit it themselves. And the claim happened to be Catavi, one of the richest tin mines in Bolivia.

With this began one of the most incredible careers in world history. Simon was lucky. He grew rich and used his wealth to grow even richer. Ultimately not only the Bolivian mines but others in Malaya, refineries in England and the United States belonged to him. He left his savage Bolivia for Paris, where as Bolivian Ambassador he married off his children to Spanish Bourbon princesses and French counts. When Simon died in 1947 he left an estate of a milliard dollars. There are certain sums of money against which even blue blood has no defence; gold ennobles. One of his countrymen, Victor Aramayo, and the German Jew Hochschild joined forces with Patiño, and the triumvirate could make the government dance like puppets according to its will. They dictated the laws of the land and these were never made except with a view to their own personal pockets. When the miners rebelled the weapons of the army were always at their disposal to mow them down. It is no wonder that the greater part of the country's revenue was spent on armaments and officers' pay. All these lickspittles of tin barons made themselves accomplices against their own people. It was they who omitted to build roads through the rich primeval forests and to wrest nourishment from the virgin soil. Why go to all that trouble when tin ensured the country a considerable income in good dollars and pounds? Naturally this tin belonged to the triumvirate and not to the Bolivian people, but since the rulers caroused at the table of these vultures, why should they think of deeds which would benefit the land and not themselves? Thus tin was always and remains Bolivia's fateful metal. Ninety-five per cent of all exports over the past decades have been from various ores. Of these tin produces three-quarters. Eighty per cent of her foreign currency comes from tin. Half of all public revenue comes from export taxes on tin. Each slice of bread eaten is paid for with tin.

But tin is an uneasy pillow. Even the mining barons whose income surpassed that of the whole country trembled before people more powerful than themselves, the buyers. Earlier it was in the main England, until the United States took over this rôle. The latter were influenced neither by Bourbon princesses nor by dying miners. Business is business. The smart merchant buys as cheaply as possible, and if Bolivia is too expensive he turns to the tin mines of Malaya, Java or the Belgian Congo. When the price of tin falls Bolivia is in mourning. Atenor Patiño, divorced by his Bourbon princess, refuses to give up his love affairs with spectacular reigning beauties, but his people far away in the Andes have to tighten their belts. The Indios are starving. The intellectuals clench their fists. They are powerless. The buyers set the price. A war breaks out in Korea and war means good business for metals. The prices rise and the tin barons rub their hands with glee. They hold back their metal "The price will go up," they say. And it rises to nearly $2.00 a lb.—nearly! For now, when the cards are running against it, the Reconstruction and Finance Corporation will not entertain free market prices. It dictates a guaranteed maximum price.

At the end of October 1952 the President signed his decree in the Catavi mine nationalizing the mines of the big companies. On the same day the placard Patiño Mines was removed by a workman from one of the finest business houses in La Paz and replaced with the name of the State mining company: The Mining Corporation of Bolivia.

There is only one fly in the ointment. This revolt against fate came too late. The destiny of Bolivia still remains a tragic one.

All mountain mines become exhausted after a time. They produce untold wealth, give birth to whole towns and provide bread for thousands, and then suddenly it is all over. Things have not quite reached this pitch in Bolivia. I had a conversation with Pierre Delaître, a French UNO mining expert who works in the Ministry of Mines. The rich veins of tin, he told me, which brought fame to Bolivia are as good as exhausted. There are however still plenty of metal seams which produce between 1.25 and 2.25 per cent, but their exploitation is no longer a lucrative affair, particularly since under nationalization the wages and pensions of the miners have increased by 50 per cent. Let the devil exploit these low-paying ores! When all the muck has to be transported to Texas and Liverpool the profit goes in freight, and when one tries to increase the concentrates, too much of the metal is lost in the washing. Should Bolivia refine it on the spot? Unfortunately there is a lack of coal. It would hardly be cheaper to transport this over the mountains, and so plans for building a refining plant were soon abandoned. No, Bolivia has ceased to be a typical tin country. Only the fact that in the case of a war its ore is the only ore that can safely reach the United States still gives these tin mines a commercial right to exist. Actually the country should change over to other ores which exist in great quantities and still slumber unexploited in the mountains—lead, bismuth, wolfram, tungsten, etc. But for this, great capital is needed and this can only come from abroad. Foreign nations, however, have not felt inclined to invest money in a land which

has just expropriated the tin shareholders. Was nationalization a
fatal mistake in the last analysis? Have they gambled and lost
future ore wealth in favour of a few worthless tin mines?

The judgment of history on the Bolivian revolution has not
yet been made and it cannot yet be seen whether the unexpected
positive development of the Mexican oil industry can be repeated
here. The beginnings were hard. The princely salaries offered to
foreign engineers had very little effect. It is prophesied that
production will fall, and then God help those who have been
responsible, whether they were guilty or innocent. And not only
that. In the expectation of being evicted the companies exhausted
the existing lodes and did not open up any new ones. As a result
the market began to stagnate. The strike of buyers was by no
means a reprisal for expropriation, but simply because the Texas
refineries were filled to bursting-point. The price of tin fell to
80 cents while production costs rose to between $1.10 and $1.25.
They had to sell at a loss. On top of this a weak attempt to
compensate the Patiño shareholders, who are half Americans,
failed. Admittedly they could never have come to terms on
compensation, since the mining companies estimated the value
of their mines at $60 million, against the Government estimate of
only $20 million. In addition to this the latter presented the
companies with a bill of $520 million for unpaid taxes, unpaid
wages and illegal Stock Exchange manipulations, so that the
expropriation balance sheet showed half a milliard dollars in
favour of the Bolivian State. An attempt was made to entice the
Americans to buy the piled-up tin reserves by putting aside a
pro rata percentage of the sales (maximum 5 per cent) for the
satisfaction of the shareholders based on the changing world
market price, but when the price fell to 80 cents this also went
west. The shareholders were furious. They insisted and threatened
that the American Government should speak to Bolivia in no
uncertain terms. The case here is very different to that of Guatemala, which is so sound economically with its coffee and bananas
and therefore almost invulnerable. Yes, quite different in Bolivia:
the revolution has brought poverty not only to the mines but
also to agriculture. The Indians who now own their own soil

hardly cultivate more than enough for their own actual needs. In the towns the people face a perpetual food shortage. "I came here to avoid the post-war chaos in Germany," a German university professor said to me, "and now it's exactly the same here as it was in Germany in 1946."

It needs only the breath of a boycott by the USA and Bolivia's revolutionary régime would have to capitulate from hunger. But America takes the opposite line. She sends more shiploads of corn to the suffering land and supports the Government with credits. Why?

Because no one knows who will succeed Paz Estenssoro and his MNR if he were overthrown. A restoration of the military such as happened in Peru is improbable here because after the *coup d'état* the army was rendered powerless and a militia was formed of mountain workers and farm hands who so far have successfully beaten off every attempt at a counter-revolution. But, on the other hand, as a result of this, the Government is robbed of its strong arm and is at the mercy of the capricious mob which even murders its own benefactor such as Villaroel at the behest of some demagogue.

And there is no lack of such dangerous characters. The Lenin of the Bolivian revolution is simultaneously Minister in the Government and union secretary. He is loved by thousands of miners round the capital. One only has to change a couple of letters of his name. His is called Juan Lechín, and if he lifted a finger thousands would emerge from their shafts armed with dynamite and rush down into the city. Therefore everyone is afraid of him and in particular the President. Is Lechín a Communist? Whenever one asked the true Communists, who form a very small active group, they curled their lips in disdain. Lechín, who began life as a miner (today he is a millionaire), has never had a thorough grounding in either Marxism or Leninism and has never belonged to a Communist group. Naturally I wanted to ask Lechín the same question. I paid him a visit in his Ministry. The appointment was for 3 o'clock, but I never had a chance of talking to him. The corridors outside his office were full of waiting people and as soon as the door was opened everyone streamed in. People sat there in chairs, on stools, on window ledges—all people with requests, complaints and reports on the Movement. At his desk, however, sat two enchanting young women from the *Golden Cockerel* night club, friends of the Minister! He is a good-looking suave man of Syrian origin with those oriental eyes from the Arabian Nights which women fall for. He put me off until the next day, but when I appeared a second time the situation remained unchanged, so I was never able to ask Juan Lechín my vital question. The reply however is quite clear. He is no Moscovite, no Leninist, but merely a simple Lechínist, a gambler for power with little ideology, a cynic who knows for certain to what extent demagogy is permissible and where the realm of reality begins. He is probably a more subtle politician than the well-meaning idealist Paz Estenssoro. The scene changes swiftly in Latin American politics. Juan Lechín has already been exiled.

Even when Estenssoro came to power under resounding Nationalist and Fascist slogans his national economic beliefs always took the upper hand and today he represents the moderate bourgeois wing of the Movement which, as far as one can use the term when describing a revolutionary Movement, could be said to be Conservative. This President, who previously thundered against the imperialist aims of foreign capital, is now only too anxious to preserve it, and if one was asked wherein the difference lay between the revolutionary Conservative Odría and the revolutionary turned Conservative Estenssoro it would be found that there is practically no difference at all, for what can be done effectively for the development of the land is in both cases very similar. Bolivia also has its eastern tropical jungle regions where the presence of oil is suspected. For years, under a Government oil company, prospecting has only progressed at snail's pace, but now Estenssoro has given a concession to the Texan, Glenn McCarthy. In order to avoid criticism by the Nationalists 150 oil specialists from Mexico were engaged to prospect independently. Thus one can reckon in Bolivia too upon a peaceful coexistence of native and foreign oil exploitation. When the yearly million dollars which Bolivia has so far paid for oil imports can be saved she will already have taken a great stride forward from her chronic state of bankruptcy.

The second step will come quite automatically in the wake of oil. Both Brazil and the Argentine have an appetite for this valuable commodity owned by their neighbour and both of them are striving to improve communications. The railway line from Corumba in Brazil to the Bolivian town of Santa Cruz has been opened and another is making its way from the Argentine. Santa Cruz, situated in the middle of an almost uninhabited rich plain, is one of the future cities of the continent. At the beginning of the fifties a road from Cochabamba, the second largest Bolivian city, was built under unbelievable difficulties. When a railway track ultimately runs parallel with it a trans-continental line will join São Paulo in Brazil to Mollendo in Peru. And since, as I have already mentioned communications is the major problem in Latin America, Santa Cruz has obviously a very great future. Everything should grow on its soil, from sugar cane and bananas to wheat, for the climate is magnificent. In a few years meat which previously came from the Argentine, sugar which was imported from Peru, and rice which was imported from Ecuador, will be produced in Santa Cruz, in Bolivia's Eden. Perhaps at last its people will be able to satisfy their hunger from their own wealth, perhaps the chain of poverty-inspired revolutions will be broken. Perhaps . . .

Another urgent Bolivian problem will perhaps also find a solution. Since the unhappy Pacific war against Chile in 1880 her outlet to the sea has been closed and her imports and exports have had to go the expensive roundabout way via Peruvian or Chilean harbours—Mollendo, Arica or Antofagasta. The Chileans have no intention of handing back their conquests to the Bolivians, but here American gold may be a solution acceptable for both. A gigantic irrigation plan for the desert stretch of Chile, which is similar to that of Peru, has been envisaged. For this service Chile would return to Bolivia a corridor to the sea. Perhaps Bolivia will one day become a happy land again. Maybe. . . .

The crest of Bolivia is a true mountain pyramid. It represents the Cerro Rico, the "rich mountain" of Potosí, the country's

mountain of destiny. Legend tells us that the Incas already wanted
to bore into its depths and to wrest its wealth from it. But as
soon as they began work a terrible thunder growled from inside
the mountain and a voice called, "God is preserving this treasure
for one who comes later." The Incas apparently kissed the soil in
piety and looked for their wealth elsewhere. Since then the
mountain has been known as Potosí, which means "Noise."
Today this taboo has been finally broken. Not a blade of grass
grows on its slopes. It is coated with scree from top to bottom—
red scree which makes it look bloodstained. You can climb its
sides as high as you like, even to the crest, which is well over
15,000 feet. Shafts yawn everywhere. Could you look into its
innards with X-rays you would see a labyrinthine picture of veins.
Often the greedy moles cross each other's path below the ground
and the lawyers down below in the little town of Potosí wrangle
about the subterranean rights. I felt almost sorry for the martyred
and tortured earth. The whole day cable railways climb busily
up and down the mountain and carry their freight to the refineries
at the foot of the Cerro. Countless hands and machinery are busy
here. They may belong to a small contractor who with a few
helpers has dug his own shaft with equipment that has not
changed very much since the days of the Spaniards. Women sit
in their cave huts in front of piles of stone beating it by hand with
heavy hammers and carefully sorting out the glittering fragments.
Or at the big Unificad, a mine which once belonged to Hochschild, you can descend by diesel locomotive into the very bowels
of the mountain, reaching the very depths where the heat of
120° Fahrenheit and a moisture of 95 per cent make clothes un-
bearable. The men stand here naked behind their compressed air
hammers while water is sprayed on them by one of their colleagues
from a hydrant. After five minutes they fling away their tools
exhausted and their mates take their place at the steaming stone.
Even if they have more powerful lungs than one's own, it must
be hell in this stifling heat. Even if this penance only lasts eight
hours a day and no longer thirty-six at a stretch as in the days of
mining capitalism, it is hell. Our guide, the engineer, pointed to a
grinning clay figure in a niche that looked like a ghost in the

light of our miner's lamp. It was the devil, and now for the first time I realized his constant presence. Every time we climbed up a rough ladder to another level among the veins we met a similar idol. *Tío Diablo* the Indians call him. He owns the ore which they haul out of the depths, and since they do not dare to carry it away without making their peace with the rightful owner his image is everywhere. Sometimes you see paper flags adorning the shafts and red-brown paint smeared on the entrances. It is not actually paint, but the blood of oxen which are sacrificed each year to the Earth Mother Pachamama, whose quivering heart is burnt somewhere in the depths.

I do not know which was worse, the heat and the twilight of the depths, the sharp blinding sunlight that seared our eyes outside, or the wind which cuts you like a knife on the mountain face where there is not the smallest corner of shade. I climbed down to the hutments, old unadorned buildings divided by partitions, where the workers live. They are not dwellings in the normal sense of the word, merely places to sleep and congregate. When the weather is fine the women sit outside in their shawls, surrounded by a pale brood of children. Nowhere will you see a blade of grass, not to mention a tree. Scree and sand, red and yellow dust with the blue sky above. A few chickens wander in and out of the house doors. With a shudder I stuck my head into one of these dark holes. The single flame flickering inside lit up the calendar of a Virgin with a pierced heart. I read the inscription: *Santo Corazón de Maria*. Below it was a no less encouraging slogan: "*Mejoral* takes away the worst headaches."

No, this mining town is not a pretty sight. Dust, nothing but dust everywhere. All the men and all the buildings are powdered with it. You will find drums which crush the booty and rattling sieves which sort it out. But then among all this brutal machinery there is some more fragile which conjures the metal fragments from the common stone and prepares the titbits for the furnaces of Liverpool and Texas.

Out of muck and dust, misery and disease, arose one of the most wonderful towns of Latin America. In Lima I realized that I felt deathly weary of the same museum-like colonial architecture, but here in Potosí, where ugliness and death grin so implacably behind the beauty, I was transfigured by a mysterious ennoblement. Here no borrowed splendour spoke to you from the walls. The native masons with their chisels more than elsewhere obeyed the ancient laws of form created by their race.

Potosí was a great city before silver flowed from the shafts, incomparably greater than today. As many as 120,000 people lived within its walls. The zeal of Christian missionaries has taken care that it does not lack for Houses of God, but today the mint, whose walls still stand defiantly on the plaza, has degenerated into a museum. Tourists are amazed at the mighty wooden machines which once formed and imprinted the wealth of Spain. Their toothless wheels and cogs driven by patient serfs seem the very personification of an overpowering, shattering destiny.

THE ARGENTINE

Meat and soil

THE Argentine is the land of surplus. The pampas stretches out before you like a green sky with the piebald cattle twinkling like stars on the horizon. They hardly need to stir. The fodder sprouts thick and high under their jaws. They merely have to open them and they cannot possibly consume it all. You never see a cattle stall. Summer and winter, day and night, they live on the meadows. Here the bulls and the cows mate and the calves are born without any men in attendance. Wealth propagates itself to infinity. Then, if you travel through the seas of corn, you see nothing but gold fields stretching for hundreds of miles, trembling beneath the caress of the wind. You will hardly meet a soul. At most you will find a fine property surrounded by a green wood breaking the monotony of the endless plain. Trees enfold it as though it must be protected from the onslaught of the boundless space. When you visit one of these *estancias* you feel thoroughly at home. As in the saloon of an ocean liner you can forget for a moment the waves outside, but as soon as you go out on the deck you are once more a prey to the boundless. Black earth which is never exhausted and which can always be renewed by rotation, stretches for hundreds and thousands of miles. What a blessed land!

The herd you have just seen stampeding is only one of hundreds and thousands which haunt the pampas throughout the day. One morning they come to their goal, the slaughter house. This is a marvellous event for the cows, for they are given a cooling bath. They blink happily in the fine spray of rain from friendly hoses which wash the dust off them, and their happiness is only at an end when a brutal stab drives them on to the ramp that carries them down like luggage into the hungry maw of the slaughter yard. The ramp is death.

They do not want to be hustled after their morning bath, but an electric goad prods them forward, and when at last they reach the top floor, where the steam of blood rises to their nostrils, they rush into the alley with a last burst of desperation. There stands a stocky butcher with his copper hammer. He raises it with great elegance like a golf club, but instead of making a graceful curve it comes down with a dull blow on the forehead of some beast which totters clumsily after so graceful a beginning. When all of them have been felled the side walls of the alley open and they fall helplessly to the floor. Each of them is caught by the hind legs with a hook and given over to the slaughterer's knife. Cows—stacked in rows like women's dresses in a wardrobe. The first slaughterer slits their throats, the second opens their foreheads as though they were Indian gods, the third—but spare me the gruesome details of mechanized murder. The smell of blood makes you feel sick. You cannot escape it. Nearby are rows of sheep bleeding to death without an anæsthetic. They stare with open, almost indifferent eyes at the sharp knife which slits the vein beneath their wool, and die without protest. I could not help admiring the pigs, the only beasts which, conscious of their martyrdom, ended their lives with heroic squeals. A pig every twenty seconds, exactly as in the case of the cows. The work is completely mechanical. The carcases slip through holes to the lower floor, are sprayed, pressed into boxes and eventually hang, frozen stiff and unrecognizable with an almost painful elegance, in the cellars. From this polar night you escape with a shudder into the heat of the quayside. The funnels of the refrigerator ships are smoking as they wait for their freight.

Meat is the lifeblood of the Argentine. When you stay on an *estancia* you will undoubtedly be invited to a so-called *asado*. Flames rise almost to the ceiling from a trench below a spit on which half an ox is being roasted. Servants watch this slow grilling and turn the joint over the fire. There are two dozen guests and the meal seems quite out of proportion. How can they possibly eat it all? You need not worry. They fall on the pieces which are cut off like beasts of prey. Here you do not eat meat sandwiches but meat with a small piece of bread.

Meat and soil, an eternity in which man is forgotten. That is the myth of the Argentine as it always has been. After the arrival of the Spaniards on the pampas the horses and cows increased so enormously that the few men among them hobbled the cattle and killed them merely for the tongue or the hide and let the rest rot, since they were worth so little.

In the middle of the nineteenth century only 2 million men lived in this enormous country. Rosas, the famous and infamous *caudillo* who created the first central government and almost rooted out the Indians, made his supporters and financiers kings over distributed State property. In the United States the wise Homestead Law of the nineteenth century limited the parcels of distributed State land to 64 hectares—a healthy small farmer holding. In the Argentine people looked down their noses at a property of less than 4,000 hectares. The invention of barbed wire ended the chaos of the pampas. Thoroughbred herds and cornfields piled up wealth in the coffers of the *estancieros*. Refrigerating plant and fast ships turned the Argentine into one of the most important larders of the world. Refugees from the over-populated countries of Europe flocked to this paradise. Almost half of them were Italians, closely followed by the Spaniards. Even today the Argentine people bear an unmistakable Italian imprint. Even the Spanish they speak sounds like the aria from an opera. The areas under cultivation increased with the influx of workers and the land rose constantly in value. In a few years it doubled itself without the *estancieros* having to raise a finger. Their country houses became castles and palaces grew up in Buenos Aires. "As rich as an Argentine," was a current expression throughout the world. I was told that in the La Plata casino landowners threw 1,000 peso notes over their shoulders on to the roulette table, since they meant so little to them.

However, it is not the old Spanish nobility of the highlands who live according to old patriarchal standards; this *nouveau riche* aristocracy has developed an equally exclusive class-consciousness. Princes and counts are not good enough for them. They intermarry and this oligarchy becomes even more hermetically removed from the common people. Admittedly the heirs split the *estancia* kingdom among their large families, but even so the 2,000 ruling Argentinian families still remain one of the most formidable feudal clans known to history. Even more than their older peers from the highlands they have planted their roots in Europe. A *première* in Paris will be discussed in Buenos Aires as though it had taken place in the next town.

And what about the people? The peon on an Argentine estate never went hungry like the Indio in the barren Andes valleys, but he too was almost a slave, treated paternally as a minor if the master was good, and like cattle in a joyless barracks when he fell into the hands of a brute.

The Argentine is obviously different from the other South American countries I have described. At the turn of the century the land began to be industrialized. This was very unwelcome to the oligarchy which preferred to sell its products overseas— particularly to England—and to buy cheap industrial wares in exchange. But the trend of history slowly forced the Argentine out of its purely agrarian position. Ancillary industries began to spring up—tinned meat factories, distilleries and textile under-takings. By the first World War a politically conscious urban middle class had grown up, and this middle class presented the Argentine with its first revolution. In the 1916 elections the radical Hipólito Irigoyen came to power, a man who for the first time demanded social reforms. But even his party did not escape the unhappy law of the revolutionary: the shameless corruption of his followers opened the doors to a counter-revolution. In 1939 the oligarchy once more seized power. It reacted with even more brutal oppression since history had obviously turned against it. Its ruthlessness was fundamentally already a *rigor mortis*. In the meanwhile industry expanded and a new type rose among the middle classes to become a political factor: the workman. When on June 4th 1943 a military revolt swept the oligarchy from power, the hour of this new class had struck. The officers' cabinet in-cluded a new department previously unknown in the Argentine, a Ministry of Labour. At its head stood an almost unknown Colonel called Juan Domingo Perón.

This young officer had for many years been Military Attaché

at the Argentine Embassy in Rome. He had seen for himself what power a skilful demagogue like Mussolini had been able to draw from the revolutionary potential of a numerically strong, poor and uneducated proletariat. He had also learnt the two methods necessary to mobilize these masses: the first a positive one, namely social reform, and the second a purely negative one, nationalism. The small Ministry of Labour, despised by his military colleagues, was to become the cornerstone of a new régime. From here the working Colonel launched his secret weapon—increased wages for farm and factory workers. The simple folk flocked to him, and when the military government, afraid of his growing influence, arrested him in October 1945 it was already too late. The workers streamed into the squares of the capital and forced them to release him. Four months later Perón was elected President of the Republic.

Nationalism in the Argentine has an individual, almost luxurious character. Mexico nationalized her oil and Bolivia her tin mines because they hated the idea of presenting the substance of a country on a plate to foreign capital. Nationalization was a life-and-death struggle in which the old owners were defeated and expropriated. The Argentine, too, in the time of its fabulous expansion had swallowed up large quantities of foreign capital—in particular the railways with £267 million of English capital, the telephone company, the tramways and gasworks. But already since 1933 limitation laws had reduced the profits to almost nothing, and when Perón with patriotic pride nationalized the railways they were already not much more than old iron which the smiling English capitalists exchanged at a good price for the Argentine meat during the war. Perón would not let himself be cheated. He was no robber, and thanks to the prosperous war trade the coffers were full of bullion. The new wielder of power jeered at the opinions of patriarchal economists who wanted to hold the gold in reserve for leaner years. He plunged his hands into it, bought the foreign companies and began to whip up the slow industrialization to a fantastic tempo.

The 5,600 million good pesos ($1,200 million) worth of currency reserves of the year 1946 had shrunk in October 1952 to a fraction of their value (according to international exchange about $150 million), and instead of the expected prosperity a crisis arose in which the régime nearly collapsed. Hardly anywhere in history has a land lapsed peacefully in so short a time from such heights of prosperity to such depths. How was this possible?

It was simply the result of a planned economy where the planning strayed into fantasy and the chimerical aim of becoming a great power threatened to lift the land out of its traditional proportions. The Minister for Economy, Miguel Miranda, created a government buying organization, IAPI (Instituto Argentino de Producción y Intercambio); this Institute bought wheat and meat from the *estancias* at ludicrous prices which brought tears to the eyes of the farmer. It was sold abroad at colossal prices which sent shivers down the spines of the buyers. The profit was dissipated in cheap credits for industry: factories sprang up in the suburbs of Buenos Aires. These were the industries which were to bring about Perón's great dream— *independencia economica*, economic independence. His economic logic was disarmingly simple and mercantile: We must produce everything ourselves, and keep in our own country all that good money which previously flowed abroad.

But the martyred agriculture took a terrible revenge. The farmers saw no sense in tilling their fields and the amount of ground under cultivation fell in ten years by 60 per cent. Ruthless export together with a series of lean years reduced the heads of cattle to a dangerous low level; instead of the normal stocks of 45 million head of cows and oxen only 28 million trotted about on the pampas. Even had the farmers wanted to develop the land they would have been unable to do so. Industries and the pleasantly active life of the cities attracted the *peons* in their thousands. Very soon the serfs' quarters of the *estancias* were empty and the ban on tractors imposed by a government obsessed with the idea of autarchy paved the way. The most important thing was to make them yourself. The Argentine builds railway wagons and tractors, builds jet aircraft from the blueprints of a German professor and tanks—the Pulqui 1 and 2. On an island in lake

Nahuel Huapi, in the national park of the country where each
summer thousands of tourists flee from the terrible heat of Buenos
Aires to their villas and luxury hotels, an atomic plant stands, a
grey hideous dangerous thing which it would have been far
better to have banished to some remote wilderness. But of course
it has to be in the public eye. After a few months the President
announced to the astonished world that the winning of atomic
energy from materials other than uranium had been achieved
and that the industries of the Argentine would soon be running
on fabulously cheap current from this new energy. And a few
years later the famous Austrian atom scientist Ronald Richter,
who had brought about this miracle, was chased from the
country as a charlatan. He was not arrested or fined, although
he had made the President the laughing stock of the whole
world. It seems as though the great mountebank had a certain
professional sympathy for his atomic colleague.

The loneliness of the spiritual man

BUENOS AIRES. I had already been there a few days
and had still seen nothing of the city. It was strange, but
I had no wish to go out. "Another day I sighed as I woke
up in the morning. Another day to get through. What shall I
do?" I have never asked myself this question in any other city
except Buenos Aires. The air is leaden. I would get dressed and
go out on the balcony. Below lay a green *plaza* with children at
play. In the centre a tree whose branches sheltered a few lonely
dreamers. . . . To my right the harbour cranes towered like
prison bars. In the distance smoked the funnel of an ocean giant
and behind that . . . no, it was not the sea, although you would
think so. What yawned there with its bleak horizon was the Rio,
the river, or should I say the collection of rivers from the north
which seek their mouth here. It is not blue like any respectable
river. Its reddish water creeps towards your feet insidiously as
if millions of men lay there bleeding. But it is not human blood.
The hills of Paraguay loose their red earth into the stream, and

it flows red down to the sea. The dredgers in the river have to work like fiends in order to rescue the reputation and the significance of Buenos Aires—the largest harbour of South America, the largest town on the Continent.

Not only that. Buenos Aires is a cosmopolitan city. Open any page of the telephone directory and names from all parts of the world are jumbled together. Go to the nearest newspaper stall. You can hear German, English, French, Russian, Polish, Czech, Yiddish and Hebrew: the same in the bookshops. You would think you were in London or Paris, yes, particularly Paris, for the Latin character, the whole air of nonchalance, permeates everything. Why then did I feel so dreadful in the mornings? Why this paranoia? Did the fault lie within myself? Had I tired of this continent after such a long visit? But all the other Europeans feel this way. They all sigh. "I walk through the *Calle Florida*," a very rich woman admitted to me, "and look in the shop windows where all the treasures of the world are displayed. The most costly jewels glitter in the jewellers' vitrines. After two hours in New York I am laden with parcels. Here I never buy anything. I don't know why."

As I have already said: the air is leaden. The façades are greyer than anywhere else and the streets more macadamized. There are parks and trees on the avenues but they give you no pleasure. There are operas and concerts, wonderfully printed periodicals for art and literature, packed halls where you can listen to the wisdom of Indian Yogis, picture galleries, modern experimental theatres and yet . . .

"And yet one feels that it's not true," said an elderly distinguished gentleman who sat next to me one day at a Spanish performance of Anouilh's *Antigone*; "the same feeling that you get when looking at waxed flowers—sinister, such a perfect resemblance, and yet they have no perfume."

I had spoken to my neighbour in Spanish. His unusual accent caught my ear. Born Argentinians cultivate a melodious opera-like tone which fundamentally is closely related to Italian (half the population actually comes from Italy). "You're French," I said, and I was right. Although my neighbour had been an industrialist here for many years, he always tried to keep in touch with his old country by frequent journeys to France. He had only returned a few weeks before from Paris. "That is the difference between France and here, you see," he went on. "Even an insignificant creation is enhanced in Paris because it is ennobled by the importance of the atmosphere. Here, on the contrary, the most important act will peter out uselessly because it remains isolated, because it is stifled in this restless, spiritual vacuum. I never felt this so strongly as on my last trip, and I have never returned with less pleasure.

"It was not homesickness—on the contrary, I might even say that it was an almost uncomfortable sensation, the sensation the prodigal son must have felt in front of his father. Now as regards worldly success, I could not possibly be called a prodigal son. I've piled up a mass of money here, but when I stood on the Ile de la Cité for the first time after landing in France I suddenly seemed to hear a voice whisper in my ear, 'You're a failure. A complete failure despite your millions overseas.' I walked along the Seine, watched the booksellers feeding the birds behind their open showcases, saw a young artist couple in the Tuileries canoodling on a snow-covered bench, and the host of trifles which enrich the daily life in Europe. The voice kept on repeating, 'Tu es un raté, rien qu'un raté.'

"After all, what is this city, what is this country, what in fact is South America? Don't you ever get the feeling, which has tortured me for many years, that you're living in a vacuum? You live among men who look like any of my countrymen from the south of France, men who read books and write articles in the papers, go to the university and become professors, and yet who are not men in our sense of the word. Somehow they are anonymous. After half an hour you have forgotten what their faces look like. They don't register at all.

"Any taxi driver in Paris has more colour, more personality, than a Minister or a professor here, not to mention the writers, painters and muscians who abound in Europe. I admit, you'll find plenty of literary men in South America. They write books, sometimes quite good ones, and they are slated or praised by the critics. But tell me, has a single creative thought which has emerged from this continent set the world alight? Not a single one. To get back to the anonymity of the people here. Their thoughts too are anonymous and lacking all originality. Try and understand me. God knows I don't think much of Jean-Paul Sartre, but no one can deny that he has found a formula for the spiritual condition of our age and has become a kind of barometer of our feelings. Apart from him you find a hundred unknown men who live outside the hub of our present-day problems, and I think that these unknown men convey just as great a cultural atmosphere as the big guns. They all thrive from the same humus. If you feel lonely in Paris you only have to go to the nearest bistro. At the counter you'll find a man you've never seen before and will probably never see again. You'll talk to him for a whole evening on the most intimate questions and leave him without ever learning his name. All that is missing here. The whole spiritual awareness is lacking. All these thoughts went through my head as I wandered along the Seine with that constant voice in my ear 'Tu es un raté avec tes millions.' "

"So to a certain extent you live the life of a hermit in the wilderness?" I asked.

"Precisely," replied the Frenchman. "Here you can make innumerable superficial contacts but no deep ones. So few understand the real art of living. But a man is never self-sufficient. He lives from his surroundings which give him support, and from the responses he gets to his impulses. It's terribly difficult to live in this new world as a kind of eclectic. Your surroundings will win in the long run. They penetrate your soul irresistibly, however much you resist them. When I see your countrymen or mine here, I nod in silence like a doctor who puts on a Hippocratic mask for a patient. They are almost without exception fat pashas. You can almost see the undigested gold giving them fatty degeneration of the heart. They too have become anonymous. They're a banking account, that's all. Sometimes when I look at them I say to myself in terror, 'Am I going to become like that? Am I already like that?' And I often feel the paralysis caused by easily won prosperity, feel the tempter whisper 'Do like the others. Be comfortable. That's the way.' So life becomes a constant defence against spiritual ataxia. I know one day that it will conquer me too. One day I shall no longer consider myself a failure. I shall become a pasha like all the others. I shall play a little golf in order not to grow too fat and belong at last to this country, this soulless bloody Continent."

"But South America, you know," he went on, "does not remain without influence when you've lived here long enough. And then, besides, the old Europe is on its deathbed, everything jitters in the face of a menacing danger, menacing because you no longer have the energy to combat it. I tell you, the urge I have to get away from here is only a destructive vacuum, the failing spirituality, a symbol of a biological childishness which is having its effect on me. One cannot possess both the freshness of youth and the wisdom of age, and I am fully aware of the impossibility of wanting to discard over here the whole burden of our thousand-year old European modes of thought."

"This had been almost one of those Parisian evenings of which you spoke," I said when I bid him goodnight. "We have discussed the deepest possible subjects without knowing each other's names. Allow me . . ."

"No," said the stranger. "Don't let us destroy the pleasure of the unknown. Just call me Monsieur X," he said jokingly. "What I've said to you any other thinking European here or in any other South American country could have told you, unless of course he has already become a pasha."

The USA, friend and foe

THE cement with which the mortar of the Peronist empire was mixed was the antagonism against the United States and their southern hemisphere politics. There are certain enmities which are almost necessities on geographical and psychological grounds. Thus the tension between the Argentine and the USA did not first come to light in the frank speech which the American Ambassador, Spruille Braden, levelled at Perón's rising star, but is almost as natural and necessary as the age-old enmity between Spain and England, between the Latin and Anglo-Saxon powers in the old world. The Argentine, although far removed from being a world power, considers herself as such and since, despite the far greater economic potential of Brazil, she is militarily more powerful and dynamic, she feels herself called upon to achieve a hegemony of the continent, a hegemony that to a certain extent must tread on the toes of the United States.

Already in the first World War Irigoyen made himself popular with the people because he refused to enter the war on the side of the Americans; the Peronist dream of a Spanish Christian third neutral power between the presumably mutually destructive North American and Soviet Russian imperialists was only a more elaborate orchestration of the same melody. Actually the Perónist anti-American melody bore a striking resemblance to communist propaganda. One only had to open a copy of *Verdad*, a weekly magazine which is printed in Spanish, a hostile imitation of the American magazine *Vision*, in order to find all the untruths and falsehoods which have been manufactured behind the Iron Curtain. Certainly after the spring of 1953 the whole economic system of the Argentine threatened to collapse under the mismanagement of the Government, and shortly before Dr. Milton Eisenhower made his journey through Latin America there was a sudden change in the tone of Perón's press. President Eisenhower was fêted as a great soldier and as a man of fine instincts who could understand the problems of his soldier colleague Perón.

South America cannot develop its economic potentialities without capital. There are only two possibilities—to accumulate her own capital and sink it in the necessary plants, or to go hat in hand for help abroad. However, in the same breath that they demand such aid there is talk of their right to the treasures of their own soil: in the face of such Nationalist behaviour the foreign capitalist will be inclined to look upon even mutual assurances as a kind of fat bait which conceals a treacherous hook.

Even the necessary means of accumulating this wealth, the essential technical capacity to develop it, more or less comes to grief, or has so far done so, on account of the Creole character which possesses neither sense of economy nor the discipline vital to efficiency in business undertakings. In this respect the vices of the Spanish colonizers have almost developed into a national trait: it may of course be an Indian heritage, that curious habit of "bluing" the economies of a whole year in one single fiesta. Or again, is it merely the tradition of feudalism which enjoyed a vast property and later, thanks to the increasing value of the soil, found that it could lead a life of almost unlimited extravagance and go quite unpunished. All these together may have produced a mentality in which nearly all values are purely imaginary. The instalment system which functions quite normally in the States exists in South America, but on a far less serious level. In Latin America the mills of justice grind so slowly that proceedings against a debtor cost a fortune or are so complicated that most of the buyers stop paying after the fourth or fifth instalment. The tradesman is therefore compelled to raise the price of his wares so that he comes out of the deal without loss, with a marginal profit of 150 per cent to 200 per cent. The client who pays his full twelve months' instalments is naturally the "mug". In practice therefore nobody does what the law demands. This need to raise prices through uncertainty obtains not only in business. "An investment that is not paid off in ten years," one business man told me, "will be looked upon as a bad debt." Even the corruption of the politicians is based upon insecurity, for no one knows whether he will be able to return to normal civilian life. He may even be exiled and he must therefore pile up as much wealth as he possibly can. And this wealth vanishes just as quickly as it was amassed: the figures of savings bank accounts per head of the population in the United States and in Europe is a hundred times greater than in countries of proportionate size in Latin America. The reserves, however, which the individuals in power pile up mostly find their way to foreign banks or are invested in giant apartment or business buildings, where the profits are enormous. The slow systematic building up of a long-term business does not suit the Latin American. He prefers to leave that to the foreigner. His speciality is not creation but the *coup*. We must never lose sight of this, despite any exception that might prove the rule.

Above all, then, they need the foreigners and in particular the rich Americans, however little they may love them. Here is the point where the psychological and the economic side of anti-Americanism meet. They label as "lacking in finesse" the business mentality of the Gringo, even that successful sobriety they would so dearly love to possess in order to transform their megolamania from the realm of fantasy into reality. From this feeling of impotence and servility is born a paradoxical behaviour. On the one hand a spoiled child's fist is raised when the United States sends milliards of dollars to Europe and Asia to prop up unstable countries against the communist flood. "And they send their brothers of the same hemisphere nothing or alms under Point 4, so that the majority of the American money is spent on the luxurious life of the American experts." But when a large American company really wants to talk business the cry is immediately raised of American imperialism which only thinks in terms of exploitation. Sometimes, as I have already said, the same people use this double talk. Their synthesis is plain: they want foreign gold, but as far as possible without foreign control and without strings attached. Best of all they would prefer a gift, something in the nature of a Marshall Plan.

One cannot really deny the justice of such wishes. As long as England was the financial and industrial centre to which Latin America turned, an industrial boom soon started in the raw-materials producing periphery because the British Isles, lacking in raw materials and food, immediately let their wealth flow out again for imports, but when the United States, far less dependent on imports, became the fatal power for Latin American economy, the boom waves did not rise so swiftly or so high. Exchange conditions between industrial—this applies to both Latin America and the USA—and the agrarian raw-material producing countries developed, apart from temporary fluctuations, in favour of the former—*i.e.,* the Latin Americans had to deliver more wheat, meat, coffee or mineral ores in exchange for a motor-car, a refrigerator or a typewriter. It also became more difficult to obtain the machines needed for their own industrialization. Why should not the controls and subsidies with which the industrial countries support their home politics also be possible on an international basis? This is the question the Latin Americans ask. Why won't they guarantee the prices of copper, tin, petrol, wool, etc.? Why not remove the tariffs with which the United States bolster up their home production? Is the hemisphere not to a certain extent a closed entity in which the weak have claims on the consideration of the strong, because in certain respects the latter are dependent upon them?

Practically all the coffee and 85 per cent of the sugar consumed in the United States comes from Latin America, not to mention mineral ores, 70 per cent to 80 per cent of bauxite and tungsten, a good part of the tin, bismuth, lead, copper, magnesium and chromium. Were America to be plunged once more into a war enemy U-boats could destroy their communications with other raw-material producing sources in Africa and South-eastern Asia, and thus Latin America would become incomparably more important for her neighbour's economy than is the case today. And it is this very moment which many Latin Americans anticipate with a certain resentment. For next time, many of them say, we will not deal as altruistically as we did when we put our whole natural wealth at the disposal of the Allies. They sold their products at limited prices, but when with their dollars they wanted to buy heavy machinery there was none available, and after the war the prices had risen so high that the accumulated dollar reserves lost a great part of their former worth. Much of the anti-Americanism springs, justly or unjustly, from this trauma—they feel cheated by the foreign companies, by the American Government and by destiny itself. There are certain platitudes that you will hear repeated from the Rio Grande as far south as Chile: "We are willing to renounce the gifts under Point 4. If we were paid fair prices for our products we should get along far better."

The United States should undoubtedly take this mood into account. Private capital obviously would hardly be tempted to sink sufficient funds in such nationalistic, unweeded and inflation-impregnated soil. Investments in Latin America must often be considered not so much from the yield as from their political necessity, and since in fact these Latin Americans view the private profit motif with distrust, the American Government should think about granting the necessary credits. Bolivia is a perfect example of how, through economic support, even a basically anti-American revolution can have its teeth drawn. Dilly-dallying and failure to take risks will only foster *Perónismo* in its original nationalistic and anti-American aspects. It is possible that Latin America will be lost economically to the United States. This is already visible in trade, where the West German Republic is taking more and more plums away from the Americans. The German exports to Latin America rose in 1953 from $30 million to $400 million, and the visit of the German Minister of Economic Affairs, Erhardt, to the major Latin American capitals gave an impetus to this upward movement. Old relationships come into play and are encouraged, but the basic reason lies far more in a greater market elasticity, generous credits and long-term re-payments. Great Britain, on the contrary, who in 1914 ruled a third of the Latin American market, sank in 1952 to 6 per cent and in 1953 to 4 per cent. Currency controls make it difficult for South American clients. They cannot get pounds, and further-more the Germans are not hampered by armament expenditure and can deliver more cheaply.

The latest competitors are the Soviets and their satellite countries, both as buyers and sellers. At a moment when the Argentine had difficulty in selling its meat, leather, wool and linseed at acceptable prices on the world market the Russians took $150 million worth. In exchange coal from Poland, machines and rolling stock from Czechoslovakia and Hungary were sent. An importer in Ecuador who has ordered wares from these countries for some years praised the cheap price because the State Board of Trades of those countries can make practical export calculations without bothering about the prices current in their own countries. The Argentine example has attracted the greedy and envious eyes of the whole continent. Uruguay even exported beef to Russia at a higher price than England paid. Chile dreamed of sending its unsold copper to Russia and its saltpetre to China (naturally without success). Brazil, however, bought Russian wheat via Finland because her dear neighbour the Argentine asked a higher price for it, although her silos were almost bursting. Only the future will show whether trade with Russia can be further developed or whether it is merely to be looked upon as a method of propaganda. In any case the whole muddle shows one thing quite clearly. If the United States are prepared to let Latin America slip out of their hands there are others who are only too ready to pick her up.

CHILE

The triple paradise

WHY is it that everyone in this country is not a poet? Chile is the most indolent of the South American lands. Her fields are a riot of flowers and the blossoms assail even the houses like a flood. White egrets cry in the tree-tops and are never shot. Their presence is considered lucky and no one kills them. Vines grow in the plains with heavy bunches of grapes. The Argentine and Peru also try to court the God Bacchus, but nowhere does the wine turn out so nobly as here. Chile's soil and the sun create sweetness and luciousness which make the grapes rival the best French varieties. Even the Creole vice, intoxication, is more pleasant here than anywhere else. They do not get drunk on spirits but on the juice of the grape. Wine is akin to poetry. It is no coincidence that this soil produced the finest lyrics in the Spanish tongue; Gabriela Mistral and Pablo Neruda are children of this land.

In the centre of this Garden of Eden lies the capital, Santiago, a not very exciting but very pleasant city. It is the fourth largest of the continent and yet it has managed to preserve more provincial intimacy than Lima or Bogotá. At midday I paid a visit to the central *Plaza de Armas*, where it is particularly agreeable to rest under the shade of mighty trees among old grey statues. It is not easy to find a place, although the flower beds are flanked with benches. Hundreds of people sit here—old men, young girls and portly matrons enjoying the sun. When you open your *El Mercurio* people look over both your shoulders and immediately start a conversation. The two old churches are pretty even if they do not compete with the ostentation of the other colonial capitals. In any case it is not the artistic treasures that arouse a feeling of well-being in Santiago, but the whole paradisal atmosphere of the asphalt streets and the tall buildings.

On the first evening the visitor stands on a hill which rises in the centre of a sea of houses, the Cerro Santa Lucia. On the far horizon, pale pink in the blue dusk, tower the giants of the Andes chain. The city itself is only 1,700 feet above sea level, but the mountains seem higher than anywhere else. The flight from Argentine Mendoza to Santiago is only a short hop. You leave at 1 o'clock and arrive at 1 o'clock, thanks to the difference in time. On the way the aircraft skirts the mighty protective peaks which lie there like powerful wild beasts. Above them all towers Aconcagun, the highest mountain in South America. The Swiss Alps look like finely chiselled sculpture in comparison with these rough-hewn blocks, planted by some Divine landscape gardener. It is not so much their beauty as their imposing forms which take the breath away. Here in Santiago they have lost their terror. Their contours do not cut the air like knives as in La Paz. They shroud their white tops in a veil of gauze from below—the smoke of factories, the sweat of men and beasts and the breath of meadows and woods. We have left behind the supernatural inhumanity of the Bolivian Altiplano. Height, breadth and climate have all become amiable and boundless, pleasant as I have already said.

No other land offers such vast contrasts as Chile, and although the majority of its inhabitants live in these gentle valleys, the sources of its wealth lie in the north and in the south, which holds untold possibilities for the future.

One day I took a plane to Antofagasta, the harbour city in the north. I had heard it mentioned countless times in Bolivia because most of the imports and exports pass through here. This time the flight was not straight through the Andes. Our silver bird felt its way at about 30,000 feet, following a green valley flanked on both sides by the ice giants. After an hour the meadows and woods disappeared from below. Rock and sandy regions swallowed up the trees and suddenly we were above a desert, the same desert I had crossed on my trip down the Peruvian coast, a moon landscape without rain. The airfield where we landed comprises only a wooden hangar, a flag-pole and an asphalt runway, a black band in the desert. After half an hour's drive we came to the town. A stormy desolation built as a resting-place for dead ore, for tin, copper and saltpetre, but not for men. A 193-mile-long canal carries the water to it—far too little even for human needs, and thus even the trees and the flowers are rationed. Only a few cactuses stand in gloomy independence outside the city: the fog in the air gives them sufficient nourishment. And then the desert once more, soft rolling sand where for hours you will meet no traces of man. After two or three hours, however, you come to the strange conical hummocks which resemble giant mole-hills. The remains of houses betray the trace of former inhabitants, but from the broken windows and the nakedness of the walls they must have been abandoned a long time ago.

In the old days, my companion told me, small holders dug saltpetre from the earth. The gigantic mole-hills were the result of mining saltpetre, but the houses—that was the custom—were merely abandoned as useless once the region had been exhausted.

What an ironic story! Only a few feet below the sand lies a mineral which elsewhere is used to manure the fields, and here are no plants. One only needs a bulldozer to clear away the crust and below lies six feet of saltpetre. Until the first World War—i.e., until the German Jew, Haber, discovered the secret of artificial nitrate, Chile had made a good income from this easily won wealth. Ninety-five per cent of the whole world's needs was supplied from here and its export comprised 75 per cent of the national revenue. For Chile this discovery meant one of the great economic tragedies in its history.

Suddenly a thick cloud rose in front of us as though the desert were on fire, but on looking closer we could see what looked like a large industrial town ahead. It was Pedro de Valdivia, one of the most modern works of the Anglo-Lautaro Nitrate Company. The smoke was a cloud of dust from the ore crushers which prepare the mineral in chemical baths. Together with the Maria Elena plant a million tons of saltpetre is won yearly, 65 per cent of the total production of the country. The company is 75 per cent American and three-quarters of its products are sold to the

United States. The small white heaps we saw being tipped into sacks and loaded on lorries were still preferred by the farmers to artificial nitrate. Nevertheless the directors of the company are not happy. They can make very small profits in their competitive struggle with the artificial product, and this indifferent yield is a source of continued bitterness between the Government and the unions. The actual raw material should last for ever, for saltpetre in different strengths lies under the desert along the whole 450 miles of coast. The small holders whose workings we had seen needed concentrates of at least 15 per cent. The modern plant extracts from minerals down to as low as 7 per cent concentrate.

And once more we were in the desert without tree or bush. Gradually we drew closer to the mountains on the horizon. At one spot we crossed a river, which meant a few yards of greenery, huts and men. Then the cool of evening caressed our faces. We climbed to 9,000 feet and we were at our goal: Chuquicamata, a jumble of tasteless buildings and a flickering furnace on the slope. Chuquicamata is for Chile what Cerro de Potosí is for Bolivia— the magic mountain of wealth. But here the metal is copper. Wherever you dig the whole mountain is of copper ore. In 1915 mining began with a mighty eruption which has resulted in a gigantic one-sided mountain—one mile long and three miles wide. It falls in countless terraces like the rows of a huge amphitheatre, and on each terrace are small-gauge electric railways, which from the distance resemble children's toys. Tiny figures hurry about the terraces. A loud explosion and a piece of the terrace thunders down to be loaded. The mountain is gradually being eaten away. Five hundred million tons have already been carted off, but even if the plundering continues at the same rate the magic mountain will last for another hundred years. The Anoconda Company, which owns Chuquicamata, has invested $90 million in a new plant for treating ore with a smaller metal content. Today Chuquicamata produces no less than half the entire Chilean copper, which a few years ago amounted to a fifth of the world production.

Until a few years ago. . . . The fact that the percentage has fallen from 20 per cent. to 13 per cent and will perhaps fall to 10 per cent is causing the American engineers of Chuquicamata great anxiety. . . . Copper which had replaced nitrate as the life product of Chile (70 per cent of her entire foreign currency came from its export) became a dangerous toy for power-crazy politicians, and the foreign companies (the Anaconda and the Braden company) could only suffer as a result of it. When the Korean war raised the prices of metal, the Chileans boldly terminated their contract with the United States, which had guaranteed them a market for a great part of their production at a limited price, because they hoped to get more for it on the world market. However, when prices fell at the close of hostilities the Chilean Government demanded an exaggerated price from all interested parties, until the growing piles of unsold copper once more drove them to Washington for help. That was the paradox of the Chilean situation: in Washington they begged and demanded consideration in the name of continental solidarity. In this country the American companies were the golden geese which had to be forced to lay their golden eggs. Not only did the Government take a fifth of the proceeds for itself, and tax the profits of the company to 75 per cent, but they also sold the company the Chilean pesos it needed for working expenses at double the price they would fetch in the free market. Not to mention the insatiable demands of the communist-organized unions. Chile became one of the most inhospitable countries in South America, not only for the mining companies but for all foreign capital.

And then the south! A night journey by express train takes you there, and once more the landscape has undergone a wonderful transformation. Once more it is primeval landscape, no longer a hostile desert but, on the contrary, one which offers itself with open arms to the bold colonist. Don Walterio, a Swiss, invited me to visit a farm on Lake Rupanco which he had enlarged by extensive clearance. The fires were still smouldering on newly won fields from which in the coming years tons of wheat would be produced. A few Coihue trees had been left to guard against drought and erosion. As in a picturesque English park, their lonely branches spread out as though they were still reaching towards a forgotten neighbour. Here and there a withered or burnt branch from some undestroyed tree seems to curse God and man that it had become a cripple. Each tree had become a kind of personality. They adorned the landscape as far as the town—memorials to the primeval forest which a few hundred years ago still knocked at its doors.

Each seed here possessed a devastating fertility. All the flowers and fruits of the old country yield threefold on this young soil. Someone imported blackberries and soon they grew in profusion over all the fields. Had they been allowed to grow unhindered they would have turned Osorno into a sleeping beauty's castle. But since the conscientious Germans are not prepared to slumber they let the goats wrestle with the branches. Goats are not kept for milk here—why should they be, when there are hundreds of cows—but merely for this almost military defence task. There is preference for billy goats, because they are difficult to steal on account of their strong odour, which mingled with the scent of the flowers, carries hundreds of yards.

Don Walterio studied geology, botany and zoology as a hobby, and while we drove in his jeep through this romantic region where a host of calves grazed on all sides, he gave me his version of the millennial geological formation.

I could imagine the extinct volcanoes which lift their snow-capped heads as though they enjoyed the blue sky, as smoking cones changing the course of rivers and creating that wonderful mosaic of lakes which has earned this region the name of "the Chilean Switzerland." It could just as well be called the Chilean Japan, for Monte Osorno towers above the lakes with all the classic beauty of Fujiyama. Other craters fell in, leaving one sharp jagged point like a decaying tooth—Puntiagudo.

Don Walterio had invited the German missionary Father Meyer to give the scattered settlers on Lake Rupanco the rare opportunity of seeing a priest. By motor boat we entered the little bay where his farm lies and looked along the lake bank for some traces of human habitation. Whenever a clearing on the wooded slopes and a homely hut betrayed the presence of some peasant the boatman made for the bank and the Father gave a high shrill call like a Swiss peasant yodelling. When some head peered out of a window or from the bushes on the hillside he cried in a stentorian voice, "Any couple to be married or any children to be baptized?" The reply, whether in the negative or the affirmative, was usually much more boorish than the friendly offer deserved. These men and women, who live so cut off from the world, do not like humans, in fact they are almost hostile to them. Only a small path leads from their hut to civilization and they have long since ceased to take the long walk to church in order to arrange their personal matters with God.

When Don Walterio and the Father climbed up to baptize some child I remained in the boat and tried to engage Pepe the boatman in conversation. By his features I saw at once that he belonged to the old native race of the Araucanian Indians who had been the lords of the country before the arrival of the Spaniards. According to the anthropologists they never reached such a high degree of civilization as their northern relations the Incas, Mayas and Aztecs, or their forerunners. But this had made them far more dangerous opponents. These warlike peasants knew how to give a sharp rap over the knuckles to the invaders, and at last they contrived to be left in peace in these southern forest regions. What the weapons of the Spaniards did not achieve, the diseases, alcohol and the gold of later pioneers finally accomplished. Today this proud ancient race has shrunk to 100,000. Had the Chilean Government not turned some of their settlements into reservations they would long since have disappeared from the plains and have retired to the solitudes of mountain slopes. They have become museum exhibits like their North American brothers, and they too eke out a melancholy and picturesque existence with Government subsidies and a contract to produce hand-woven ponchos and other objects of folk art. Some, like Pepe, enter the service of their new white masters and the girls go as maids into the town. In their heart of hearts they still feel that they are the true rulers of the land. With Pepe I came up against this same dumb, obstinate defence, the same basic mistrust I had experienced among the highland

Indians of Mexico and right down south as far as Bolivia. He
looked with obvious anxiety at the smoke from the clearing
bonfires which drifted here and there down the slope, and he
only started to listen when I brought the conversation round to
the heroic deeds his ancestors had accomplished against the
Spaniards. He was illiterate and could not have read them anywhere, but the myth of the "True Race" has been passed down by
word of mouth from mother to child.

Our ultimate goal was an island which was for sale. Don
Walterio wanted to inspect it, because he proposed to stock it
with deer and turn it into a shoot. It covers about a square mile
and today only a few cows inhabit it. What magnificent country
where you can buy an island and turn it into a place for sport.

A few days later I crossed one of the most beautiful lakes in the
whole neighbourhood, Todos Los Santos, on my way to the
Argentine frontier. The melted snow which trickles down from
Osorno and Puntiagudo troubles its depths, changing them to a
milky white. Even in summer it remains cool and mysterious.
There are no landing stages and the steamer occasionally stops
in the middle of the lake and drops its passengers into a small
boat. Here too the whole bank is wild, with an occasional house
or park, but certainly no village which it would pay to visit.
Travellers find it very similar to Lake Rupanco: the first feeling
is one of unbounded joy, a primitive feeling of uncontested
mastery that any wild beast must have when it enters a still
unexplored game preserve. After all, does not man himself feel
the primitive urge to seize his own kingdom and be master there
with his brood.

But this intoxication of solitude does not last long. After a few
hours' journey the need for companionship gets the upper hand.
It is the instinctive need to find traces of one's fellows. You crave
for human works that will give you a yardstick in order to measure
Nature. The old church, for example, standing on the top of a
cliff, the arch of a bridge over a ravine. . . . Admittedly the ant-
like cultivation with which the civilized world is beginning to
disfigure the lake shore bans us from the natural paradise we are
seeking, but a paradise without Adam is no paradise, because

where there is no path to a neighbour the vastness encloses you like a prison.

No hotels have been built on Lake Todos Los Santos. Sometimes, when the ship rounds a cliff and comes to a breath-taking new view of rock and ice, one wonders why no enterprising spirit has built a tourist resort here where the gentle sky bird Osorno or the powerful choleric, glacier-armoured Tronador could wish the visitors Good morning. A Swiss *hotelier* should put in an appearance. Now, in Peulla, where we spent the night, the hotel keeper is a Swiss, the son of that old Roth who years ago opened the region to tourists; buses and ships linked it to Argentine territory via Bariloche. But Peulla, which lies at the end of the lake without a view, is no more than a resting-place for the night. Roth junior sighed at my suggestion. "Nobody would come for their holidays to a lonely hotel with no attraction but the scenery. That applies not only to Chileans but in general to all South Americans and possibly to all the Latin races. They like to spend their holidays in a hive of activity, the louder and noisier the better. The love of nature is a luxury enjoyed by the Anglo-Saxons and the Germans."

There are plenty of Germans in Southern Chile. Anyone passing through Osorno or Valdivia will see fair-haired Germans and hear German spoken almost as though he were in a small German provincial town. The Moorish flat roofs have disappeared and tiled gables rise in the air. When you visit one of the houses you will be overwhelmed by German *gemütlichkeit* in all its characteristic aspects. I might say that in many respects the German atmosphere here is more aggressively stressed than in Germany itself. This is not only the case with the Germans. Foreign colonists preserve their national traits and sport them like a flag. German, French and English traditions become a programme and pass from the instinctive into the self-conscious. This results in a further curious peculiarity: they are all inclined to cling on to old attitudes which have long since paled in their own ·countries and have been replaced by others. Like their compatriots in Southern Brazil who at the end of 1952 could celebrate the centenary of their arrival in the country, the

Germans of Chile, even at the time of the Weimar Republic, had remained basically royalist and national. It was not particularly difficult for Hitler to dye their black, red and white souls brown. From this German core organizations of a more or less avowed National Socialist hue directed their influence upon the Chilean population. Their task was all the easier since German instructors to the army and the police had instilled an unmistakable Prussian spirit with its attendant sympathies. Even today the cut of the Chilean uniform, although in the meanwhile American military experts have taken the place of the Germans, reminds one of the old Wehrmacht, particularly when worn by a young lieutenant from Osorno or Valdivia.

This is why Teutonism in Southern Chile has been far better preserved than anywhere else on this continent. The German not only feels that he has been born in a similar landscape to his homeland, but also among a people of similar mentality. Not for nothing have the Chileans been called the "Prussians of South America." This is denoted by a certain warlike sobriety in their character, their readiness to accept discipline and the military ability which in all disputes has earned them the reputation of invincibility among their neighbours. Perhaps it would be more accurate to call them the "South American English," for much in the Chilean character can be explained by their insularity, an insularity that is no less effective because the barriers that cut Chile off from the outside world are giant mountains and deserts. Before the era of the aeroplane the Chileans were a race living at the end of the world on a small snake-like strip of coast. Their existence never allowed them to form a true centre nor to know the peace of a territorial centre. The sea was not only the natural means of communication inside the country, as in the case of the Norwegians, but also their egress. It was a long way to other countries and they could only be reached by rounding the Horn. For Chile the world lay at the rear and ahead was nothing except the vast empty expanses of the Pacific. Shipping was therefore a natural profession. The Chilean character bears the imprint of geographical ostracism, of the continual need for breaking out of their solitude and fighting a way to the world, far more than of the inherited martial savagery and love of freedom of the Araucanian Indians. The Chileans are therefore the least South American of all the South Americans, if by this term one means that element of fantasy, of inconstancy and of Latin charm. They are almost Nordic in their heaviness and in their melancholy. My suggestion of re-christening them the English of South America finds support in the fact that many English or Scottish emigrants succeeded in what the Germans never attempted, namely of finding their way into the Chilean aristocracy and of assimilating themselves so completely that the social register of Santiago and in particular the harbour city Valparaiso teems with Anglo-Saxon names. Today on some lonely property one can meet with a MacDonald or a MacPherson who in black Andalusian garb rides to the fiestas and cannot speak a word of English. The realism of the Chileans also preserves them from that inferiority complex which is one of the basic traits of this continent and which shows itself in an imaginary *grandezza*—a *grandezza* which recoils from the slightest breath of criticism as though it were a painful insult. Self-irony, on the other hand, is one of their most outstanding characteristics. A statesman as swollen-headed as Perón would here very quickly be deflated, because the Chileans love to laugh at the weaknesses of their great men with a satire not unlike that of the French. It is significant that the satirical newspapers, which in the neighbouring countries lead a very precarious existence, are in Chile the most influential and popular political publications. Chilean politics, although not entirely free of revolution, are very near to Parliamentary democracy and are only surpassed on this continent by those of Uruguay.

Black eyes—Red hearts

IT must not be thought that Chile is free from the social problems that exist throughout Latin America. The contrast between the "haves" and "have-nots" is just as striking here as in the feudal kingdoms where the heirs of the Spaniards came into conflict with the subjugated Indians. Here in Chile, of course, it is not a question of antagonistic races. The cowherd, the *huaso* and the *roto* who has left the land and vegetates as a proletarian in the city slums may, if white skin were a sign of nobility, claim ancestors as noble as many of their employers. But white men, too, can be paupers and illiterates. According to statistics 90 per cent of the arable land forms part of the enormous *haciendas* or *fundos* as they are called here, and the independent small farmer is quite a rarity. If only the land were at least subjected to an intensive agriculture, but here too the average landowner is a spendthrift who, as his father did before him, lets his land be administered and merely casts a rapid eye at his bailiff's accounts. While in Chile far more cultivated land is available per head of the population than in California, Switzerland or New Zealand (to quote similar countries), the production per head is only half as great as in Switzerland, only a third of that in California, and the yield per acre is five times smaller than in New Zealand and sixteen times smaller than in Switzerland.

When on his return from exile the poet Neruda was asked what attracted him most in his fatherland, he said without a thought, "The peaches. There are no peaches in the world like the Chilean." In actual fact a visit to the fruit market is a revelation. Everything grows so magnificently in this blessed soil if you take the trouble to plant it. Despite the oxen and the calves on her meadows, despite the wheat fields through which you travel by train, Chile has to use a great part of its currency for food, instead of using it productively for industrialization.

And here we have the fundamental problem of this beautiful land. Chile, too, is in search of a new mode of life, and this mode is obviously industrialization. In this respect she is in a better starting position than her large neighbour the Argentine, because, thanks to her mineral wealth, she has remained more independent of agriculture. Nature has presented her with everything the Argentine strives for in vain—iron ore, magnesium, coal—*i.e.*, the bases for a heavy industry. American loans made possible the building of the $100 million Huachipato steelworks, next to Volta Redonda in Brazil the largest on the continent, with a production of 300,000 tons per annum. The 140 North American technicians who got the work going in 1915 have by now been reduced to fifteen indispensable chief engineers. Chileans have taken over all the other positions and even the *rojos*, who at the outset caused their superiors great anxiety by their irresponsibility, have proved magnificent workers. Even the chickens which originally lived in the bathrooms of the modern settlements have been banished to a somewhat more normal dwelling-place.

In other fields too, in textiles, metallurgic and mechanical industries, great progress has been made during the post-war pears. Today the mining and industrial workers form a quarter of all labour. It is clear that these powers must of necessity shake the conservative social structure of Chilean society; that the conflict between feudalism and socialism must find here a very fruitful soil. In actual fact Chile was the first land in the western hemisphere to elect a People's Government in 1938 based on a coalition of all the left-wing parties, from the Progressive Liberals and Radicals to the Communists. Their President, Aguirre Cerda, harboured the most magnificent plans for an improvement of education and health services. One of his most important works, the value of which is still disputed even today, was the *Corporación de Fomento*. With the help of foreign credits, this institution attempted further development through the creation of State subsidized and controlled industries. In actual fact this *Fomento*—as the Corporation is called for short—has been instrumental in bringing red tape and State control into Chilean economic life, with the consequent inflation and errors in trade policy, as a result of which private capital, instead of building up the land, has taken flight. Although *Fomento* has done a great deal—Huachipato is one of its achievements—it has also proved a great hindrance.

When I asked a Conservative official in Santiago why the Labour Government had been so little revolutionary even under Cerda's successor, he smiled slyly and said, "Nosotros los rodeamos." This means that the traditional powers in Parliament represented by the Conservative and Liberal parties are, thanks to their political experience and to the fact that they represent the ruling classes, somehow always able to retain a hold on the President and to bend him according to their will. It is almost a natural law that the Chilean Presidents have to go to the under-dog for support and later have to serve even more faithfully the interests of the top dogs. This was the case at the end of the twenties with General Ibañez, who as President played the strong man and fascist dictator. It was the same later with the Progressive Radical Alessandri Palma, who found himself forced to suppress the workers' strikes with a strong hand. An even more out-standing example was the betrayal of the last Labour President, Gonzalez Videla, who in 1946 was elected with the help of the Communists. When in the flush of victory they became too obstreperous a law was passed in 1948 for the protection of democracy, banning the party, and 23,000 known communists were struck from the electoral roll. In the 1952 election, when General Ibañez tried to stage a comeback, he did not officially enjoy the support of the left, who put up their own candidate, but he produced a programme that must have rejoiced the heart of every communist. He demanded State control and nationaliza-tion of the copper and nitrate mines; he attacked the military pact signed by his predecessor with the United States by which Chile agreed to deny her copper ores to the communist bloc in return for American war material, and he promised to lift the communist ban imposed by his predecessor. But no sooner was he in office than things took a very different turn. The realities were stronger than demagogy. The trend which started after many years of painful experiences with Perón became manifest under Ibañez in the first few months of his presidency. He too began to scream for American capital and a ready American market for Chilean ores.

Nor did he dream of repealing the law for the protection of democracy, since in view of the vacuum into which his government programme had fallen and the avalanche of the rising cost of living, the communists were a growing danger.

Communism in Chile largely conforms to the general characteristics of the nation, as I have described them. The remoteness of the country with its back towards Europe makes Santiago feel almost lost in space. When I spoke to a young Chilean about the menace of Soviet-Russian imperialism he replied with an almost compassionate smile. His countrymen sit in a stage box looking at a performance of world history. What is going on in Europe and Asia was an exciting spectacle and from this æsthetic point of view—to a certain extent *sub specie æternitatis*—police terror, the oppression of opinion, and concentration camps are dismissed as trivial details or products of imperialistic propaganda, as opposed to the great emancipation of China and Russia—the apotheosis of these two vast nations by their own efforts. For here people have the maddening and powerless feeling of being an economic colony of the United States; this inevitably drives the young intellectuals into the ranks of the communists and the fellow travellers. Communist propaganda therefore thrives in this twilight of progressive sympathies without too openly revealing its cloven foot. In Santiago, for example, a very smart magazine, *Vistazo*, while professing impartiality, always prints a few plums of a pro-communist and anti-American nature even when dealing with such a jejune subject as the sex transformation of the former G.I. Christine Jorgensen. I visited the paper out of curiosity and met a nest of rabid communists. The editor had just returned to Chile from Czechoslovakia via New York and could not be enthusiastic enough about the free and happy atmosphere of Prague, while, according to him, in the States all the citizens expected a visit from the F.B.I. every time there was a knock on the door. But *Vistazo* takes good care not to betray the true spirit of its editorial board. It leaves crude propaganda to the party paper, *El Siglo* (for some curious reason it has never been banned), and with its pernicious seed reaches a far greater public than it would do otherwise. Again, there is a superb art journal *Pro Arte* which in a completely cosmopolitan setting displays an outspoken weakness for the cultural achievements of the Soviet Union. Not to mention whole pages allotted to the great Chilean poet Pablo Neruda as a platform for his æsthetic and political views.

Were there no Pablo Neruda possibly the communist influence would not be half so strong among the Chilean intellectuals, but one can imagine what would happen in Anglo-Saxon circles were T. S. Eliot a communist. . . . One can be of two minds as to the merit of Neruda's poetry. Its trend towards the rhetorical rather than the truly lyrical often make it seems trivial compared with the æsthetic drama of his earlier poems of the Spanish Civil war—he was Chilean Consul in Madrid at that period. Now it contains trite slogans of the political struggle. The poet who in early youth wrote some of the most beautiful love poems in the Spanish language wrote hymns to the heroes of Stalingrad during the second World War. His anarchic, individualist nihilism burns with brotherly love for the worker. In 1945 he entered the political arena as communist Senator for the North. He was propaganda chief for Gonzalez Videla in his presidential election. After the latter's betrayal he inundated him with all the most injurious insults his poetical genius could master. As a result of this he was deprived of Parliamentary immunity and only escaped prison through flight. The police only made a half-hearted search for him, because one really could not fling the most important Spanish poet in gaol. But his game of hide and seek with the police hounds of reaction was a magnificent poetic martyrdom. With a valid pass from the Government he crossed the Andes in secret and fled to Paris and Mexico. The fruit of this exile is his *Canto General*, a collection of poems in which the barren political song only echoes from afar—for example, in the *Heights of Machu Picchu*, where he sings the praises of the small ants who raised this monument of stone, the unknown Inca slaves unjustly forgotten in the brilliance of the great. Here is something like a true socialist hymn. If only he had continued in this vein.

Neruda lives in a small attractive house in a suburb of Santiago with his wife and beautiful young secretary Marguerite Aguirre, who herself is one of the most talented of the Chilean poets. It was extremly difficult to make an appointment with the poet because the telephone system in Santiago is one of the most abominable in the whole of South America. It is easier to get a

call through to someone in Bombay than to your nearest neighbour. I found Neruda to be a more narrow-minded doctrinaire
than the satirical Diego Rivera in Mexico. Perhaps the realist
socialism demanded by the party line is less suited to lyric poets
than to fresco painters. In his behaviour Neruda is more haughty
and self-conscious than Rivera, and as holder of the Stalin Prize,
less susceptible to bourgeois sentimentality. "I have grasped,"
he said to me, "that a poem is only of value when it can be
relayed over a loud speaker to ten thousand listeners." I looked
at him in horror. His bald head and large melancholy eyes
reminded me of a Byzantine mosaic. He was in deadly earnest. I
protested and pointed out that he had written his best for the
eclectic taste of aristocratic minds; that he was too subtle an artist
to court the masses and lose his own individuality. His wife
nodded eagerly and I felt that even the poet agreed in his heart.
He replied with an unbridled diatribe against the imperialists who
enslaved the world in the name of cultural freedom. From then
on no conversation was possible. Politeness forbade me to let
him know how wretched I found his latest verses which embodied
these theories.

Chilean communism follows the general Latin American
pattern; the *rojos*, who as the real sufferers of the bad old days
should be the most radical, are less permeated than the intellectuals.
The communists have firmly installed themselves in key positions
in the unions, particularly in the coal and nitrate mines, which
have a membership of some 35,000 men. The copper and railway
workers' unions are for the moment dominated by socialists and
Falangists, a left wing Catholic and rather pink group. In the
central organization of the unions the communists have only 5
out of 25 representatives, but here again they are all in key positions. Their following in the whole country can be judged by the
last presidential election, in which out of a total electorate of
950,000 the communist-supported Senator Allende only gained
25,000 votes. Even when one reckons the 23,000 barred from the
polls by Gonzalez Videla, the communists do not number 10
per cent. But since, as I have already said, they control key
positions in the unions and often a certain non-communist

following, they could at the decisive moment cripple the land with strikes, and particularly in the event of a war between Russia and the United States disrupt the vulnerable export of copper. In the past years several magnificently co-ordinated general strikes have brought trade and activity to a complete standstill, and it is not difficult to see in this a kind of general rehearsal staged by the extraordinarily capable secret directors. In the spring of 1953, for example, mines, factories and banks closed for twenty-four hours when Clotario Blest, head of the largest union, cursed the President as the betrayer of his country and was subsequently arrested. Blest himself is not a communist but a typical product of that unworldly objectivity which I have already mentioned exists among Chile's intellectuals. He is a devout Catholic and an enthusiastic reader of Thomist philosophy. In 1952 he was invited to Moscow with other union leaders. The hook with which the communists caught him was disguised with an unusual bait. The Thomist was taken to an impressive Easter celebration of the Orthodox Church which convinced him absolutely of the Soviet goodwill. Thus the Christian Resurrection echoes to a certain extent in the knocking on Chile's door by the Revolution. No less remarkable than this aspect of the communist movement is the story of their competition with Perón. The remarkable thing is that it deals less with men than with women, for whoever observes Chile must never leave the women out of account.

I could not help exclaiming as I walked along the streets for the first time. After an hour I took refuge in a dark café to be rid of the sight of women. I was tired of quizzing them. What shall I speak of first? Of their slim gazelle-like figures, the soft oval faces, the dark eyes, or the natural complexion that gleams like a peach? Grace is to be found elsewhere, of course, perhaps a softer and more sensitive grace than in this tropical paradise, but real beauty demands more than pretty forms. It demands a personality that flashes from the eyes, an ego that enchants you, and in my opinion the Chilean women possess this more than any of their sisters in South America. Whether it derives from the courage of the Araucanians or from English and German blood, whether. . . . But why bother to dig for the roots of beauty. We should merely enjoy its existence. As foreigners we should rejoice that they like to enchant us, with a preference for the registry office. There must obviously be a fly in the ointment. Since they have such strong personalities they have understood how to play a political rôle. Naturally the Chilean women share the fate of their sisters in the other Latin American countries and even in Spain. Their voice is only valid in the sanctity of the home. For them the ways of man are obscure and troubled. That he guards her fidelity with jealous eyes, that he enjoys the love of other women, she knows for sure, but she does not rebel. On this point, which for women of other latitudes is the most important, she yields without a protest. The man needs her just as he needs a telephone or a fountain pen in his office. Inconstancy is to a certain extent a necessary concomitant of marriage. Should she she take her revenge by being unfaithful? Not a bit of it, for woman, Spanish tradition tells us, is a superior being to man, due to her ennoblement through motherhood. So she submits to her fate. Neither her dignity nor her security will ever be jeopardized. How pathetic and insignificant is the emancipated wife as she exists in the Anglo-Saxon countries, seen from this perspective. She wants an equal voice in political business, demands the vote, and is prepared to exchange for it that secret exaltation which the Spanish and the Creole woman enjoy in their passive inviolability.

But such is the way of the world. The old values fall because their meaning grows empty and they are no longer understood. Even Latin America has been attacked by the concept of female emancipation. Only a few countries still remain where the weaker sex today does not go to the hustings.

Now, in Chile something remarkable occurred. The women who first seized the banner of equality were nearly all lawyers and intellectual ladies, very European or American-minded and unsympathetic to the ideas of the true Chilean woman and mother. They demanded equality in voting and they obtained it. They demanded equality for the woman in the administration of the conjugal fortune, and in actual fact today Chilean men must have their wife's signature on any transaction. The most beautiful of these beautiful ladies was sent as the Chilean representative to UNO! The second became Minister of Justice. Truly the women could be satisfied, but sometimes it is not beautiful ladies who make history. The party to which the Minister of Justice belonged was roundly defeated in the next election. The victor, however, General Carlos Ibañez, during the whole campaign had at his side a woman of about forty who was twice a grandmother and did not attempt to disguise the fact. It was she who aroused the masses to blind enthusiasm when, with her raw sensual voice not unlike that of a French *diseuse*, she began to rant against the robbers in the ministerial seats of the previous Government. She succumbed to passion, burst into uncontrolled sobbing and flung out her arms as though she were being pilloried. Her very name was symbolical, María de la Cruz. No name for the prophetess of a new and better existence could sound sweeter. María the Mother of God and the Cross, both symbols of that faith which has captivated this earth with its magic. She was not beautiful when she stormed—all mouth and wrinkles—but she possessed a passion which knew how to arouse an echo in the depths of the people's souls. María dug her own grave. On hearing her rave ecstatically of altruism and neighbourly love, who could ever doubt her integrity? One day, however, it was learned that María, despite her idealism, had not hesitated to accept considerable sums of money as graft. She also aroused the fury of her compatriots when she sponsored the advances of General Perón, and represented Chile on a State visit to Buenos Aires, where she was received with great pomp. It was all very well for the ruler of 16 million Argentines to declare that he had no intention of annexing 6 million Chileans, that he looked upon the new bonds of friendship far more as an annexation of the Argentine by Chile. . . .The Chileans understood all too well the real meaning of these honeyed words and their wrath fell on María. The women's party collapsed. Their leader was thrown out of the Senate to which she had previously been elected and disappeared for a while into oblivion. But such a demagogic talent could never be silenced in obscurity. A few months later she returned to the toil of political life and no one knows what direction the waves of emotional excitement she knows how to evoke with such mastery will take. For Chile's soil and Chile's women are volcanic, and unfortunately so is Chile's social and political situation.

URUGUAY

A South American Switzerland

TAKE a ship one evening in Buenos Aires, let yourself be lulled to sleep by the drone of its engine, and next morning you will wake up in Montevideo, in a completely different world. The same red water of the Rio Plata still gurgles beneath the keel. Cows, sheep and cornfields look exactly the same as on the other bank, and yet with your first breath you seem to be breathing a different, freer and happier air. Uruguay is known as the "Switzerland of South America" and it really lives up to its name.

You must of course take this with a grain of salt, for in spite of everything we are still in South America and its virtues and vices will be noticeable at first glance. For example, take the famous hospital which towers twenty storeys high from the middle of a park—a gigantic hospital built to house so many patients that half the city would have to be ill in order to fill it, so appallingly gigantic that it has taken twenty-five years to build and is still unfinished. People suddenly realized that it was too ambitious and that they had not enough money to equip it. The famous clinic has therefore remained unfurnished with empty spaces behind the windows, and heaven knows when it will ever be put to its proper purpose—probably when humanity is no longer in need of hospitals. The guides let the tourists admire the giant and sell them postcards of it. To a certain extent it has become a monument to South American *hubris* which at the first urge tries to rise to infinity without the humility of knowing small, systematic and enduring effort. The same faulty relationship to reality lies in another phenomenon. No Latin American State is complete without those poor wretches and cripples who sell the State's lottery tickets. "*Sale hoy.*" It is the monotonous cry of lonely melancholy birds in a stony forest.

"*Sale hoy*" they call the whole year round, for the lottery is permanent. I have stood in the Argentine resort Mar de Plata, and in Chile's Viña del Mar, with a slight feeling of discomfort outside the chilly walls of the casino where the *estancieros* gamble the profits of their harvest. Easy come, easy go, is their motto.

Tiny Uruguay lacks the famous gambling hells of her rich neighbour, but there is plenty of gambling all the same. It has become such a passion with this race that even the widow's mite will be sacrificed to the goddess Chance. Their particular game of hazard is called *Quiniela* and the money is staked on any two-figured number. The lottery publishes the winning numbers twice a week. The obsession of the Uruguayans for this game of chance is so strong that on the days of the draw the amount of food consumed decreases, for they would rather go hungry than forfeit their stake. During the past few years they have now found an accessory to this operation which is taken very seriously. Other countries may have gambling hells, Uruguay has a gambling saint. I think the story is worth telling here. On the 3rd July 1882 the Italian Benedictine monk San Cono was canonized by the Pope. Now, by chance two years before a few Italians had emigrated to Uruguay from his birthplace somewhere in Calabria and were so proud of their saint that they built a chapel to him in their village, Florida. These simple folk hit upon the idea of using the birthday of the saint—*i.e.*, 03—in the Quiniela. They won three-quarters of a million pesos—a considerable sum of money. The story became known. Soon hundreds of devout gamblers visited the altar of San Cono and covered his cloak with gold pieces to court his favour. What followed was pure sorcery: the miracle continued. 03 appeared again on his next birthday in the draw and soon things came to a pitch where the runners of the lottery refused to take bets on this dangerous number. But now people staked with equal success on other numbers—for example 07, the number of letters in the saint's name, or on 12, the century in which he had lived, or on 26, the house number of his chapel. On his birthdays whole busloads of pilgrims drove to Florida and his Italian officiants did magnificent business, such good business in fact that the Church thought it high time to start investigating this saint and to look into his origins. Now, the Uruguayan Government is anything but devout and keeps away from the priests as far as possible, even at State ceremonies. Easter week is officially known as the Semana de Turismo. The judgment of the law which the Italians invoked to their aid followed this trend. It decided that religion was a purely private affair and every citizen was free to implore as many saints as he pleased and look upon them as his own personal property. Thus the ingenious Calabrians could continue to pluck the increasing number of banknotes from the cloak of their gambling patron saint.

Uruguay's second great passion is 'soccer.' In a population of 2½ million there are no less than 2,000 football clubs and 65,000 amateurs, not to mention professionals who are shuffled about like priceless pedigree cattle and at times sold for enormous sums to other clubs without their having the least say in the matter. Near the uncompleted giant hospital lies a completed giant stadium to hold 60,000 spectators: it has long since grown too small for the mobs who throng the turnstiles every Sunday. In actual fact their presence in the stadium is not altogether necessary. The voices of commentators and the radios roar full blast throughout the streets of the city, and if the stadium is applauding a goal the whole city rejoices at the same time. On the streets, in the cafés, a single cry goes up, "A goal!" The sympathies for the rival clubs are in the family tradition. The two largest, the Nacionales and the Peñareles, play a similar rôle to that played by the Montagues and the Capulets in medieval Verona. Should a son dare to question his father's sympathies he would be thrown out of the family. This passion has increased fourfold since the well-deserved victories in the football championships of 1924 in Paris, 1928 in Amsterdam, 1930 in Montevideo and 1950 in Rio de Janeiro. On the last two occasions, when the winning team returned home, cages with canaries hung in the streets of Montevideo as symbols of the defeated Brazilians, Uruguay's most dangerous rival.

But I can hear the reader ask, what has this curious people to do with an enlightened and almost sober land like Switzerland? Well, in spite of everything, quite a lot. Uruguay too owes its

independence to the envy of two neighbours, Argentine and
Brazil, neither of whom will cede to the other the control of the
La Plata estuary. Thus a small country is guaranteed against the
covetousness of two others. This is even more important since
the Uruguayans, as opposed to the warlike Swiss, shy from
military service as a cat shies from water. Only the dregs form
the standing army of 8,000 men, and it is almost heart-breaking
as an instrument of power. During the last World War, when
general service was introduced, a cry of terror ran through
the whole country. Of the 62,000 men who were called up,
18,000 presented themselves, and even these were so ingenious
in dodging the column that only 18 completed their military
training. What could they do? You cannot lock up a whole
country for desertion. Things went badly, so the authorities closed
both eyes and trusted in the *Pax Americana* which the United
States had brought to the Latin continent, a trust which even the
growl of despots in Buenos Aires has so far been unable to shatter.

In 1952 there was a great deal of comparison with Switzerland
when Uruguay, as the only Latin American country, threw the
presidential system overboard and subscribed to a collegiate form
of government on the pattern of the Swiss *Bundesrat*. Now, here
is a case of that grain of salt which, when judging the Swiss
character of Uruguay, is particularly spicy. This democratic land
is basically just as far removed from a true democracy as any of
the Indian countries of the Andes. Here too a host of rich old
families will be found which rule the fate of the land and the
nation. Of these families the Batlles have always been the un-
crowned kings of Uruguay. In their dynasty the power passes
quite naturally from father to son. In hardly any other country
of this continent has this *caudillo* system been so well preserved,
and one can with reason describe Uruguay as being the most
progressive as well as the most conservative country in South
America. Here at last we arrive at the innermost secret of these
small people—it is simultaneously progressive and conservative,
exactly as, under somewhat different circumstances, Switzerland
has found her magnificent stability in this curious synthesis. It is
the basis of its uncompromising happiness; for in this respect the

Batlles were wiser than their colleagues, the arrogant *estancieros* beyond the La Plata. At the beginning of the century one of them recognized the signs of the times and granted his people social laws which must make even the most advanced European nations turn green with envy. In this way he stole the very fuel from the revolutionary locomotive. It never got under way and thus the kingdom of the Batlles still endures today. Towards the end of the first World War the same wise Batlle introduced something approaching the Swiss Bundesrat into Uruguay, although a President still made all the important decisions. This President— not a Batlle this time—was the man who in 1933 did an unheard-of thing, something which progressive Uruguay thought was impossible—he threw out his Bundesrat colleagues and once more ruled alone.

Now, on our journey through Latin America we have seen the different aspects of the presidential system and how pliable it can be made to suit each individual folk. Where a strong hand is necessary fate gives them a General. Where democratic enlightenment reigns the President becomes a true patriarch with a constant ear for public opinion. Thus Uruguay was no unhappier under the new order, and when eventually it reverted to its Bundesrat the reason was far from being merely political. The grounds were a family dispute. One of the Batlles did not want to give the Presidency for the next term to his more able cousin. He did something quite unheard of. He allied himself with Herrera, his own family's greatest rival, a friend of all the dictators from Mussolini to Perón. He promised his party a majority of seats in the Bundesrat and thus the democratic constitution was christened with the blessing of the authoritarian worshippers of dictatorship and to the regret of all true democrats. Politics in the South American Switzerland can even be as crazy as this. Whether the position can endure is very doubtful. Naturally there will be no revolution. A revolution would only break out in Uruguay if the Bundesrat put a ban on football.

BRAZIL

Millionaires with an inferiority complex

"THIS is the only place in the whole continent where I really feel at home," a North American friend said to me one day in São Paulo. "This is a bit of the States in South America." We were looking from a window on the thirty-sixth floor of a skyscraper hotel and below us black streams of cars glided soundlessly—for the noise did not reach to our level—through the geometrical avenues which run between other skyscrapers like ravines. Next to these monsters of cement and glass huddle those modest houses which fifty years ago were the pride of São Paulo. Their façades are crumbling without anyone bothering to repair them, and when you enter one the damp air assails you at the doorway. Today they live on their past fame—or possibly one might say on their decay. The storied parvenus next door, the skyscrapers, lay down the law, above all for the freehold prices of this city which is already vying with Manhattan. São Paulo is a city with a craze for expansion, and it expands in all directions faster than anywhere else in the world. Every hour a new house is completed. The population rises giddily. In 1890 it was a miserable 60,000; by 1920 already half a million; on the eve of the second World War, 1,300,000, and today nearly 2½ million. In the last ten years alone it has increased by 67 per cent and over the same period industrial production has increased five-fold.

What is the reason for this monstrous rise? Why do all the energies of this vast country, Brazil, seem to have been concentrated in this one spot? The city has to thank the Jesuit Fathers, who, in 1554, looked southwards from Rio de Janeiro for a favourable place to build a mission in the jungle. This city, which today has become one of the mightiest strongholds of Mammon, owes its pious Christian name as well as its origin to the zeal of

these holy savers of souls. It is not surprising that the place pleased
the Fathers. They found wonderful fruitful red soil when they
cleared the jungle. The rivers brought down water in adequate
quantities. Fresh breezes cooled the foreheads of the workers as
they still do today. São Paulo lies on a plateau about 2,000 feet
above sea level. When you drive along the magnificent new
motor road to the harbour the gentle undulating terraces stop
short as though cut with a knife just as suddenly as the heights of
La Paz. The eyes look down from the plateau on to a gleaming
silver bay, and on the descent, round bold hairpin bends, you get
a whiff of burning tropical heat. Hardly have you got out of your
car in Santos than you want to lie down on account of the moist
hothouse heat. Even the most energetic man here eventually
becomes an idler. In São Paulo, however, the air is almost like a
tonic. People remain alive and active, and this is no modern
phenomenon. Even in the past centuries an extraordinarily
enterprising society ruled here. For love of adventure they forced
their way along the coast zone to the spots which the Portuguese
colonizers had claimed. Half explorers, half pirates, they drove
jungle paths into the hinterland in quest of gold and other riches,
advancing into closed regions which so far had been inhabited
by shy primitive Indians. It was these *bandeirantes* of São Paulo, as
they were called, who first discovered Brazil as a country and
therewith began a process of infiltration which today in the age
of the aeroplane and the bulldozer is reaching its last phase.
The *Paulistas* are the most active men in Brazil, and they proudly
dub themselves the locomotive which pulls the other nineteen
States of the Federation. The State of São Paulo earns half
the total revenue and produces the same proportion in taxes.
More than half the coffee production of the whole country
is harvested here (no less than a quarter of the total world
production) and the same applies to the other agricultural
products—wool, meat, bananas and, most important of all,
electricity.

As though the Jesuit Fathers had foreseen the dams and pipelines
which have become almost in the nature of things, the rivers
running from the high plateau of São Paulo do not run directly

into the sea, but make a long detour through the interior from Paraná to Buenos Aires. Human cunning has known how to exploit this. The Canadian Light and Power Company, known locally as *The Light*, has built two gigantic dams from which the waters fall 2,100 feet to the plain of Santos, generating a million horse-power. Were this source of power not in the neighbourhood, who knows whether or not São Paulo, despite its healthy climate, might not have been a modest, perhaps dying, provincial town?

Agriculture, on which its wealth was based, is going gradually downhill. Fifty years ago one could walk through the coffee plantations at the gates of the city. Today you have to drive at least 60 miles to see a single coffee bean—and then it is in an agricultural experimental institute—for the fine soil is exhausted very quickly. At the outset, when the virgin forest was cleared, the harvests were prolific as in a Garden of Eden, but from year to year they declined. What is the answer? Manure? It is hardly a paying prospect and only a few planters will take the trouble, for further inland is new jungle only waiting for the axe to give endless unexploited space. Why bother, then, about exhausted soil? In this respect the planters are the Don Juans of the earth, always on the quest of virginity with a smile of contempt for the aged. I travelled by bus from Uruguay to São Paulo. It was an endless journey, endless not so much in miles but because of the perpetual emptiness with rare human settlements like islands in a green ocean. But it is "No more" instead of "Not yet" which is written over this wilderness of vegetation; it is the melancholy of abandon. Here and there you see a few horses grazing, or a pine tree raises its straight branches like a Jewish candelabra against the evening sky. What a strange country is Brazil. How youthful and old at the same time, how fresh and worn out at the same time. It cannot be taken in at one glance, and although I describe my impressions here I realize that I should need to write a whole book about Brazil, for it obeys its own laws. In Mexico one senses Lima, in Bogotá one senses Buenos Aires. Despite all local discrepancies they all belong to the Spanish world. In Brazil one senses no neighbours. It is the centre of a single continent, a world in itself with a great future ahead of it, such as no other community in South America.

. The frontier mentality which drives the settlers over further into the interior in search of virgin soil has pushed the plantations and ploughed lands ever further from São Paulo. They have wandered beyond the State frontiers and are eating into the jungles of their western neighbour, the State Paraná. Here the wealth lies virtually on the ground or rather in the soil. Three to five times more coffee grows here on one stalk than in the tired São Paulo earth. Spluttering and fractious, halting at every station like a tired horse, an engine with rickety wagons rattles into the interior. In the corridors are piled trunks, cases and bundles of unshaved, wild-looking young men travelling with women and children to Londrina. A thousand use this line every day on average. The whole train is scarlet as if splashed with blood and the men are red too, for the soil which is crushed like dust beneath the wheels and trickles through all the cracks is bright red. When you spit, your spittle is red. Londrina is the same colour. It was founded twenty-two years ago as a frontier town in the battle between civilization and the jungle, but today it has long outgrown its origins. It has become a boom town of 45,000 inhabitants with all the features of the inorganic—tall concrete buildings above unsurfaced roads. Maringa, 60 miles further on, has grown in six years from nothing into a small town of 20,000 inhabitants; another dozen miles further on a few lights shine above scaffolding, the beginnings of another town. Whoever has money to buy land here can sell it the following year for double the price and even lay down a plantation with a few thousand of the 25 million coffee bushes which are planted each year in Paraná. In a few years he will probably possess an airfield of his own from which he can survey his own little kingdom. The red earth is as evasive as ether. When the weather is dry, it rises in clouds into the air. When it rains, the roads crumble under the wheels of the vehicles. Only the air is safe.

The virgin soil of Paraná has other vices. The ground mist often descends like a shroud over the jungle clearings and destroys the green leaves with its frosty bite. In the wintry July of 1953 the coffee pioneers were hit by a particularly serious frost disaster which reduced their harvest to a quarter of its normal size. The plantations looked quite ghostly; leafless branches stretched their twigs like witches' brooms to the sky, and only at a certain height on the slopes in a straight line as if drawn by a ruler was the green monotony rescued from the frost. This catastrophe, which rocketed the price of coffee throughout the world, somewhat curbed the expansive urge in Paraná. The ruined plants had to be renewed and many a coffee Don Juan began to think with some melancholy of his more constant love—in other words, the safe hill of Sao Paŭlo near the sea where frost is unknown. People are beginning to wonder if this used soil could not be revivified with manure, and in Campinas, about 50 miles north of São Paulo, Carlos Arnaldo Krug, the director of the State Agricultural Institute, described to me the methods which he and his colleagues have envisaged in this respect. According to him, it is necessary to replace the one-sided exploitation of the soil by a combination of cattle and poultry breeding which gives natural manures to increase the effect of artificial nitrates. This combined farming has already been adopted by a number of planters, and thus coffee is not only fleeing towards the jungle but is returning in modest proportions to its old region.

In the meanwhile the city of São Paulo has discovered and carried out another mission. Thanks to the rich electric current at hand, it was predestined to be an industrial centre. Two-thirds of all the industrial products of Brazil are produced here. Admittedly factories have sprung up in the outlying suburbs of Rio, but all the trump cards for the future lie with the *Paulistas*. The best possibilities of future sources of energy lie in their kingdom, although at the present time São Paulo is so short of electricity that it has to cut off the current a few hours each day. In the neighbouring State of Minas Gerais it is estimated that 13 million tons of iron lie under the soil, and the steel works of Volta Redonda, which are only in the development stage, will one day make possible a flourishing heavy industry. In a wide circle round São Paulo there is no lack of other raw materials, and only the fact that Brazil possesses inferior quality coal prevents it from becoming a South American Pittsburg or Birmingham.

One is almost tempted to say that São Paulo is basically an international city on Brazilian territory, rather than a true Brazilian city. Only one out of five of its inhabitants can boast of two Brazilian parents. On the other hand, exactly as with the operatic Spanish of the Argentine, we find Portuguese ennobled to a kind of classic melody. For São Paulo, like hardly any other South American city, bears the imprint of Italian emigration which began at the beginning of the nineteenth century and in the thirties of our century had passed the million mark. Among the soulless skyscraper ravines will be found some vestige of an Italian small town: men sitting in a *cafeteria*, nibbling cakes and *panettonis* or slicing a *pizza*.

But in the vegetable market clipped and tongue-twisting Portuguese rings out dynamically and the slanting eyes of Japanese glitter from behind mountains of tropical fruit. The *Paulistas* look upon this strong East Asiatic group in their city with both laughter and tears. They are pleased because they are industrious workers and magnificent growers of vegetables, and thus their kitchens never lack green vegetables throughout the year. They are distressed because they are the only group which clings to its own customs and puts up an iron resistance against any attempt at assimilation. A part of them went so far as to refuse to admit the Japanese defeat of 1945. They insisted that the American occupation troops were prisoners placed there to rebuild the towns they had destroyed. These obstinate Nationalists went so far as to convert their more intelligent fellow citizens by acts of terror into accepting their version of world history and to murder as traitors those who would not accept it. The motives of many of these terrorists were admittedly not purely patriotic. They had made high wagers on the victory of their fatherland and were trying to get out of paying ruinous sums of money by simply ignoring the trend of history.

In the racial mosaic of São Paulo we must not forget the *Turcos*. This is the name given to the Syrian and Lebanese Christians who emigrated here from their uneasy Moslem surroundings. They are the craziest acrobats in the whole dizzy, unscrupulous, crooked atmosphere. I met a *Turco*, who shall be nameless, who a year ago bought a textile factory with $12 million debts and who is now worth $20 million. No one asks where this money came from. Just as Paraná recalls the Wild West of the United States, the financial adventures of the great Moguls—the Vanderbilts, Rockefellers, Morgans, etc.—are being repeated in the commercial world of São Paulo. Here wealth is being earned by all means and every opportunity is exploited quite shamelessly; price wars, cut-throat competition for the elimination of competitors, the creation of monopolies, and all the practices of an unfettered Liberalism, are here the rule. The profits are astronomical. In the textile industry, for example— to revert for a moment to my friend the *Turco*—they are sometimes 400 per cent. In São Paulo today there are already 500 dollar millionaires and a thousand more are not far removed from this enviable category. But this Eldorado of the go-ahead business man also has its weak side, because the high profits put up prices and the cost of living index shows a general rise. A refrigerator in São Paulo costs three times as much as in the United States, and foreign competition is countered with high duties instead of with rational measures.

The richest and most powerful man among the industrial barons is Count Francisco Matarazzo, known to his friends as Chicinho. He owns not only a factory, not only a whole trade, but a vast business empire comprising no less than 300 branches which employ 30,000 workers and a similar number of clerks. All in all, Chicinho is lord over a quarter of a million men and is in receipt of the largest personal income in the world—$50,000 a day. What does he produce? It would be easier to say what he does not produce. The IRM (Indusrias Reunídas Matarazzo) produces all the elementary objects which men need for everyday life—textiles, jams, sugar, flour, meat, fats, spaghetti, salt, table oils, paper, cellulose, alcohol, porcelain, sacks, candles, etc. There is hardly a civilized house in Brazil in which you will not find a tin, a bottle or a packet bearing the name Matarazzo.

How does such a man become a multi-millionaire? It is perfectly simple. Chicinho's father had no conception of his future glory when in 1881 he arrived as a 17-year-old youth in his new homeland and sold bananas on the streets. The sausage factory which he finally started was already called the Companies Matarazzo. A flour factory followed and everything ensued quite simply on the principle that Matarazzo never let his wholesalers make any profit. Flour was transported in sacks, so he needed a sack factory. From jute he went over to wool and from wool to artificial silk. To bring down the production costs he introduced aetznatron and thus got his foot in the chemical industry. The need for vegetable and animal fats compelled him to enter the soap industry. In order to get cheap packing material he launched out into the cardboard and glassware industries; to transport his own goods he bought his own engines and ships, and to finance the whole concern he ultimately founded his own bank. On the death of the old man in 1937 this law of natural expansion was continued by his son. He, too, was a modern Midas and everything he touched turned to gold. A few years ago he bought a farm for his weekends. Today the *Fazenda Amalia* is a gigantic undertaking with 15,000 employees, pedigree cattle, a sugar cane plantation and countless subsidiary activities. The man cannot touch anything without reorganizing it and cannot organize anything that does not succeed.

And with wealth comes honour. The father in the first World War, by provisioning the Italian Government, was given the title of Count, and when the *Conde* sits beneath a genuine Rubens it is difficult to see a trace of the ancestral banana salesman in this typical business man with the fat double chin. One tries to find the amusing side of this man, some light side despite the Rubens and the generous gifts to museums and other cultural institutes. Fundamentally Chicinho fails both in culture and in business. He is no Henry Ford and no Morgan, who in their way were artists. He is a notorious miser who pays his workers lower wages than his competitors because he can afford to do so, thanks to his power. But above all he lacks that which plays so great a rôle in the Latin races—joviality, the smile which can bridge so many

differences. The visitor finds himself regarded almost with hostility by a pair of short-sighted eyes behind thick glasses. One feels
that this man with the biggest income in the world feels insecure
behind his million dollar wall because he knows that he cannot
buy love, that he has not once been able to arouse the admiration
of the Patiños or been taken seriously by the old aristocratic
families. Chicinho has never really shed his father's sausage
factory, and this social insecurity applies not only to him but to
nearly all the other Italians, Arabs, Germans, Jews and men of
other nationalities who have risen to millionaires from nothing.
The villas of these *noveaux riches* are marvels from the Thousand
and One Nights. Take for example the 37-year-old millionaire
Francisco Pignatari, who built a house for his bride with two
Turkish baths, a shooting gallery and other sports grounds with
an enclosed swimming pool 120 yards long. At one end of
this pool there is an artificial waterfall, and if you pass through
it you find yourself in a neon-lit cocktail bar.

There are also villas with private theatres and music rooms in
which the most famous artists play to a chosen public. A productive patronage results from this millionaire intoxication
inasmuch as the money to a certain extent supports culture. For
example, São Paulo possesses the only museum for European art
worthy of the name in South America. All of it was bought over
a period of a few years on the initiative of a very strange man
who represents the adventurer type of *Paulista* in a far more
amusing manner than Chicinho. Assis Chateaubriand has no
factories and no millions—in fact, nothing but debts, but in his
way he is no less powerful than the *Conde*. His name denotes
French nobility even as little as does the Italian title. It is a
pseudonym, for Assis is a writer and a journalist, the owner of
twenty-eight newspapers, five magazines, nineteen radio and
two television stations, and—most important of all—he possesses
an all-embracing dossier of various true or imaginary misdeeds
of the rich *Paulistas*. These dossiers are to a certain extent his
capital. When he needs money no one dares to refuse him, for
the press in Brazil gossips about the weaknesses of its great men
with unbelievable gusto. Robber and murderer are here quite

commonplace epithets which never call for a libel action. The only man who stands up to Assis is Chicinho. He lends him no money and quite stoically takes in his stride the appalling attacks and revelations, even when, on the marriage of his daughter, which rivalled that of any princess in pomp, he had to read a sensational account in Assis' papers about her former life. Or when one morning he found a horde of people in front of his office—Assis had published that the Count had made such enormous profits that he had decided to distribute a considerable sum to the poor—and anybody who needed money had only to apply.

The money which Assis obtains from his rich countrymen is spent in magnificent activities. He founded, for example, private flying clubs throughout the country in order to develop the aviation qualities of the Brazilian youth. One day he announced at a fund-raising party on his yacht that he wanted to found three schools in Brazil on the pattern of Groton in Massachusets, in order to produce a spiritual elité in a real "Rolls Royce School". It was also Assis Chateaubriand who presented São Paulo with an art museum in his newspaper building; it houses marvellous exhibits from medieval Sienese through Rafael to Vincent Van Gogh and Modigliani. Naturally we must not forget the Portinari Rooms.

Candido Portinari, whose style hovers between a monumental realism reminiscent of Rivera and the stripped vision of a Picasso, is one of the names which has brought Brazil into the international realm of art, together with Oscar Niemeyer and other young architects under whose hands the theoretical seed of Le Corbusier has sprouted in an almost tropically graceful luxuriance. The buildings which São Paulo built to celebrate its 400-year anniversary were breath-taking fantasies of concrete, steel and glass. Between them, however, spread a garden such as exists nowhere else in the world. Alfredo Burle-Marx, who designed it, sought to reconcile the modern abstract formula and the wildness of the Brazilian jungle. Whole expanses are covered with coloured tiles, circles of beds and squares full of unknown flowers which he discovered in the jungle; with twinkling brooks and white footpaths. It has lost all contact with the French or English

garden. It is an abstract garden inspired by abstract painting.
Burle told me that his work swallowed untold sums of money.
It was only possible in São Paulo. That is the right setting for
the ostentatious, even the crazy, for in the crazy there is room for
the creative artist.

The most beautiful city in the world

THE Redeemer stretches out his arms as though he were
about to fly; as though the universe tears so irresistibly at
his heavy body that no power of gravity can hold him back.
When you go out on the terrace beneath these stone wings—it
is crowded at all hours of the day by tourists—you are for a
moment quite bewildered. You have often heard that Rio is the
most beautiful city in the world and you may have felt sceptical
at the use of so many superlatives, but now you know that it is
true, so true that the power of this view takes your breath away.
Two thousand feet below you lies the city, or rather the countless
small cities which comprise it. Like an eagle in its eyrie the
escarpment of Corcovado rises almost vertical above its centre.
Around it zigzag other cliffs no less bizarre and romantic, against
the sky and the sea. At your feet the breakers of the houses beat
against the hills and mingle with the jungle that girdles the cliffs.
The view is not unlike that of the ruined city of Machu Picchu.
It possesses the same magnificent kinship between nature and the
work of man, with one difference, that here it is alive.

Here lived a Kaiser. Not one of those Spanish viceroys who
made Lima and Mexico mere copies of their Spanish homeland.
You will also find churches and monasteries in Rio; not the
proud citadels of God of the Spanish world, but almost modest
village buildings in which you can feel the calculating intelligence
of commercial builders. Thus colonial Rio, the Rio of the
Portuguese, is far less the heart of this city as elsewhere the
Spanish is the kernel. Rio lives far more outside that age since it
has outgrown the mother-country without a struggle and its
refugee king became an elected child of its colony; outside

the nineteenth century, too, with its refinements and already crumbling façades. By the law of increase Rio has outrun the status of a small Lisbon and without a war of secession has become the new capital. It has never known the hatred or that little-man-trying-to-be-a-big-one feeling which strikes you at each corner of Buenos Aires. On the broad pavements are mosaic arabesques and the tree-lined avenues furnish you with perpetual shade so that your feet seem to be walking on cushions. In addition to this there are cafés at every corner filled the whole day with gossipers. It is elegant, magnificent indolence and therein lies Rio's nobility.

And just as a lord can allow himself the luxury of wearing a torn overcoat because his aristocratic bearing is revealed in every ell, Rio too allows itself the luxury of filth and poverty. The rich escape elsewhere to remote residential quarters far out of sight of the poor. There you will find the luxury villas where an apartment costs £100 a month, while just below on the hills with exactly the same ravishing view over the sea *favelas* can be seen among the trees. These are the troglodyte dwellings of the negroes with corrugated iron roofs and rusty tin walls which cling like swallows' nests to the hill. Only with great difficulty can you reach them up small winding paths. Your panting lungs crave for fresh air and to be free of the stench of drains and excrement. Should you turn back? You have a lasting memory of the dark hostility with which the slum dwellers of Lima or Mexico look upon the more fortunate Gringo. But here no bitter envy greets the unbidden visitor. Inquisitive heads are stuck from all the windows. Curiosity quivers in all these beings. They want to gossip and joke and you find something of the sunny un-class-conscious nature of this proletariat in the whole race. The Portuguese strain gives them a more cosy nature than is to be found in the Spanish.

Even your relationship with officials is a real pleasure here. They are so amazingly agreeable. Actually I made an illegal entry into the country. I had omitted to obtain a Consular visa from the Brazilian Embassy in Montevideo, which is needed by any foreigner. "Swiss citizens do not need one," I declared to the Customs officer at the frontier. "Don't they really?" he replied

with some surprise. "Of course not," I insisted. At this he made
an inimitable gesture with his hand, a mixture of doubt, tolerance
and laziness, and said, "Well, go through then."

Of course the person who has to live in Rio or anywhere else in
this country sings another tune. At the beginning of your visit
you will always be asked: "Do you like it here?" There is usually
a note of compassion in your hostess's voice. "Well, you've only
been here a week. You don't know it like we do." And then she
starts. "There's no water. There's no electricity. The road sinks
just in front of the door into such a deep hole that you'd think
they wanted to build an underground railway. The post office
hasn't taken on any more staff for twenty years, although Rio has
expanded beyond recognition. You simply don't get parcels
from abroad any more. They pile up in a gigantic warehouse
under the mountain and now and then a postman grabs half a
dozen or so in order to surprise the addressee after the delay of a
year or more. Every evening you will meet mile-long queues in
the avenues waiting for a rare bus. They would get home much
quicker on foot. The ancient open 'Bond' trams rattle along like
prehistoric monsters through the streets with clusters of men
hanging on to them. The conductor climbs like an ape over the
passengers' heads and collects the fares like a free church offering
without ever giving you a ticket. . . ."

The floor seemed to steam, or perhaps my eyes deceived me
as on a lazy summer day. From the gallery you could only half
make out the people below. Actually there were no longer
individuals, only a sea of shaking heads and bodies. Here a black
skin powdered white, there a white skin painted black. Crinkly
heads, blonde permanent waves, dominoes, false noses or merely
the blank mask of complete trance. Manifold are the faces of
carnival and all these thousand faces formed part of a single body,
formed part of that seething rondel below, revolving in its slow
monotony. The Samba was not born in this hemisphere; Africa
screams in its deafening roar. Screams. . . . Now you realize it:
all these men in that sea below are howling in unison with wide
open mouths. Not only their limbs quake as though obsessed in

a St. Vitus dance, their souls are engulfed by the rhythm of the melodies that beat ceaselessly in your ears.

Occasionally the drummer in the band grows tired and waves to his deputy. The latter approaches gently, takes over and continues in the same eternal rhythm. Thus the trance is not broken for a single second.

I suddenly became aware of another peculiarity—many of these men danced alone. They came here without women and without a companion. They merely joined the bubbling broth of heads. A hand is stretched out to them and they clutch it without knowing to whom it belongs; they let themselves be led without knowing where they are going. No one belongs to anyone else and all belong to each other. Thus the gestures of this intoxication do not lie in the embrace or in the complicity of "mine and thine." Next to you a male or female fellow traveller is dancing. You are seized by the hips from behind in a column of three, five or eight and whirl your way through other columns. The discipline of the dance step has long since ceased. You wobble in short steps forward because no conscious form remains.

There is a bar where the overheated can get a cool drink, but they swallow orangeade or beer, and these same men who are quite sober, in the next five minutes will once more be lost in the mob, the mob which lives in the music and in the supernatural power of the collective gesture.

Even perversion is ennobled here through grace. Who can enjoy this carnival more than a homosexual who does not shrink from wearing women's clothes, but on the contrary can at last become himself. You will find hundreds of perverts at these dances. Artificial bosoms on countless male chests, countless boys' heads wearing ringleted wigs. . . . Effeminate youths stand like marble statues on the tables at the fringe of the theatre, their heads adorned with tall coronets and their sexless limbs with a chain mail of diamonds like show window dummies at Christmas. They carry a wax figure of the beheaded John in their outstretched hands; they remain impassive while the obsessed crowd rages round them. No gesture disturbs their pose. They are surrealists in a Cocteau film.

Many people told me that Mardi-Gras in Rio had lost much of its magic. In the old days society, which now confines itself to exclusive balls, reigned with their magnificent masks in the streets of the inner city, while the people enjoyed their noisier fiesta in the suburbs and were banished to the *favelas*. It may be one of the social symptoms of our age that today this tremendous rift is apparent. Rio, for the traveller who visits here in her normal everyday garb, is an elegant white city, but at carnival time she is black. The carnival belongs to the negroes. They may starve and wallow for a whole year in filth, but for these three days they are the kings and all the wages they have earned in a modest day as a dock worker or a servant girl are dissipated. Princely brocades cover their black limbs, silken dresses are embroidered with wonderful flowers or fantastic figures. Like jungle weeds, their crinkly hair gives birth to the most fabulous creations. It is woven into the strands of a basketful of bright flowers, or a ship rides with full sail upon black locks. It is the deepest desire of the coloured soul—at least for a brief moment—to imitate the white lord and to steal his power by the splendour of his costume: but here the bitter irony with which the Indian overplays his mimicry, turning it to parody, is lacking.

This chaotic feast lasts for three days. For three days no single citizen is capable of a normal thought. The Samba rules. On the fourth day work only begins at midday and with it the care for the morrow does not dampen the noisy intoxicating finale.

Carnival does not rage in Rio alone. It is the national *fiesta* of this country and its magic increases the further north you go into those tropical provinces where Africa with its black men streamed across the sea to the neighbouring continent. Not voluntarily of course. A similar thing happened here as elsewhere: the frail jungle Indians whom the Europeans masters constrained to work broke under their compulsion like tender china figures. Brazil, too, knew the tragedy of the black slaves, their sorrows and their liberation by the decree of an enlightened ruler. Here there was no revolt and no war. This would have been altogether too alien to the Brazilian spirit of tolerance. Thus no deep-rooted hatred has split the races and poisoned the atmosphere as in the United

States. Admittedly the light-skinned Brazilian does not particularly admire the negro. There are certain unwritten discriminations which must be observed, and you will look in vain for a black skin in the diplomatic corps, among the higher ranking officers, or in key administrative positions. The silent supremacy of the white race is expressed in jokes. A drop of white blood, they say, is enough to make a negro a white man, but 95 per cent. black blood will never change a white man into a negro. A Brazilian of quality will never extol his black great-grandmother or grandmother who brought a touch of the tarbrush into his family, but will revert to his Indian ancestors, for these wild men of the primeval forest were real men, noble idlers who preferred to die rather than to survive by work. One cannot talk in Brazil of a renaissance of the Indios as in Mexico; too few of them have survived, and even the last few melt like snow before the sun as they do in the jungles of Ecuador and Peru under advancing civilization—but their biological heritage is preserved with that touching reverence one always devotes to vanishing beauty. The negro merits no such respect. He is there, healthy and indestructible.

General opinion, which is almost invariably wrong, endows the negro with great erotic prowess. Would a Brazilian girl allow herself to be seduced by a negro? Ridiculous! On the other hand, to sleep with a white man is the dream of every negress—and she gets her wish. It is made easy for her, since the ban which reigns throughout Latin America protecting the young girl from masculine contacts before her marriage has in Brazil become an almost inpenetrable armour plating. Not so however with the negress. The Brazilians make a present of her to their youthful Lotharios. From her womb will be born those children who during the course of the centuries produce a mixed race. Thus the relationship between white and black is here almost tinged with the tenderness of boy and girl love.

And since give and take ensues without the bitterness of inferiority complex and contempt, a bridge is built. In the southern States of America, however, the rift only deepens into a more bitter hatred.

An important reason for the lack of racial conflict in Brazil is actually the lack of any written code. Only a few years ago a decree was issued stating that each hotel or theatre that forbade the entrance of a negro would be fined. It is significant enough that the negroes were the ones who felt furious about this decree. A negro lawyer in Rio explained to me that such legislation puts racial discrimination on a legal footing and gives it a foundation from which racial hatred can develop. It would be far better to ignore individual cases of discrimination which can occur than by punishing them and bringing up the subject for public discussion. In other words, let sleeping dogs lie.

Official statistics speak of a numerical balance between black and white, a balance whereby the white side tips the scales. But they are wrong. Anyone who knows the superior reproductive power of the negro—above all in the country—must know that Brazil will not become lighter but darker. On the other hand, perhaps the lack of racial darkening can be traced back to the indolence of the blacks upon whom no demands are made; even this indolence allows social rifts to appear which may of necessity one day lead to a racial war. The whites own the richest parts of Brazil, namely those lying south of latitude 20. These States of Minas Gerais, Paraná, Santa Catarina and Rio Grande do Sul comprise only a sixth of the whole Brazilian country (incidentally Brazil is equal to the United States with a second Texas added), but more than half the population lives in this region and among them almost all the European immigrants. The most important mines and water power are awaiting exploitation and most of the capital streams in here where the heart of Brazil beats. The home of the blacks, however, is the north—Pernambuco, Recife, Bahia. Here the mixed world of Rio has finally been transformed into an African colony. But the white sugar plantation owners here rule a beggarly illiterate starving mass from which only a few of the more cunning and enterprising elements occasionally manage to break loose and journey in quest of the fleshpots of the south. The south goes on developing, but the north stagnates.

As in the case of the Indios of the Andes, there is every ground

for attributing this less to the lack of enterprise of these negroes
than to their century-old neglect. American and European
engineers who have to work with white and black Brazilian
employees naturally complain loudly of their laziness and
thoughtlessness, independent of colour, but praise their gifts of
improvisation and adaptability which always makes them ready
to cope with a new situation. If from youth they were given the
favourable conditions of life such as European workers enjoy,
many people maintain that there would be little comparison
between them. The negro worker is in general considered to be
clumsy, but to have more powers of endurance than his white
colleague. What he loses in the morning he usually catches up
in the afternoon when the heat lays the white man low. Thus,
viewed objectively, Brazil has little to fear from the "negroizing"
of the country. The mixture of black blood can, on the contrary,
be of great service to the vitality of the country if it can weather
the shoals of political and social tension.

A South American China ?

"**G**OOD night, gentlemen," said the small man with the
big head and the features that reminded one of Franklin
D. Roosevelt. It was five o'clock in the morning of
August 31st 1954. Getulio Vargas, the creator of modern Brazil,
was taking leave of his Cabinet after being hissed by an indignant
public and abandoned by the army. He was preparing himself for
the long night. For three hours he wrote his will, and then put a
bullet through his heart. Even in his downfall, at the end of a
career which at its height brought him adoration and at its
depth an attempted assassination, Getulio made his exit like a
tragic hero. His final speech was an explosive mixture of compassionate grief and demagogy, just as his life had been a mixture
of greatness and political artistry. "The foreign capitalists have
combined with my opponents to encompass my downfall, the
downfall of a friend of the people," he complained. "But to
those who think they have defeated me I reply, I was a slave of

the people, and today I find release in eternal life. But these people whom I served as a slave will never be enslaved. My sacrifice will burn for ever in their souls and my blood will be the price of their redemption. I have fought against the plundering of Brazil. I have fought against the plundering of the people. I have fought with my breast bared. Hate, infamy and slander never destroyed my spirit. I gave you my life. Now I bequeathe you my death. Nothing remains. In all serenity, I take my first step towards eternity and leave this life to enter history."

What magnificent Latin American rhetoric! It did not fail to have an effect. The people, who had been reduced to poverty under his picaresque policy, were aroused to almost as great a passion as the Colombian masses displayed at the death of Gaitán. The newspaper offices of the opposition were wrecked, businesses were looted and private property set on fire. The police had to protect the American Embassy with machine guns and tear gas. They fired on the mob. It was forgotten that, a few days before, one of the most popular journalists and critics of government policy had been murderously attacked by members of the presidential bodyguard and one of his friends, an Air Force officer, murdered and that the chain reaction of assassination reached Getulio's camp (probably instigated by his son Lutero). Exactly in the same way as the Argentine masses forgot their reduced standard of living at Evita's bier, the flickering light of the great people's tribune flared up once more. A strange coincidence: in no other country of this hemisphere did the collapsing social revolution come to a more tragic end than here in mild Brazil.

One talks of *Peronismo*. By rights it should be called *Getulismo*. The Argentine General has unjustly usurped a political discovery made eight years before him by Vargas when in 1937 the latter dissolved Congress and created the *Estado Novo*, an authoritarian democracy with all the trappings of Fascism—muzzling of the press, secret police and political jails. He consolidated the people's victory over the feudal plutocracy of the coffee barons, presented the workers with a social code, a minimum wage and a forty-eight-hour week, and to the women he gave emancipation.

The nationalism which accompanied its twin brother socialism was a creation out of nothing; Getulio was the first to instil in his countrymen, who previously wrangled as *Paulistas*, *Cariocas* (from Rio) or as Northmen, the concept of *Brasilidade*. Even worse than this: one was now a foreign German, Italian, Syrian or Japanese. On my trip through the Rio Grande do Sul I visited cities and villages where even more than in Chile the settlements seemed as though they had been transplanted on a magic carpet direct from Germany.

Their nationalist-tinged Teutonism was firmly anchored in their own schools, choirs and sports clubs. One could meet men in the Brazilian jungle who did not speak a single word of Portuguese and only understood German. Hitler welded their colonies into a dangerous instrument of imperialist megalomania, splitting Brazil between Germany and Italy. Vargas, in spite of his admiration for his German colleagues, was forced to act. Portuguese became the compulsory language in the schools; Portuguese was sung in the choirs and used in the sports clubs. American air bases threw a protective roof over the land. A Brazilian expeditionary force fought under General Clark in Italy. In Puerto Alegre a word uttered aloud in German brought the police into action. Today in Blumenau and Joinville, German nationalism smoulders in the hearts of the older generation, but their sons have become Brazilians. Mixed marriages, previously the exception, have today become almost the rule.

With this new creation of a national conscience, Vargas carried through an administrative centralization which broke the threads of the individual States and concentrated them in Rio. This was not accomplished without a bitter conflict. But Brazil became a reality.

The year 1945, when a wave of democracy rolled across Latin America, brought the first fall of the dictator. Unlike the second, it was almost melodramatically mild. Getulio capitulated gracefully to an army *coup d'état* and retired to his ranch in the Rio do Sul, from whence in 1930 he had ridden at the head of his gaucho army and seized power. Had he only remained there! But an overwhelming election victory brought him back to office in

x

1950. As Chile proved in the case of Ibañez, fallen dictators make bad democratic presidents. Today their task is even more difficult. All the tribulations we met with in the Argentine plague Brazil, overcrowding of the cities and rising prices in agricultural production to the point where competition is impossible. Vargas tried similar antidotes to Perón: he decreed a minimum price which almost ruined the coffee export industry. The national debt—the 800 million dollar reserves accumulated during the second World War had been frittered away—rose to giddy heights, and bankruptcy was only averted at the last moment thanks to American aid. The currency sank visibly day by day. Trade was in desperate straits, but Vargas did nothing decisive. He tried to put everything right by a deceptive euphoria of optimism. The plantation owners and the big Rio merchants, who love free enterprise, found an attentive ear, as did the *Paulista* tariff-conscious industrialists. In the same breath as he told the Minister for Economy, Aranhe, to preach austerity, he tried to cajole the workers by doubling the minimum wage. And the more rapidly the country rushed towards the abyss, a prey to strikes and corruption, the more rein the helpless President gave to his nationalist demagogy.

Nothing could have been more absurd than the triumphant acclaim of the Brazilian oil question. The geologists believe that a third of the country is oil-bearing, that perhaps one day Brazil will be among the foremost producers, ranking with U.S.A., Venezuela, Saudi Arabia, Iraq and Persia. But here too Brazil is a land of the future which, as the Brazilians say ironically, never comes. The wealth lies unexploited and undiscovered beneath the soil. Only a hundredth of the oil this gigantic country could produce is taken out of the ground. The rest is imported from Venezuela against good currency—the very currency which is urgently needed for capital purchases such as machinery. Why does Brazil not follow the example of Venezuela and Peru and sign a contract with powerful companies, sharing the profits with them?

A wave of indignation ran through the country at this thought. "The oil belongs to us" was the slogan used to prevent the national property being delivered into the hands of the "imperialists". Parliament decided to found a half-State, half-private company, and this *Petrobras* was to be responsible for oil prospecting. No foreigner, even if he were a naturalized Brazilian, could own shares in this company—not even Brazilians who had married foreign wives. "The more national the better," Getulio is supposed to have said when he signed the ridiculous decree. The result was that the "imperialistic" oil companies as importers from Venezuela earn as much as would the producers. *Petrobras*, suffering from lack of capital, goes ahead with heart-breaking slowness; each year the petrol consumption rises by 20 per cent. with a proportionate wastage of currency.

We must trade! This vast land, which could feed 500 instead of 56 million men, suffers from undernourishment—a deficit of 260 calories daily. On the other hand, 30 per cent of the harvests rot in the fields because an antediluvian transport system cannot cope with them. A quarter of the cattle driven to the slaughterhouses die on the way from hunger and thirst because the train takes ten days to cover 200 miles. What other solution remains open, except the hated foreigner? Brazil, despite her nationalism and as opposed to that impertinent urchin the Argentine, has always been the little Lord Fauntleroy flattering Uncle Sam and sitting obediently in his lap. His growling outbursts have merely been jealous requests for particularly expensive presents. A joint Brazilian-American Commission has worked out a development programme with a 220 million dollar credit from the World Bank and the Import-Export Bank which will open the way to economic prosperity.

Like everything else in this land, communism is also quite uncontrollable. No one knows exactly how many party members there are. The Government say 40,000 to 60,000, the communists claim 130,000. The party is forbidden, but no one stops five communist newspapers from appearing daily in the largest cities. The party leader Luis Carlos Prestes has his house searched by the police, but the newspapers continue to publish his manifestoes. People suspect quite rightly that the communist leader would not be arrested even if his whereabouts were known, for his popularity

stretches far beyond communist circles. He was already a swash-
buckler of almost mythical prestige when in 1924 a military
putsch failed in the south and he led his troop northwards on an
adventurous journey through the jungle and reached the sanctuary
of the Bolivian frontier. This brilliant rearguard action with fifty-
six successful clashes with a superior opponent has become classic
war history in Brazil and is studied by all young cadets at the
Military Academy.

The greatest chance for Brazilian communism lies in the fact
that it has sympathizers among the highest ranking officers of the
army. How could the preserver of the national safety operate
against a new rebellion when communist newspapers would
probably be found in the homes of that small circle of initiates
with access to secret army orders, as happened in November
1951? Only as a result of the energetic protests and threatened
resignation of one of the most popular loyal Generals did the
President in March 1952 sack the crypto-communist General
and President of the Military Club, Estillac Leal, who had
sabotaged his purge of the Officers' Corps. Since then this task
has gone forward under the leadership of more responsible
officers, but even in January 1953 we find that the army Judge,
Amador Cisneiros do Amirál, to whom the cleaning up was
entrusted, was also a fellow traveller and skilfully squashed any
evidence against colleagues of his own creed. And where in all
this tremendous elasticity can one find a strong-point from
which the struggle against communism could be waged? The
entire youthful intelligentsia, the government administration,
the unions and the press have been indoctrinated. They have, and
yet again they have not, for can one ever nail them down ideologically? Politics here is a jungle. You can wander through its
paths without noticing a living creature and yet only a few yards
away jaguars and wild boars crouch behind the leaves.

And this is not perhaps an exaggeration. According to reports,
somewhere in the actual jungle of the Brazilian hinterland, like
Mao Tse-tung of old in Yunnan, Luis Carlos Prestes sits in a red
capital. In a giant triangle stretching from Rio to Natal and into
the Matto Grosso on the Bolivian frontier thousands of armed

guerrilleros stand ready in their lairs to break into the carefree Brazilian daily life, perhaps during one of the general strikes staged ·by the complacent unions. For years news of these hidden red armies has flickered through the Brazilian press. They are everywhere and nowhere. They bob up here, they bob up there. They are either bandits who have never heard the name of Stalin, or farm hands who have rebelled against some inhuman plantation owner, burning his house over his head and distributing his land. The whole nation holds its breath when an alleged communist headquarters is discovered on an island on a tributary of the Paraná and is attacked by the police and the army. The surprised inhabitants turned out to be peaceful citizens of a nearby village who had built their week-end bungalows there. Thus in all probability many of the communist shadow divisions are really no more than ghosts. When dubbing Brazil the South American China one must always take into account that the comparison is inept on various counts. China hungers because it is over-populated, because an equally poor though industrious and ingenious people to a certain extent lives on the borderland of its true potential; it seeks a form of escape in the inhuman hyper-organization of the communist system. Behind Brazil's hungry people lie thousands of miles of virgin soil. It only needs someone to sow them, and if someone other than the communists took the initiative out of their hands. . . . But who will do it?

Envoi

MY last day in Rio arrived and I should like to invite the reader once more to follow me along the quays of its incomparably beautiful bay and watch the yellow light of evening climb up the white cliffs of houses and vanish into the darkening blue haze. The cable railway climbs busily to the top of the sugar loaf mountain. When the shadows engulf the city and the electric lights gleam in semi-colons around the bay—punctuation marks between which you can see nothing—the view from above is a dream we all yearn for in our hearts. Below on the quayside stroll the lovers; each pair is in close embrace some distance from the next as intimacy demands. It is as though some artist had placed statues on the banks of the shore. Two young people cling to each other in hopeless resignation. They wear wedding rings and an indissoluble marriage chains them to another. Not far away a seedy young man of the underworld takes a banknote from a pretty frivolous creature and sticks it boorishly into his pocket without a word of thanks. Next come two young things so deeply in love that they want to melt into each other. Melancholy rules all these lovers on the seashore. In their longings I could feel more misery than happiness. It is probably true that happy couples have no need to wander home-less on the quayside. Perhaps too this is on account of my own melancholy, because tomorrow I am leaving and I do not know when I shall see this continent again, this continent I love and hate like no other. Its artistic profusion arouses greater enthusiasm in me than even the cultures of the Far East; and its barrenness drives me almost to a pitch of despair. This continent, so near and so remote from God, tragically ranting like Dionysus. South America! For its children the Indios, whose rightful ownership for centuries has shown in the deep wrinkles of their faces, it is the land next door to heaven, where the terrifying gods demand the bloody quivering heart and man succumbs in terror to a transcendental fate. Then there are the milliard figures in the commercial ledgers; the packets of shares on the London, New York and Zurich Stock Exchanges. South America is synonymous with minerals, meat, petrol and coffee. It is the continent of the future—no longer the future of its own people but of the others, the foreign calculators who understand organization and work with the regularity of alarm clocks. Its own children, however— not only the Indians but those who have lived long enough there to have put down their tap roots, try in vain to copy that other victorious spirit, to wrest the magic formula from the foreigner and to usurp his power. Fundamentally they do not understand him even when they think they do. They sit upon the greatest material wealth of the globe and grieve in a dream for an imaginary world. They call themselves pathetic beggars on golden stools, and this is exactly what they are. And they will remain so until they lift their eyes from the ground to the sky which is so close to them.